Teach Yourself

VISUALLY™

Flash® CS4 Professional

Visual

by Keith Butters

WILEY

Wiley Publishing, Inc.

Teach Yourself Visually™ Flash® CS4 Professional

Published by
Wiley Publishing, Inc.
10475 Crosspoint Boulevard
Indianapolis, IN 46256

www.wiley.com

Published simultaneously in Canada

Library of Congress Control Number: 2008942703

ISBN: 978-0-470-34474-3

Manufactured in the United States of America

10 9 8 7 6 5 4 3 2 1

Trademark Acknowledgments

Contact Us

For general information on our other products and services please contact our Customer Care Department within the U.S. at 800-762-2974, outside the U.S. at 317-572-3993 or fax 317-572-4002.

For technical support please visit www.wiley.com/techsupport.

WILEY

Wiley Publishing, Inc.

Sales
Contact Wiley at (800) 762-2974 or fax (317) 572-4002.

Praise for Visual Books

"Like a lot of other people, I understand things best when I see them visually. Your books really make learning easy and life more fun."

John T. Frey (Cadillac, MI)

"I have quite a few of your Visual books and have been very pleased with all of them. I love the way the lessons are presented!"

Mary Jane Newman (Yorba Linda, CA)

"I just purchased my third Visual book (my first two are dog-eared now!), and, once again, your product has surpassed my expectations.

Tracey Moore (Memphis, TN)

"I am an avid fan of your Visual books. If I need to learn anything, I just buy one of your books and learn the topic in no time. Wonders! I have even trained my friends to give me Visual books as gifts."

Illona Bergstrom (Aventura, FL)

"Thank you for making it so clear. I appreciate it. I will buy many more Visual books."

J.P. Sangdong (North York, Ontario, Canada)

"I have several books from the Visual series and have always found them to be valuable resources."

Stephen P. Miller (Ballston Spa, NY)

"Thank you for the wonderful books you produce. It wasn't until I was an adult that I discovered how I learn — visually. Nothing compares to Visual books. I love the simple layout. I can just grab a book and use it at my computer, lesson by lesson. And I understand the material! You really know the way I think and learn. Thanks so much!"

Stacey Han (Avondale, AZ)

"I absolutely admire your company's work. Your books are terrific. The format is perfect, especially for visual learners like me. Keep them coming!"

Frederick A. Taylor, Jr. (New Port Richey, FL)

"I have several of your Visual books and they are the best I have ever used."

Stanley Clark (Crawfordville, FL)

"I bought my first Teach Yourself VISUALLY book last month. Wow. Now I want to learn everything in this easy format!"

Tom Vial (New York, NY)

"Thank you, thank you, thank you...for making it so easy for me to break into this high-tech world. I now own four of your books. I recommend them to anyone who is a beginner like myself."

Gay O'Donnell (Calgary, Alberta, Canada)

"I write to extend my thanks and appreciation for your books. They are clear, easy to follow, and straight to the point. Keep up the good work! I bought several of your books and they are just right! No regrets! I will always buy your books because they are the best."

Seward Kollie (Dakar, Senegal)

"Compliments to the chef!! Your books are extraordinary! Or, simply put, extra-ordinary, meaning way above the rest! THANK YOU THANK YOU THANK YOU! I buy them for friends, family, and colleagues."

Christine J. Manfrin (Castle Rock, CO)

"What fantastic teaching books you have produced! Congratulations to you and your staff. You deserve the Nobel Prize in Education in the Software category. Thanks for helping me understand computers."

Bruno Tonon (Melbourne, Australia)

"Over time, I have bought a number of your 'Read Less - Learn More' books. For me, they are THE way to learn anything easily. I learn easiest using your method of teaching."

José A. Mazón (Cuba, NY)

"I am an avid purchaser and reader of the Visual series, and they are the greatest computer books I've seen. The Visual books are perfect for people like myself who enjoy the computer, but want to know how to use it more efficiently. Your books have definitely given me a greater understanding of my computer, and have taught me to use it more effectively. Thank you very much for the hard work, effort, and dedication that you put into this series."

Alex Diaz (Las Vegas, NV)

Credits

Project Editor
Sarah Cisco

Senior Acquisitions Editor
Jody Lefevere

Copy Editor
Kim Heusel

Technical Editor
Jon McFarland

Editorial Manager
Robyn Siesky

Business Manager
Amy Knies

Sr. Marketing Manager
Sandy Smith

Manufacturing
Allan Conley
Linda Cook
Paul Gilchrist
Jennifer Guynn

Book Design
Kathie Rickard

Production Coordinator
Erin Smith

Layout
Carrie A. Cesavice
Andrea Hornberger
Jennifer Mayberry

Screen Artist
Ana Carrillo
Jill Proll

Illustrators
Ronda David-Burroughs
Cheryl Grubbs

Proofreader
Linda Quigley

Quality Control
David Faust

Indexer
Potomac Indexing, LLC

Vice President and Executive Group Publisher
Richard Swadley

Vice President and Executive Publisher
Barry Pruett

Composition Director
Debbie Stailey

About the Author

Keith Butters is a founding partner and executive creative director at The Barbarian Group. He has over 10 years experience architecting, designing, and programming for the Internet. Some notable and award-winning Web sites that Keith has worked on include several projects for Volkswagen of America, Comcastic!, the Method "Come Clean" site, and the Subservient Chicken. Visit The Barbarian Group's Web site at www.barbariangroup.com to learn more and to see a full portfolio.

Author's Acknowledgments

Thanks to the team at Wiley Publishing, especially Jody Lefevere and Sarah Cisco for working with me on this book, and for their patience.

Thanks to all of the barbarians, for continuing to be an inspiring collective of the most talented and interesting people I have ever known.

And, a special thanks to Melanie for her love and support, and for trying to keep me on track with the writing of this book.

Table of Contents

Click here to see the fighter plane in action!
START

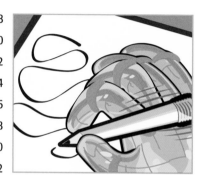

chapter 3 Modifying and Positioning Artwork

chapter 4 Working with Text

Table of Contents

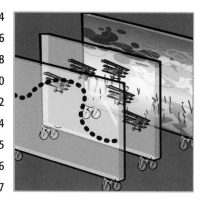

chapter 7 Working with the Timeline

chapter 8 Working with Symbols and Instances

Table of Contents

 **Adding Interactivity with User Interface Components**

chapter**12** **Integrating Sound**

Table of Contents

 chapter **13** **Adding Video**

 chapter **14** **Loading External Elements Dynamically at Runtime**

chapter **15** **Publishing Flash Movies**

How to use this book

Do you look at the pictures in a book or newspaper before anything else on a page? Would you rather see an image instead of read about how to do something? Search no further. This book is for you. Opening *Teach Yourself VISUALLY Flash® CS4 Professional* allows you to read less and learn more about the Flash program.

Who Needs This Book

This book is for a reader who has never used this particular technology or software application. It is also for more computer literate individuals who want to expand their knowledge of the different features that Flash has to offer.

Book Organization

Teach Yourself VISUALLY Flash® CS4 Professional has 15 chapters and 3 appendixes.

Chapter 1, **Getting Started with Flash**, introduces you to the Adobe Flash application and its user interface. It also demonstrates how to set up a new Flash document, test it, and save.

In Chapter 2, **Drawing in Flash**, you learn about creating vector artwork using the Flash Drawing tools.

Chapter 3, **Modifying and Positioning Artwork**, shows you how to create more complex artwork by customizing lines, creating gradient fills, and using transforms.

In Chapter 4, **Working with Text**, you go through the steps needed to format type, including paragraph formatting, kerning, and leading.

Chapter 5, **Importing Artwork**, teaches you how to use images and illustrations that were created in other applications like Photoshop or Illustrator.

Chapter 6, **Working with Layers**, shows you how to organize the Flash Timeline by creating new Layers and Layer groups, and by changing the appearance of your layers.

In Chapter 7, **Working with the Timeline**, you learn how to add and edit Frames and Keyframes in Flash.

Chapter 8, **Working with Symbols and Instances**, teaches you about the basic Symbol types in Flash, how to edit and modify them, and how to use them in your movies.

Chapter 9, **Creating Timeline Animation in Flash**, shows you how to create animation using Motion Tweens, Shape Tweens, and Classic Tweens.

In Chapter 10, **Adding Interactivity with ActionScript**, you learn how to change the behavior of your Flash Movie by writing Frame Actions. It demonstrates how to set properties of Symbols, and how to 'listen' for Events like mouse clicks.

Chapter 11, **Adding Interactivity with User Interface Components**, gives you the tools you need to utilize Flash's built-in components, and how to skin them to look the way you want them to.

In Chapter 12, **Integrating Sound**, you find out various ways to use audio in your projects. You also learn about the different types of sounds and how to optimize them for the Internet.

Chapter 13, **Adding Video**, tells you everything you need to know to add video to your Flash movies, including how to customize the appearance of the video player component.

Chapter 14, **Loading External Elements Dynamically at Runtime**, takes you through a series of tasks designed to show how Flash can load images and other types of data on the fly. It also demonstrates the basics of creating XML and how Flash can read data from an XML file.

In Chapter 15, **Publishing Flash Movies**, you learn about the different ways you can distribute your Flash movies. It shows how you can publish as an image, as a video, and how to embed Flash in a Web page.

Appendix A, **Flash Keyboard Shortcuts**, is a table that shows you the most commonly used quick-keys in Flash, so you can speed up your workflow.

Appendix B, **Commonly Used ActionScript Commands**, is a reference for ActionScript commands that are used frequently.

Appendix C, **ActionScript Operators**, is a reference for operators in ActionScript for tasks like mutiplication, division, and comparison.

Chapter Organization

This book consists of sections, all listed in the book's table of contents. A *section* is a set of steps that show you how to complete a specific computer task.

Each section, usually contained on two facing pages, has an introduction to the task at hand, a set of full-color screen shots and steps that walk you through the task, and a set of tips. This format allows you to quickly look at a topic of interest and learn it instantly.

Chapters group together three or more sections with a common theme. A chapter may also contain pages that give you the background information needed to understand the sections in a chapter.

What You Need to Use This Book

Using the Mouse

This book uses the following conventions to describe the actions you perform when using the mouse:

Click

Press your left mouse button once. You generally click your mouse on something to select something on the screen.

Double-click

Press your left mouse button twice. Double-clicking something on the computer screen generally opens whatever item you have double-clicked.

Right-click

Press your right mouse button. When you right-click anything on the computer screen, the program displays a shortcut menu containing commands specific to the selected item.

Click and Drag, and Release the Mouse

Move your mouse pointer and hover it over an item on the screen. Press and hold down the left mouse button. Now, move the mouse to where you want to place the item and then release the button. You use this method to move an item from one area of the computer screen to another.

The Conventions in This Book

A number of typographic and layout styles have been used throughout *Teach Yourself VISUALLY Flash® CS4 Professional* to distinguish different types of information.

Bold

Bold type represents the names of commands and options that you interact with. Bold type also indicates text and numbers that you must type into a dialog box or window.

Italics

Italic words introduce a new term and are followed by a definition.

Numbered Steps

You must perform the instructions in numbered steps in order to successfully complete a section and achieve the final results.

Bulleted Steps

These steps point out various optional features. You do not have to perform these steps; they simply give additional information about a feature.

Indented Text

Indented text tells you what the program does in response to you following a numbered step. For example, if you click a certain menu command, a dialog box may appear, or a window may open. Indented text may also tell you what the final result is when you follow a set of numbered steps.

Notes

Notes give additional information. They may describe special conditions that may occur during an operation. They may warn you of a situation that you want to avoid, for example the loss of data. A note may also cross reference a related area of the book. A cross reference may guide you to another chapter, or another section with the current chapter.

Icons and buttons

Icons and buttons are graphical representations within the text. They show you exactly what you need to click to perform a step.

 You can easily identify the tips in any section by looking for the TIPS icon. Tips offer additional information, including tips, hints, and tricks. You can use the TIPS information to go beyond what you have learn learned in the steps.

Operating System Difference

This book was written using Mac OS X Leopard (10.4.5). Depending on your system, you may need to hold down the `Fn` key to use `F1`-`F10` on many Macs. On a Windows computer, you can use the `Ctrl` modifier key where on a Mac you use the `⌘` key.

Getting Started with Flash

Adobe Flash is an excellent tool for creating rich interactive experiences for the Internet, animation, and online applications. This chapter gives you a working knowledge of the Flash authoring environment. You also learn to create, save, and customize a new Flash document.

Introducing Flash

Adobe Flash is an integrated development environment, specifically designed for creating animation, multimedia experiences, and Web page components. Flash has also become the de facto standard for delivering video over the Internet. The Flash Player plug-in allows users to view Flash in their browsers. Nearly all current Web browsers support Flash.

Create Illustrations, Animations, and Other Artwork

Flash has many of the same drawing tools as other illustration programs that allow you to create vector graphics. Vector graphics are composed of lines, curves, and polygons. Conversely, bitmaps are made up of pixels. The main benefit of using vector artwork in Flash projects is that they can be scaled larger and smaller without a loss in fidelity. And, depending on their complexity, vector graphics may download a lot faster over the Internet. To learn more about creating graphics, see Chapters 2 and 3. To learn how to import artwork, see Chapter 5. See Chapter 4 to learn about working with text.

Work with Symbols and Instances

Symbols are objects in Flash that you can reuse. These objects can be Graphics, Buttons, MovieClips, sounds, and videos. Copies of your symbols that are used in your Flash movie are called instances. No matter how many instances you create, the symbol is only compiled into your movie once. On the Web, this is very powerful, because a hundred instances will download just as quickly as a single instance. You can scale, rotate, and modify other properties of an instance without affecting the base symbol. But, if you edit a symbol, all of the instances inherit your changes. To learn more about working with symbols and instances, see Chapter 8.

Create Animation

There are several ways to animate in Flash. You can create frame-by-frame animation, use the Motion Editor, or use ActionScript to move and manipulate an object's properties. Frame-by-frame animation is used primarily for creating movements that cannot be achieved in Flash by other methods. For more on creating animations, see Chapters 8 and 9. To learn how to animate using ActionScript, see Chapter 10.

Organize with Layers

Layers are very useful in Flash for several reasons. First, you can draw, erase, and add or remove instances on one layer without affecting another layer. Second, you can hide layers (make them invisible) and lock layers (make them uneditable). Also, you can use layers for organization in a more complex Flash document. Many Flash developers use one layer at the top of their document exclusively for actions, and another exclusively for labels. To learn more about working with layers, see Chapter 6.

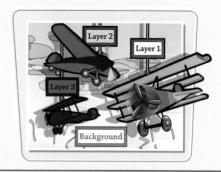

Add Interactive Elements

You can add interactivity to your Flash movies in a number of ways. The simplest is by using the `Button` object. Buttons have built-in rollover and click states. With a small amount of ActionScript, you can create a vast range of interactivity, from simple rollover effects to triggering complex animation. For more on adding interactivity to your Flash movies, see Chapters 10 and 11.

Publish Your Movies

You can publish and share your Flash movies over the Web or create self-contained Projector files. Flash movies can also be exported as QuickTime movies, animated GIFs, and a variety of image sequence formats. For more on how to publish your Flash movies, see Chapter 15.

Get to Know the Flash User Interface

The Flash program window has several components for working with graphics and movies. Take time to familiarize yourself with the on-screen elements. If you use Flash on a Windows-based computer, the program elements may look a bit different than those displayed in the following example, which was done on a Mac.

● **Title Bar**

Allows you to open, close, and minimize Flash.

● **Menu Bar**

Displays Flash menus that, when clicked, reveal commands.

● **File Tab**

The tab at the top of the work area represents the current file. If two or more files are open, you can switch from file to file by clicking a tab.

● **Timeline**

Contains all the frames, layers, and scenes that make up a movie.

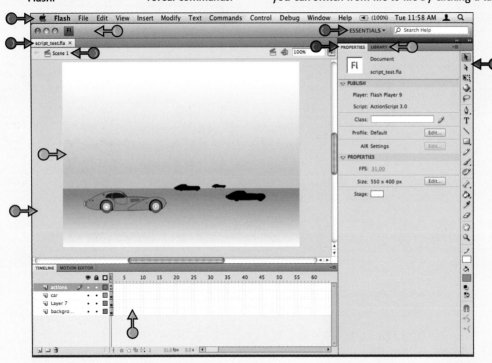

● **Tools Panel**

Contains the basic tools needed to create and work with vector graphics.

● **Current Location**

Displays the name of the scene on which you are currently working. If you are inside instances or groups, it allows you to navigate up the object hierarchy.

● **Workspace Menu**

This menu allows you to switch between workspaces and to create new ones. It is the same as clicking **Window, Workspace** from the main menu.

● **Library Tab**

Use this tab to organize and select symbols to add to your movie.

● **Properties Tab**

Use this panel to view and edit properties of the current object.

● **Work Area**

The area surrounding the Stage. Anything placed on the work area does not appear in the movie.

● **Stage**

The area inside of the work area, which is visible when you publish or export your Flash movie.

Using Flash Utility Panels

Flash utility panels allow you to organize your workspace by function and by what tools you use most often. They are all dockable to the main Flash window. So now any panel can also be a part of any of the tab sets. You can also create new tab sets.

● **Top Bar**

Click this bar to collapse a panel into its icon form.

● **Tab**

Displays the name of the panel. The tab is also the portion of the panel that you click and drag to dock, move, or break away from other tabs.

● **Panel Dropdown**

Use this menu to close a panel, get help about a panel, or to access a list of functions that affect the panel.

● **Close Button**

When a panel exists on its own, not as a part of a tab set, you can close it by clicking the Close button.

● **Minimize Area**

Click on this area of the panel to hide the content of the panel, but retain the tabs and top bar.

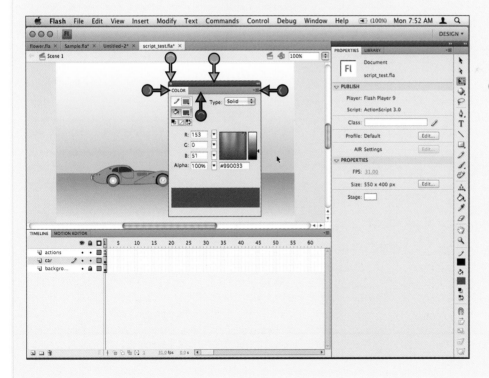

Open a Flash File

There are two main types of Flash files you can use to create Flash movies: Flash document files (.fla) and ActionScript files (.as). Flash documents are the base file type you use to create your Flash movies.

Open a Flash File

OPEN A FLASH FILE

1 Click **File**.

2 Click **Open**.

● If there are no open documents, you can click the **Open** button on the welcome screen.

The Open dialog box appears.

3 Click on a Flash file, or navigate to one you want to open.

● To enable only certain types of files for Flash to open, click here and select a file type.

4 Click **Open.**

The file opens in Flash.

OPEN MULTIPLE FILES AT ONCE

1. Click **File**.

2. Click **Open**.

The Open dialog box appears.

3. Select multiple Flash files by holding down Ctrl (⌘) and clicking the files you want to open.

4. Click **Open**.

All of the documents you selected open in tabs in Flash.

How do I switch between multiple files?

Flash has a tabbed interface that allows you to have many files open at the same time and provides an easy way to switch between files. If you open multiple files, switch between them by clicking the tabs. On a Mac, you can cycle through them by pressing ⌘ + ~. There is no keyboard shortcut on a PC.

Save and Close a Flash File

You are going to want to keep your Flash files so that you can continue to work on them in the future. Flash does not automatically save your work periodically, so it is essential to save early and often — every time you make a significant change.

Save and Close a Flash File

SAVE A FILE

① Click **File**.

② Click **Save.**

You can also press `Ctrl`+`S` (`⌘`+`S`) as you work to save changes to your file.

You can also press `Ctrl`+`Shift`+ `S` (`⌘`+`Shift`+`S`) to open the **Save As** dialog box.

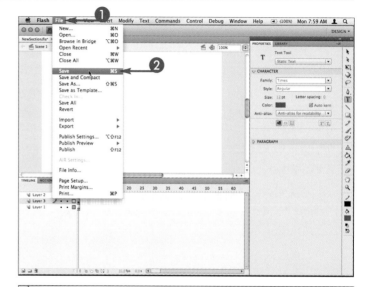

③ Type a name for your file.

④ Click **Save (Save As)**.

Your file is saved.

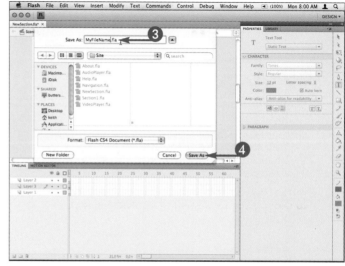

CLOSE A FILE

Save your file. See the task "Save a File" to learn how to save.

1 Click **File**.

2 Click **Close.**

You can also press `Ctrl`+`W` (`⌘`+`W`) to close your Flash document.

If you forget to save your file before closing, Flash prompts you with a dialog box to save your work.

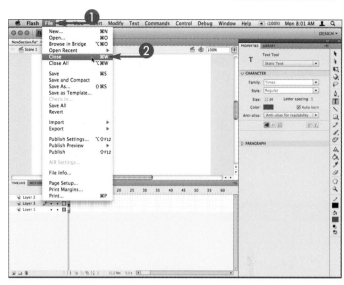

CLOSE A FILE WITH THE CLOSE BUTTON

Press `Ctrl`+`S` (`⌘`+`S`) to save your file.

1 Click the **Close** button (`⊠`) on your documents tab.

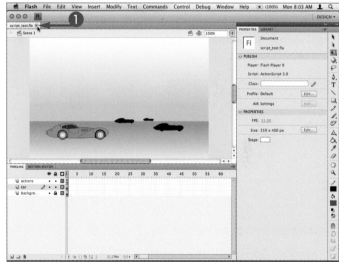

TIPS

How do I close all of the open documents at once?

If you close the main Flash window, all of your documents close and the Flash program quits. Only do this if you have saved all of your documents. Flash gives you an opportunity to review any unsaved changes, but it is preferable to not rely on the Review Changes dialog box.

Can I save my Flash CS4 file as a CS3 document?

Yes, although when you work on a project with multiple people it is better if everyone uses the same version of Flash. Click **File**, click **Save As Type (Save As)**, and select Flash CS3 Document from the Format drop-down menu. This saves your FLA file in the older format.

Save and Version Your Work with Save As

You can save a snapshot of your work with Save As. Sometimes you may want to experiment in the middle of a project without fear of not being able to get back to your last stable version. So, before experimenting, you can save a copy and always go back to it.

Save and Version Your Work with Save As

① Click **File**.

② Click **Save As**.

You can also press `Ctrl`+`Shift`++`S` (`⌘`+`Shift`+`S`) to display the **Save As** dialog box.

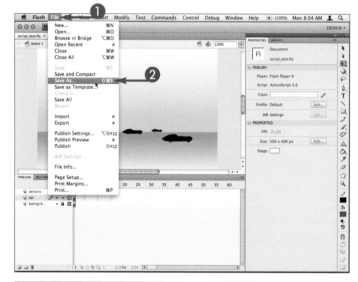

● The **Save As** dialog box appears.

③ Choose a new name for the current version of your document.

④ Click **Save (Save As)**.

You can now work with the newly saved version of your file.

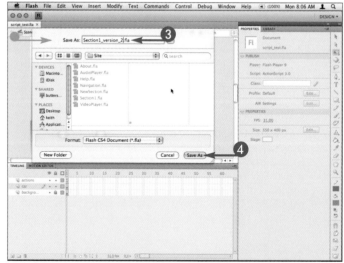

Flash files are called *documents* or *movies*. You can create a new document in Flash to design artwork, build an animation, or begin a larger interactive project. Flash movies are saved in the .fla format, so you can also refer to your flash movie as your FLA file.

Create a New Flash Document

① Click **File**.

② Click **New**.

The New Document dialog box appears.

③ Click the type of document you want to create.

● A description of each type appears here.

④ Click **OK**.

A blank document appears in the Flash authoring environment.

Organize and Save Your Workspace

You can organize all of the windows and panels of the Flash interface to suit your needs. You may want to save a few different workspaces, each specifically laid out for designing, programming, or debugging.

Organize and Save Your Workspace

1 Click **Window**.

2 Click **Actions.**

3 The Actions panel appears.

4 Click and drag the Actions panel and move it next to the Timeline tab below the work area.

● A highlight appears where your dragged panel will be docked.

Release the mouse button.

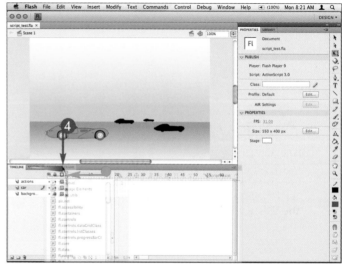

⑤ Click **Window**.

⑥ Click **Other Panels**.

⑦ Click **History**.

The History panel appears.

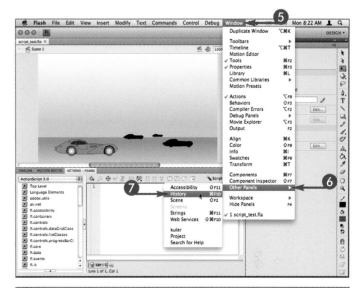

⑧ Click and drag the History panel to the right of the Library tab.

● A thin, blue border outlines the panel set where your panel will be docked.

The History panel's tab is next to the Properties and Library tabs.

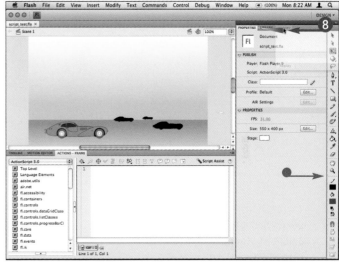

TIPS

How do I rename and delete a workspace that I have created?
Click **Window, Workspace, Manage Workspaces.** A dialog appears that has options to rename and delete your workspaces. Flash does not allow you to delete or rename the built-in workspaces, so if you have not yet created your own, the dialog will be empty.

Can I hide and show all of the open Flash panels?
When you have panels open, you can click **Window, Hide Panels** (F4) to hide everything except the Stage. After hiding the panels, you can make them all appear again by clicking **Window, Show Panels** (F4).

continued

If you work on a laptop at home, but connect your laptop to a larger display at work or school, you can arrange and save additional workspaces for those situations. Many times, you will want a workspace for working on a laptop to be more sparse than a workspace for larger or multiple displays.

Organize and Save Your Workspace

⑨ Click and drag the Tools panel to the left of the work area.

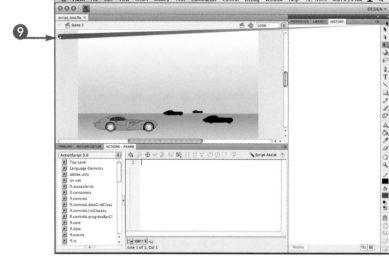

● A vertical line highlight appears, denoting that dropping the panel here docks the panel to the left.

Release the mouse button.

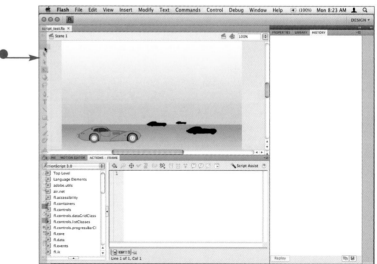

⑩ Click **Window**.

⑪ Click **Workspace**.

⑫ Click **New Workspace**.

The **New Workspace (Save Workspace)** dialog box appears.

⑬ Type a name for your workspace.

⑭ Click **OK**.

Your workspace is saved.

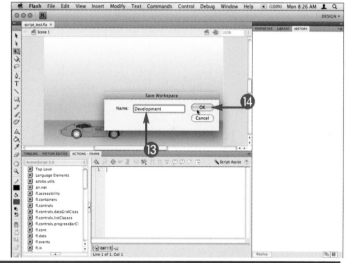

TIPS

How do I go back to the workspace that shipped with Flash?

You can always revert back to the original workspace layout of Flash. Click **Window, Workspace**, and then click **Essentials** (**Default**). Your windows and panels are restored to their default positions.

I moved around my windows and opened other panels, and now I want to get back to the workspace I have saved. How?

To revert to a saved workspace, simply click **Window, Workspace** and then click the name of the saved workspace to which you want to return. You can also click **Window, Workspace,** and then click the item that says **Reset** followed by the name of your current workspace.

Move and Zoom the Work Area

Many times you may want to zoom in to get a better view of your work or zoom out to find objects that you placed off-stage for safe keeping. The most common way to move around the work area is to use a combination of the Zoom tool, and to use the keyboard to toggle on the Hand tool for moving.

Zooming and moving your view merely changes the scale and placement of the work area. It does not affect the size and placement of your objects and artwork.

Move and Zoom the Work Area

ZOOM IN

1 Click the Zoom tool () in the Tools panel, or press **M**.

   ▶ changes to 🔍.

2 Click on the work area to zoom in.

   Flash zooms in on your view of the work area.

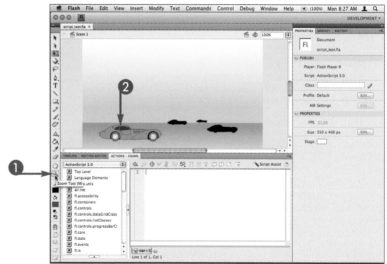

ZOOM OUT

1 Click the Zoom tool in the Tools panel, or press **M**.

   ▶ changes to 🔍.

2 Press and hold down **Alt** (**Option**).

   🔍 changes to 🔍.

3 Click on the work area to zoom out.

   Flash zooms out of your view of the work area.

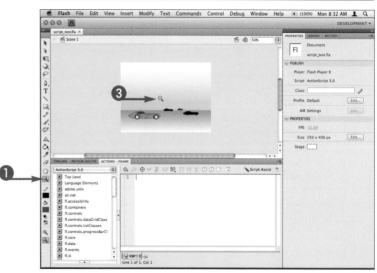

18

MOVE YOUR WORK AREA

1 Zoom in.

2 Press and hold down Spacebar.

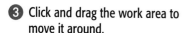 changes to 🖐.

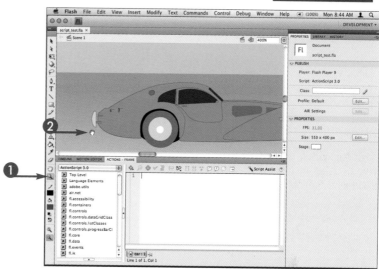

3 Click and drag the work area to move it around.

Flash moves your view of the work area. Release the mouse button and the Spacebar when you finish moving.

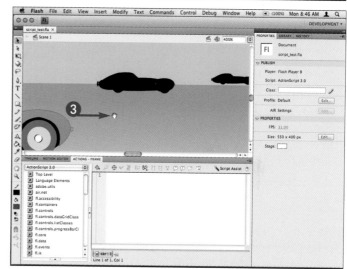

TIPS

How do I zoom to a specific magnification?
In the upper-right corner of the work area there is a magnification text field that displays the current zoom level. You can type any number from 8% to 2000%, press Enter, and your work area zooms to your specified magnification.

How do I get back to viewing my work at actual size?
There are three ways to do this. You can double-click the **Zoom** tool, press Ctrl +1 (⌘+1), select 100% from the zoom level menu, or type **100%** into the magnification text field.

Using Rulers and Grids

You can be very precise with the layout of your objects and illustration by using rulers and grids. Rulers and grids do not appear in your exported or published movie; they are just tools to aid your design.

Using Rulers and Grids

ACTIVATE THE FLASH RULERS

① Click **View**.

② Click **Rulers**.

● Flash displays a horizontal and vertical ruler in the Stage area.

You can repeat steps **1** and **2** to turn off the rulers.

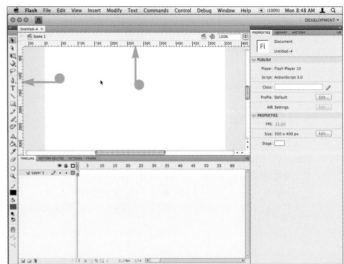

TURN ON THE GRID

1. Click **View**.

2. Click **Grid.**

3. Click **Show Grid**.

● Grid lines appear on the Stage.

You can repeat steps **1** to **3** to turn off the grid lines.

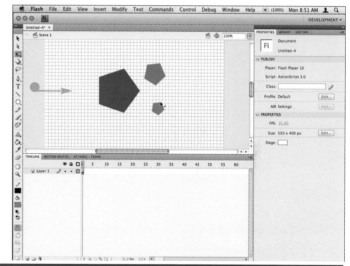

TIPS

How do I change the size of my grid squares?
Click on **View**, **Grid**, and then **Edit Grid**. A dialog box appears that allows you to change the vertical and horizontal spacing of the grid lines. It also allows you to change the color of your grid, adjust snapping, and determine whether the grid appears above or below elements on the stage.

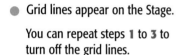

What are guides?
Guides are lines you can drag onto the Stage to help you as you move items and control positioning. You can turn on the Flash guides as another tool to help you position objects on the Stage. To display the guides, click **View**, **Guides**, and then **Show Guides**. You must also turn on the Flash rulers in order to use guides. To add a guide to the Stage, drag a guideline off of the ruler and onto the Stage. To remove a guide, drag it back to the ruler.

Work from a Template

Flash has a library of templates that you can use as a starting point. Many of these templates are for creating content for online advertising, mobile phones, and slide shows. You can also create your own templates or download other templates from the Internet.

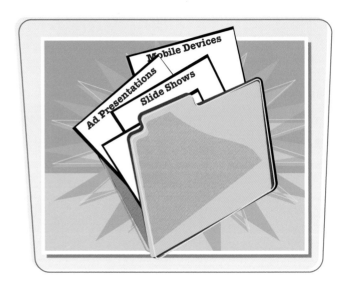

① Click **File**.

② Click **New**.

The New Document dialog box appears.

③ Click the Templates tab.

● New from Template appears as the dialog box title.

④ Click a category.

● A list of related templates appears.

● Click a template and view a preview here.

● A description of the template appears here, if one is available.

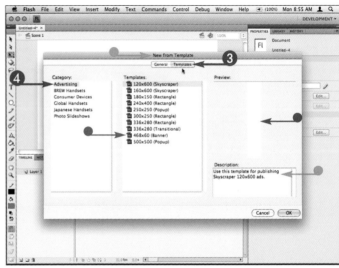

⑤ Click the template you want to create.

⑥ Click **OK**.

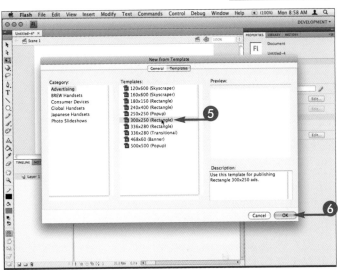

● A blank template appears in the Flash window.

You can add content to create the new file.

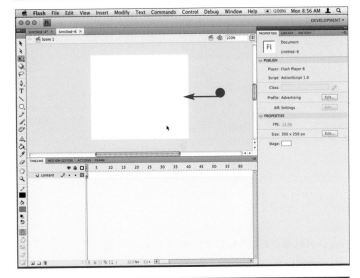

Can I make my own templates in Flash?

Yes. To turn any Flash file into a template file, click **File** and then **Save As Template** to open the Save As Template dialog box. Type a unique name for the template, select a category to save the template to, and type a brief description. Click **Save** and Flash saves the file and adds it to the templates list.

How do I save a file I create with a template?

After you finish working on the template, you can save it as a regular Flash file. Click **File** and then **Save**, and assign a unique name for the file in the Save As dialog box. To learn more about saving files, see the section "Save and Close a Flash File" earlier in this chapter.

Using the Properties Inspector

You can use the Properties inspector to see and edit the properties of the object that you currently have selected. The Properties inspector changes to reflect the properties associated with the object you select on the Stage. If you have no objects selected, the Properties inspector displays the general properties of your Flash document.

The Properties inspector acts as a panel that you can collapse, hide from view, or move. By default, Flash places the Properties inspector at the right of the program window, in a tab set that includes the Library panel.

Using the Properties Inspector

COLLAPSE AND EXPAND THE PROPERTIES INSPECTOR

① Click the panel's title bar to collapse or minimize the panel.

This also minimizes any other panels that are a part of the same tab set, and collapses them to icons.

Note: This example shows the document properties listed in the Properties inspector panel.

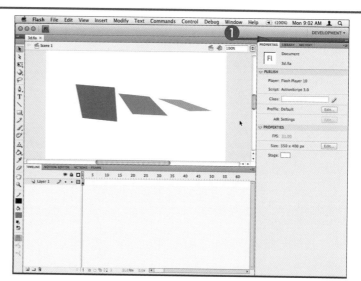

● The Properties inspector panel and other tabs collapse.

② To expand the panel again, click the panel's title bar.

● To temporarily view collapsed panels, you can click the panel name in the collapsed view.

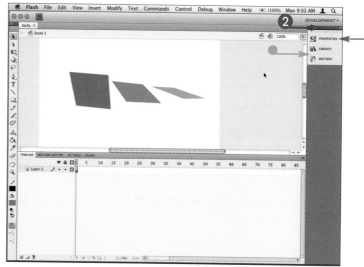

CLOSE THE PANEL

① To close the panel, click the panel drop-down button ((▾≡)), and click **Close.**

Flash closes the Properties inspector.

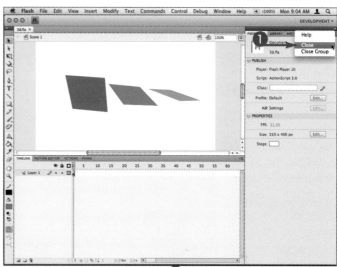

OPEN THE PANEL

② To display the panel, click **Window**.

③ Click **Properties**.

You can also press Ctrl+F3 (⌘+F3) to quickly open the panel.

Flash opens the Properties inspector.

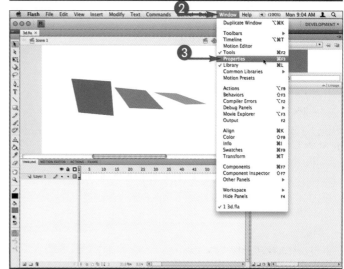

TIPS

Can I move the Properties inspector around like a normal panel?

Yes. If you click and drag the **Properties** tab, you can move it anywhere. If you release the mouse button while another part of the Flash window is highlighted, it docks there. If no area is highlighted, the Properties inspector appears as a regular panel.

Can I rearrange the tabs where I have many panels docked?

You can rearrange any tab set in Flash by dragging tabs to the left and right. Flash automatically moves the other tabs to make room for your dragged tab while you are dragging, so you know where everything will be when you release the mouse button.

Set up a New Flash Document

When you first open a new document in Flash, it is a good idea to set up your Stage size, frame rate, background color, and ActionScript version first. Sometimes, your animations or scripts behave differently than you expect after a change in frame rate. And it can be labor intensive to move all of your objects on the Stage to accommodate a new Stage size.

Everything you need to get set up is in the new Flash CS4 Properties inspector.

Set up a New Flash Document

SET YOUR ACTIONSCRIPT VERSION AND FLASH PLAYER VERSION

1. If it is not already open, open the **Properties inspector**, by clicking **Window** and then **Properties**.

   You can also press `Ctrl`+`F3` (`⌘`+`F3`).

   ● The default Publish settings appear.

   ● The default document properties appear.

2. Click **Edit** in the Publish settings.

   The Publish Settings dialog box appears.

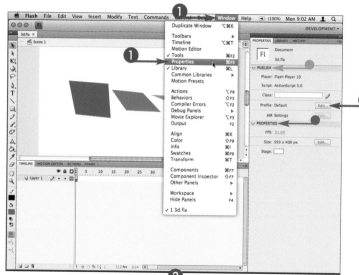

3. Click the **Flash** tab.

4. Click the **Player** menu and select Flash Player 10.

5. Click the **Script** menu, and select ActionScript 3.0.

6. Click **OK**.

   Your Publish settings are stored in your Flash document.

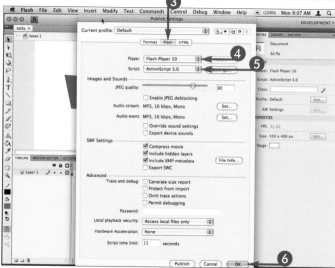

CHANGE THE FRAME RATE

1 If it is not already open, open the **Properties inspector** by clicking **Window** and then **Properties**.

You can also press Ctrl + F3 (⌘ + F3).

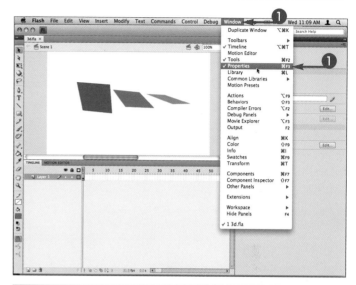

● The document's Properties appear below the Publish settings.

2 Click the number in the FPS field (frames per second).

3 Type a new frame rate in the FPS field.

This example shows a frame rate of 31.

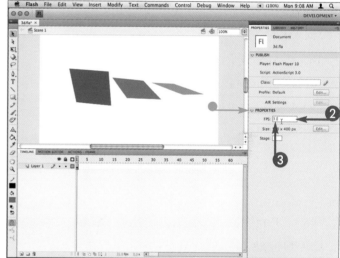

TIP

How do I save my document setup, so I can reuse it in future projects?
Click **File**, **Save As Template** to save all of your document settings as a Flash template. Then, when you create a new document, you can choose your saved template as a starting point.

continued

You can set your frame rate to be anything you want. Most of the time you should stick with conventional 31 frames per second for Flash, unless you have a compelling reason to use a different frame rate.

Set up a New Flash Document (*continued*)

CHANGE THE STAGE SIZE

① In the **Properties** inspector, click **Edit**.

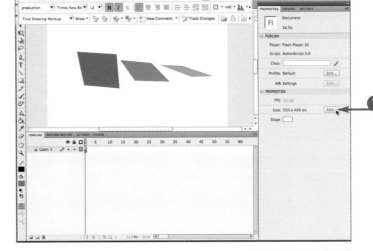

● The Document Properties dialog box appears.

② Type the height and width dimensions you want for your Flash movie.

③ Click **OK**.

Your Flash movie is now set to your desired dimensions.

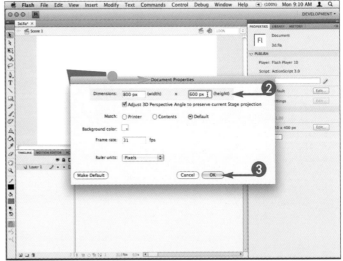

CHANGE THE BACKGROUND COLOR

① In the Properties inspector, click on the white box next to the word Stage.

● A set of color swatches appears.

② Click on one of the swatches to select a new background color.

● Your background color changes to the color you select.

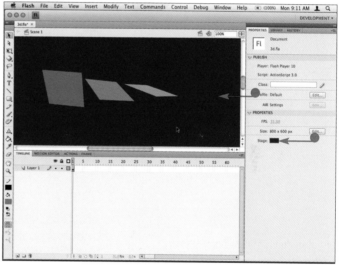

Can I change my document setup at any time?

Yes. When you work on a file and need to change these settings, click on an empty part of the Stage and then open the Properties inspector. Again, changing your frame rate and Stage size in the middle of a project may require you to rewrite scripts, edit animation, and reposition all of the objects on the Stage, so be careful.

How do I change all these settings in a single panel?

Click **Edit** next to the stage size in the Properties inspector. Most of the changes made in this section (and a few extras) can also be accomplished in the resulting dialog box.

Adjust Publish Settings

You can publish your Flash movies in a number of different formats. For Flash-based Web pages, there are a few settings that you can adjust to make your previews and tests more representative of the final output.

CHANGE BASIC SETTINGS FOR FLASH

① Click on **File**.

② Click **Publish Settings**.

- The Publish Settings dialog box appears.

- By default the Flash tab is selected.

③ Click the Player menu drop-down menu and select Flash Player 10.

④ Under Images and Sounds, click and drag the slider to set your default JPEG quality.

You can always increase or decrease the JPEG quality for better image fidelity or smaller file sizes, respectively.

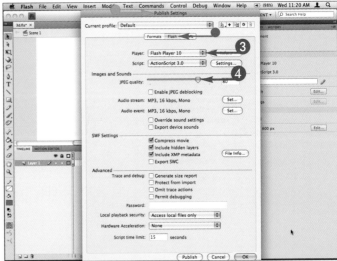

CHANGE BASIC HTML SETTINGS

1. Click **File**.

2. Click **Publish Settings**.

● The Publish Settings dialog box appears.

3. Click the **HTML** tab.

4. Click the **Template** drop-down menu and choose an HTML template.

In this example, **Flash Only** is chosen.

● You can click **Info** to get a description of the template you have selected.

● You can select the **Detect Flash Version** option to allow your HTML page to make sure anyone viewing your Web page has the appropriate Flash Player installed.

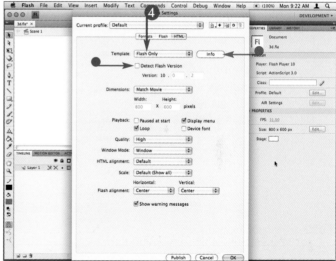

TIP

The Detect Flash Version option only allows for versions 10 and above. Why?

If you want to detect for a version lower than Flash Player 10, click on the Flash tab of the Publish Settings window, and change your player to a lower version. Then, the HTML tab shows the appropriate version number in the Detect Flash Version setting.

continued

You can set up Flash to publish your movie as a Web page. Flash exports a SWF file as well as an HTML file, which you can view in a Web browser. See Chapter 15 to learn more about publishing Flash movies.

5 Click the **Dimensions** menu and select an option.

If you want your Flash movie to remain a fixed size, choose **Match Movie**; if you want your Flash movie to scale, choose **Percent**. Or, if you want to change the dimensions of your exported SWF, choose **Pixels** and enter in your custom dimensions.

6 Click the **Quality** menu and select **Best**.

Your Publish settings are now set.

SELECT PUBLISH FORMATS AND FILE NAMES

1. Click **File**.

2. Click **Publish Settings**.

● The Publish Settings dialog box appears.

3. Click the **Formats** tab.

4. In the Type section, select the formats to which you want to publish.

● You can click here and type new names for your exported files if you do not want to use the default names.

● If you want to revert to Flash's default names, click **Use Default Names**, and Flash restores them.

● If you want to publish your files to a specific folder on your computer, click the folder icon next to the filename.

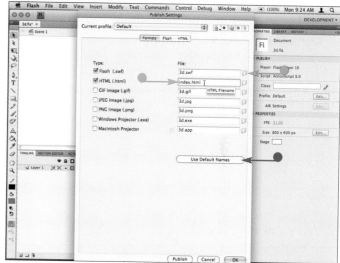

 TIPS

Can I publish many formats at the same time?
Every time you publish a Flash movie, Flash looks to see which formats you have selected in the Publish Settings dialog box and publishes them all.

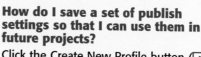

How do I save a set of publish settings so that I can use them in future projects?
Click the Create New Profile button (+) at the top right of the Publish Settings dialog box. Flash asks you to name your profile. Any settings you change become part of your current profile. You can switch between profiles by clicking the **Current Profile** menu at the top of the Publish Settings dialog box.

Test a
Flash Movie

You can test your Flash movies
at any time during design and
development. You will probably
find that every time you
complete a task in Flash, you
will want to test it to see how
everything works out.

Test a Flash Movie

TEST WITH TEST MOVIE

1 Click **Control**.

2 Click **Test Movie**.

You can also press `Ctrl`+`Enter`
(`⌘`+`Enter`).

Your Flash movie plays in a test
window.

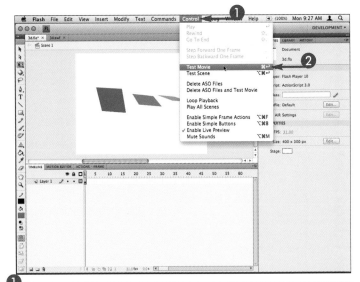

TEST WITH PUBLISH PREVIEW

1 Click **File**.

2 Click **Publish Preview,** and then
click the format you want to test.

Flash previews your movie in the
selected format.

Get Flash Help

When you need help understanding a technique or feature in Flash, you can use the Flash help system. The help system contains information and tutorials on each feature of Flash, a complete ActionScript reference guide, and a place to get additional help from the Flash community.

Get Flash Help

① Click the search box at the upper right of the Flash window.

② Type in search terms for the topic you need help with.

③ Press **Enter**.

Flash opens your Web browser and loads the Flash help system.

Note: *To go directly to the help system without searching, click **Help, Flash Help** or **F1**.*

● A list of Flash CS4 Resources appears here.

● An index of learning topics for Flash appears here.

● You can also search directly inside the help system using this search box.

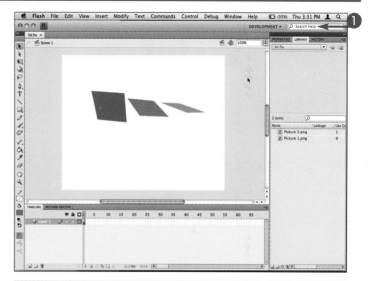

Drawing in Flash

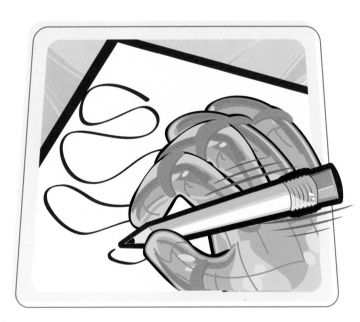

Flash puts many tools at your disposal for creating compelling illustrations, buttons, and user interfaces. These tools are similar, if not the same, as other professional-grade drawing applications like Adobe Illustrator.

Introducing Flash Drawing Tools

The Tools panel helps you create and work with graphics and text. By default, it appears docked on the far-right side of the program window. You may want to move it to the far left if you are used to other drawing programs like Photoshop or Illustrator.

The keyboard shortcut for each tool appears in parentheses after that tool's name.

● **Selection (V)**

Also called the Pointer or Arrow tool, you can use this tool to select and move items on the Stage.

● **Subselection (A)**

This allows you to select and adjust anchor points and handles of lines.

● **Free Transform (Q)**

Use this tool to scale, rotate, or skew a selected item. This tool shares space with the Gradient Transform tool (F) on the panel.

● **3D Rotation (W)**

Use this tool to rotate a symbol in 3-D space. This tool shares space with the 3D Translation Tool (G).

● **Lasso (L)**

Use this tool to select irregular shapes.

● **Pen (P)**

Use this tool to draw precise Bezier curves. This tool also shares space with tools to modify your Bezier curves.

● **Text (T)**

Use this tool to draw text boxes or edit text.

● **Line (N)**

Use this tool to draw straight lines.

● **Rectangle (R)**

Use this tool to draw square and rectangle shapes. This tool shares space on the Tools panel with the Oval (O), Rectangle Primitive, Oval Primitive, and PolyStar tools.

● **Pencil (Y)**

Use this tool to draw lines freehand.

● **Brush (B)**

Use this tool to draw with a fill color, much like a paintbrush. This tool shares space with the Spray Brush tool.

● **Deco (U)**

Use this tool to draw decorative patterns.

● **Bone (X)**

This tool is used to create objects with inverse kinematics. Inverse kinematic objects are manipulated based on bones and joints like a skeleton for an animated character. It shares space with the Bind tool (Z). Both are used in character animation.

● **Paint Bucket (K)**

This tool fills shapes with color. It shares space with the Ink Bottle (S) tool, which is used to apply strokes.

● **Eyedropper (I)**

Use this tool to copy the attributes of one object to another.

● **Eraser (E)**

This tool erases parts of an illustration.

● **Hand (H)**

This tool allows you to move around the Stage and work area. You can temporarily access the Hand tool by holding down the Spacebar.

● **Zoom (M)**

This tool allows you to zoom in on the work area for a closer look or zoom out for a larger view.

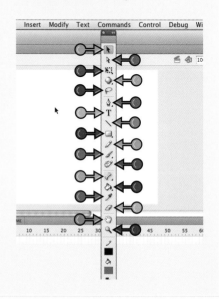

COLOR TOOLS

- **Stroke Color**

  Click this to select a color for lines and shape outlines.

- **Fill Color**

  Click this to select a color for fills.

- **Black and White**

  Resets your colors to black strokes and white fills.

- **Swap Colors**

  Change your fill color to your stroke color, and vice versa.

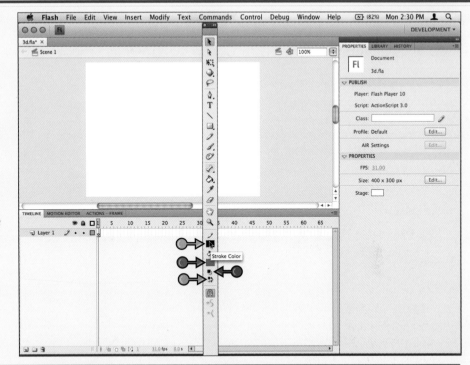

TOOL MODIFIERS

- Many of the tools in Flash have options. This area of the Tools panel displays those options when each tool is activated.

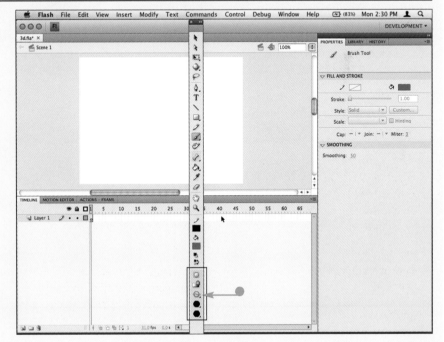

Understanding Groups

Groups are a great way to keep your illustrations and other artwork organized. They also make moving around multiple parts of a drawing easy. Understanding the nature of Groups also helps you understand more complex topics like symbols and nesting of symbols.

The Merge Drawing Model

The default method of drawing in Flash uses what is called the Merge Drawing model. Essentially, anything you draw that overlaps anything else is merged together. This can be an asset when drawing shapes within shapes or trying to cut a shape out of another. You can also combine shapes to create new and more complex ones using this model.

Object Drawing Model

Object drawing actually draws what are called groups. These groups are self-contained and are not overwritten by drawing on top of them. Flash gives these groups a bounding box when selected. You can still use groups when in the Merge Drawing model; you just need to explicitly group items on the Stage.

Nesting Groups

One great feature of groups is the ability to nest one group inside of another. For example, if you have a drawing of an apple, your apple group might contain a fruit group and a stem group. You might also have another group nested in your apple group that contains only highlights and shadows.

Arrange Groups

Because groups do not overwrite other groups on the Stage, you can arrange them. Arranging allows you to place things on top of each other, much like making a sandwich, in the order that you want them to appear.

Limitations of Groups in Flash

While groups are fantastic for creating illustrations and user interface elements, Flash does not allow you to do certain things. You cannot animate a group with a tween. You also do not have nearly as many properties to choose from as you would with a MovieClip, graphic, or button symbol.

You can draw just about any shape in Flash just by using the Line tool. For drawing precision curves, you should use the Pen tool. Lines are also called *strokes* in Flash, particularly when they form the outline of a shape or illustration.

DRAW A STRAIGHT LINE

1. Click the **Line** tool (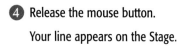).

2. Move the mouse pointer over the Stage area ([k] changes to [+]).

3. Click and drag to draw a line to your desired length.

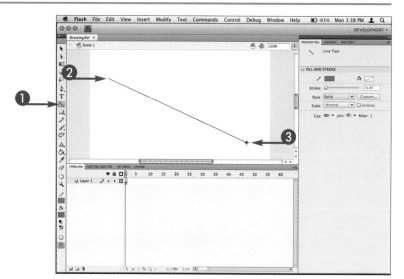

4. Release the mouse button.

   Your line appears on the Stage.

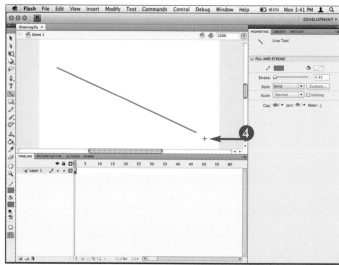

DRAW A VERTICAL OR HORIZONTAL LINE

1 Click the **Line** tool (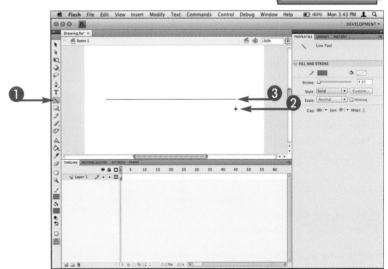).

2 Move the mouse pointer over the Stage area (changes to).

3 Click and drag while holding **Shift**. Drag vertically for a vertical line, horizontally for a horizontal line, and at an angle to create a perfect 45-degree line.

4 Release the mouse button.

Your vertical or horizontal line appears.

Note: If you click **View, Snapping, Snap to Objects,** you can also draw precise vertical and horizontal lines by dragging close to vertical or horizontal.

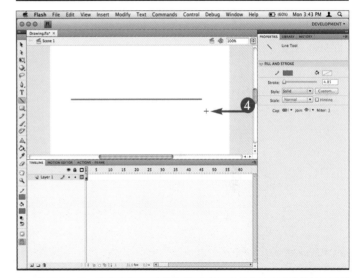

TIPS

How do I control the line thickness and style?

You modify the properties of your line in the Properties panel (**Ctrl**+**F3** / **⌘**+**F3**) before you draw. To adjust the thickness of a line, click and drag the **Stroke** slider. You can also use the **Style** drop-down menu to select a dashed, dotted, or other line style.

What do the Cap, Join, and Miter properties do?

The Cap style refers to the shape of the ends of your line segment. If you draw thick lines you will notice the ends either being semicircles or square. Modifying the Cap property allows you to control which type of line ends you get. The Join property allows you to adjust how multiple lines are connected, either as rounded, square, or mitered junctions. Mitered junctions create an angle opposite to the angle that the lines are connected.

Draw Lines Freehand with the Pencil Tool

You can use the Pencil tool to draw freehand lines. It can be very helpful if you want an illustration to appear to be hand drawn or if you want to write script that looks like it was written on a piece of paper.

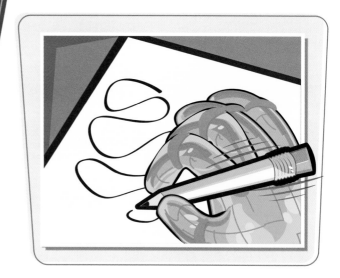

Draw Lines Freehand with the Pencil Tool

① Click the Pencil tool (🖉).

② Move the pointer over the Stage area (🔖 changes to 🖉).

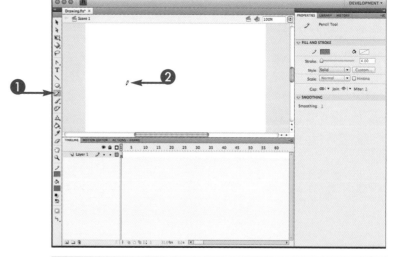

③ Click and drag to start drawing the line.

④ Stop dragging and release the mouse button.

Flash automatically smooths your line when you release the mouse.

Note: *If your line does not automatically smooth, click on the **Pencil Mode modifier** (⑤) and click **Smooth.***

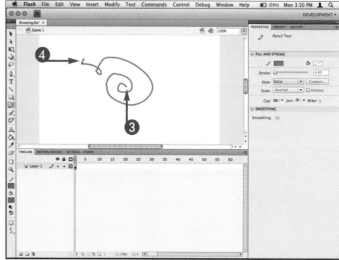

USE THE STRAIGHTEN PENCIL MODE

① Click ✐.

② Click the **Pencil Mode modifier** (⌊S⌋).

③ Click **Straighten.**

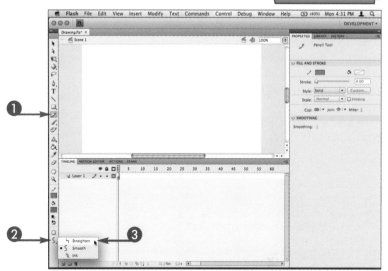

④ Click and drag on the Stage to begin drawing.

⑤ Stop dragging and release the mouse button.

Lines appear straightened.

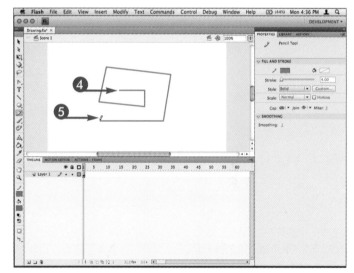

TIPS

How can I select all the segments of my freehand line?

First, you must click the Selection tool. Clicking once on a freehand line only selects a single line segment or curve. But if you double-click on a line segment, all intersecting and connecting lines are selected.

Can I draw perfectly straight lines with the Pencil tool?

Yes, but they can only be vertical, horizontal, or 45 degree lines. You can try this by using the Pencil tool while pressing and holding Shift.

Draw Fills with the Brush Tool

You can use the Brush tool to draw shapes much like you would with a paintbrush. The Brush tool differs from the Pencil tool in that it creates fills rather than strokes. Fills are contiguous blocks of color, while strokes are comprised of curves and line segments.

Draw Fills with the Brush Tool

① Click the Brush tool ( ).

● Your cursor changes to a black circle.

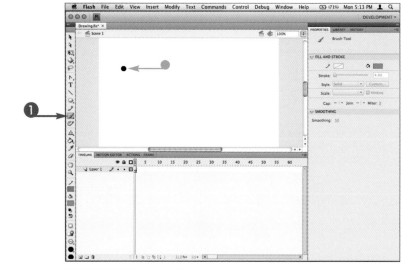

② Click the Brush Size menu.

③ Click a brush size.

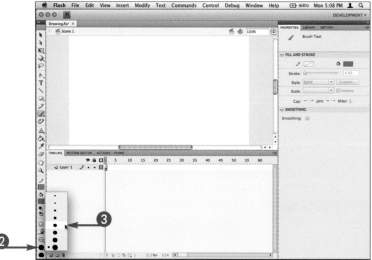

④ Click the Brush Shape menu.

⑤ Click a brush shape.

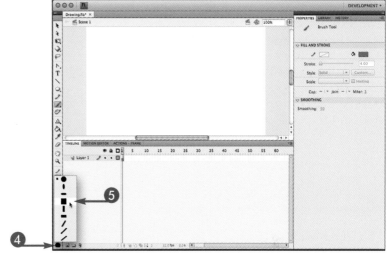

⑥ Click and drag to begin drawing.

Your fill appears as you draw.

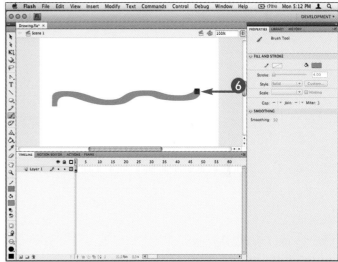

TIP

What do the different brush modes do?

You can choose from five brush modes by clicking the Brush Mode menu on the Tools panel.

Paint Normal () paints your literal brush strokes anywhere on the Stage over white space, strokes, and fills.

Paint Fills () paints white space and fills, but does not paint over strokes.

Paint Behind () paints on white space, but does not paint on top of any lines or fills on the same layer.

Paint Selection () paints only inside your selection.

Paint Inside () paints over the first fill that you click on and nowhere else.

Draw Shapes with the Pen Tool

You can draw precise lines and curves with the Pen tool. It is probably the most-used drawing tool for creating vector illustrations. You draw lines, or paths, by clicking to create anchor points, and then dragging to adjust the curvature of your line.

① Click the Pen tool (![pen]).

② Move the pointer over the Stage area (![pointer] changes to ![pen cursor]).

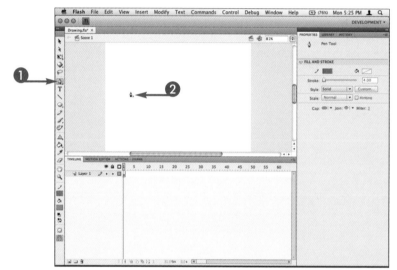

③ Click and begin dragging to create your first anchor point and handles.

④ Stop dragging and release the mouse button.

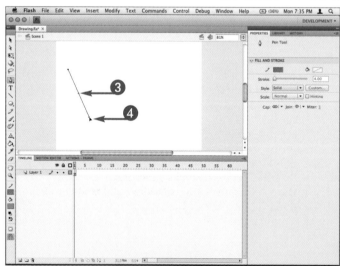

⑤ Click and drag where you want your endpoint.

⑥ Release the mouse button.

⑦ Move your cursor over your starting point.

(🔻 changes to 🔻).

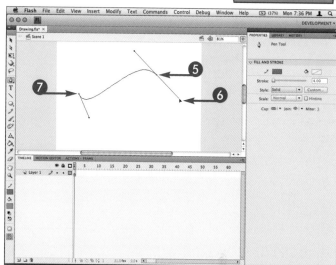

⑧ Click and drag your first point to complete your shape.

⑨ Release the mouse button.

Your shape is closed.

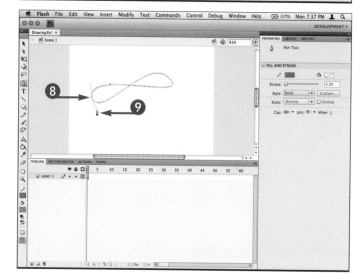

TIPS

How can I edit points on a curved line?

Use the Subselection tool (🔻) to make changes to a curved line you created using the Pen tool. Move the cursor over a handle on the line or over an endpoint of the line. Click and drag any of these points to reposition and reshape the line or curve.

Some of my lines don't have handles and are not curved. How do I make them curves?

Click and hold down the Pen tool in the Tools panel, and select the Convert Anchor Point tool (🔻). Then click and drag any anchor point on your line to create the handles and curve your line.

Draw Rectangles and Ovals

You can use the Rectangle and Oval tools to easily draw basic shapes in Flash. Although you can use the Pen tool or Line tool to create these shapes, it is much faster to use the dedicated shape tools.

Draw Rectangles and Ovals

DRAW AN EMPTY RECTANGLE

1. Click the **Rectangle** tool ().

2. Click the **Fill Color** palette ().

3. Click the **No Color** button ().

Note: You can also click the Fill Color button in the Properties inspector and select the No Color option.

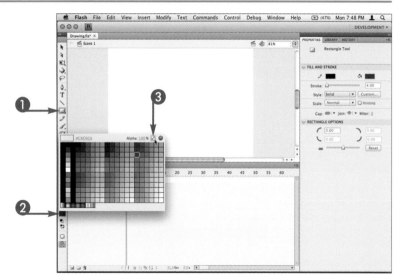

4. Move the cursor over the Stage area (changes to).

5. Click and drag to draw your rectangle.

6. Release the mouse button.

    Flash draws your rectangle on the Stage.

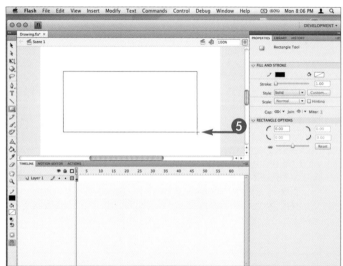

DRAW AN OVAL WITH A FILL COLOR

① Click and hold the mouse button down on the **Rectangle** tool (▢).

● A fly-out menu appears.

② Click the **Oval** tool (⬭).

③ Click the **Fill Color** palette and select a color from the swatches.

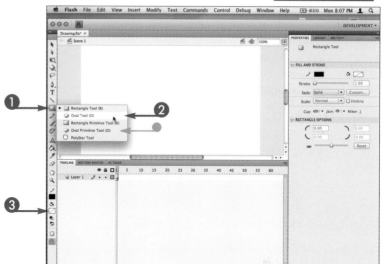

④ Move the cursor over the Stage area (➤ changes to ✛).

⑤ Click and drag to draw the oval.

Flash completes the shape using the color you selected to fill the oval.

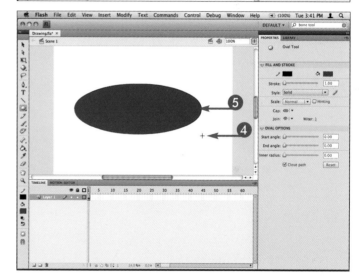

How do I draw a rectangle with rounded corners?

You can use the Properties inspector to modify the corners of a rectangle shape. If the Properties inspector is not open, press Ctrl+F3 (⌘+F3). Change the Rectangle Corner Radius setting to create the type of rounded corners you want for the shape. Click and drag the slider control to the right to designate how much curvature you want for the corners, or drag the slider to the left to create inverted corners. You can also type the radius for your rounded corners in the text field.

How do I adjust the properties of the Stroke in my shape?

You can use the Properties inspector to modify the corners of a rectangle shape. If the Properties inspector is not open, press Ctrl+F3 (⌘+F3). The Fill and Stroke options are very similar to the options for the Line tool and are adjusted the same way.

Fill Shapes with the Paint Bucket Tool

You can use the Paint Bucket tool to quickly fill in objects such as shapes. You can fill objects with a color, a gradient effect, or even a picture. The Flash color palette comes with numerous colors and shades as well as several premade gradient effects from which to choose.

Fill Shapes with the Paint Bucket Tool

ADD A FILL

1 Click the **Paint Bucket** tool (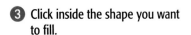).

(arrow changes to bucket).

2 Choose a **Fill Color** from the palette.

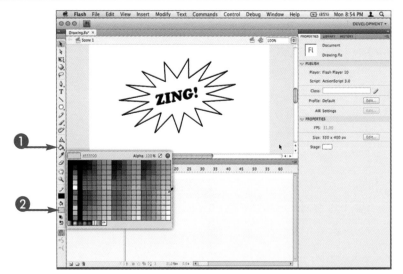

3 Click inside the shape you want to fill.

Flash fills your shape with the new color.

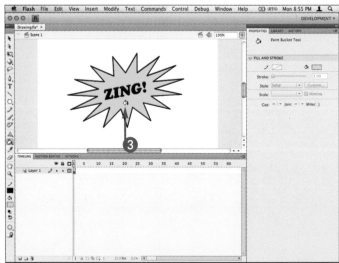

ADD A GRADIENT FILL

① Click the **Paint Bucket** tool (🪣).

(▶ changes to 🪣).

② Click the **Fill Color** palette.

③ Click a gradient color effect.

Note: *See Chapter 3 to learn more about creating new gradient effects.*

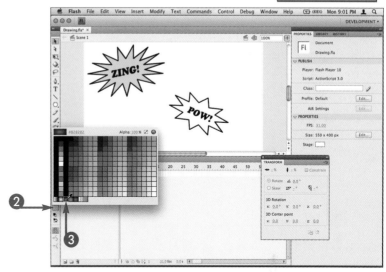

④ Click inside your shape and drag in the direction you want the gradient to blend.

Release the mouse button; your gradient fills the shape.

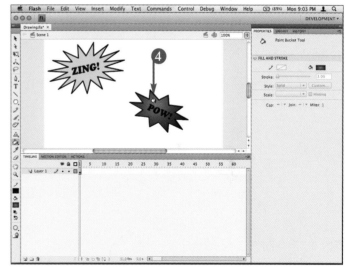

What is a gradient effect?

A *gradient effect* is a fill that is composed of multiple colors with a gradual transition from one color to the next. With Flash, you can create a linear gradient effect that blends color shading from left to right or top to bottom, or create a radial gradient effect that blends color shading from the middle to the outer edges, or vice versa.

What does the Gap Size modifier do?

When you select the Paint Bucket tool, the Gap Size modifier appears at the bottom of the Tools panel. Click the Gap Size modifier to display four settings. Selecting the Don't Close Gaps option only fills shapes that are closed. Selecting the other options fill shapes that are not closed to varying degrees.

CHAPTER 5

Modifying and Positioning Artwork

Do you want to modify and enhance your art or add complexity to illustrations? This chapter shows you how to edit, apply new fills, change line styles, and align elements to perfect your drawing.

Using the Eraser Tool

You can use the Eraser tool to clean up any unwanted lines or fill in your design. It is also useful for erasing portions of a fill and creating transparent areas or highlights.

Using the Eraser Tool

① Click the **Eraser** tool (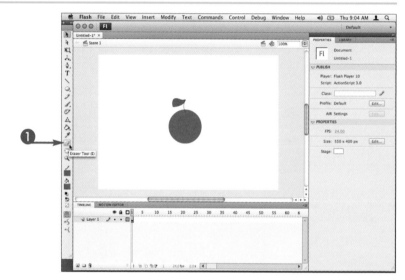).

To quickly erase entire lines or fills, you can click the **Faucet** modifier (🪣) and then click the item you want to erase.

② Click the **Eraser Shape** modifier (●).

③ Click a size or shape for the eraser.

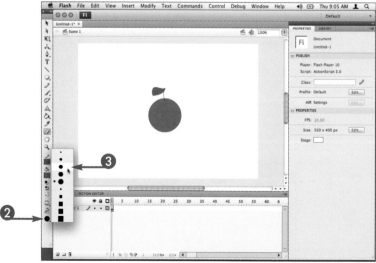

④ Click and drag to begin erasing.

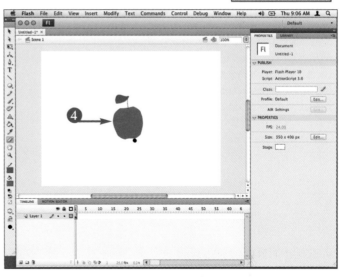

⑤ Release the mouse button when finished erasing.

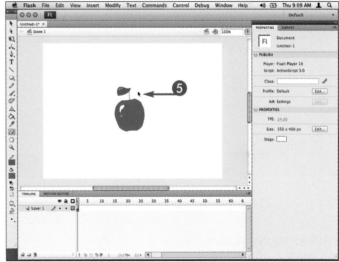

TIPS

What do the Eraser modifiers do?
You can use one of five modifiers with the Eraser tool:

Erase Normal (🖫): Lets you erase over anything on the Stage

Erase Fills (🖫): Erases inside fill areas but not lines

Erase Lines (🖫): Erases only lines

Erase Selected Fills (🖫): Does just that — erases only the selected fill

Erase Inside (🖫): Erases only inside the selected area

Select Artwork

You can use the tools in Flash to select artwork objects or portions of artwork. There are two main ways you can select art. The most common is to use the Selection tool and click the element you want to select. The second is to use the Lasso tool to draw a shape that encircles everything you want to select.

SELECT MULTIPLE ELEMENTS

1 Click the Selection tool ( ).

2 While holding the Shift key, click one or more elements that are on the Stage.

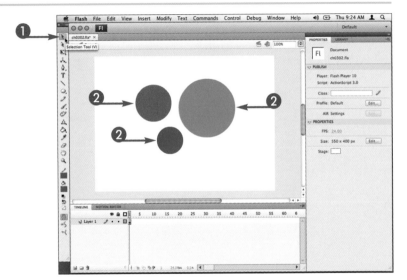

● Flash highlights each element you select.

You can move, delete, or edit the selected elements together.

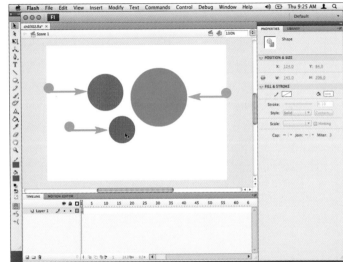

LASSO ELEMENTS

1 To select an irregularly shaped object, click the **Lasso** tool (🪢).

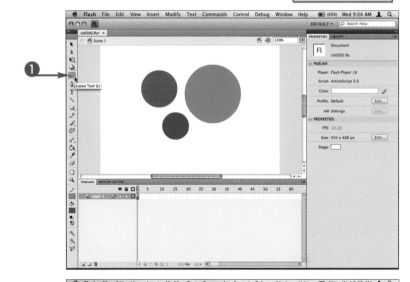

2 Click and drag the lasso around the items you want to select until you reach the point where you started.

3 Release the mouse button.

4 Flash highlights everything within the lasso shape.

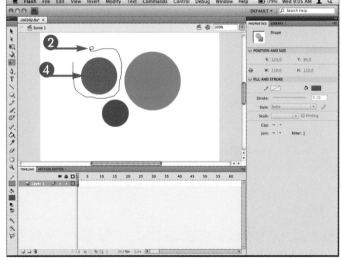

TIPS

How can I select complex shapes?
Drawing around irregular items with the Lasso tool can be difficult. For additional help, use the Lasso tool's Polygon Mode modifier (🪢) in the Modifier tray at the bottom of the Tools panel. You can alternately hold down the **Alt** (**Option**) key when using the Lasso tool to enter Polygon mode.

How do I select just a fill and not its border?
Using the Selection tool (🔺), simply click the fill to select it. To select both the fill and the fill's border, double-click the fill. To deselect a fill or border at any time, just click anywhere outside the selected object.

Change the Color of Lines and Fills

You can change the colors of the artwork you draw by using the Bucket tool and the Ink Bottle tool. When you want to replace the color of many elements at once, it is easiest to select the items you want to change and choose new colors from the Color panel.

① Click the **Selection tool** ( ).

② While holding the Shift key, click one or more elements that are on the Stage.

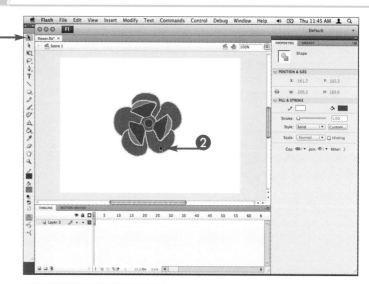

③ Open the Fill Color Picker panel by clicking the Fill Color swatch in the Properties inspector.

④ Click a new color from the swatches.

Your selected fills change to the new color.

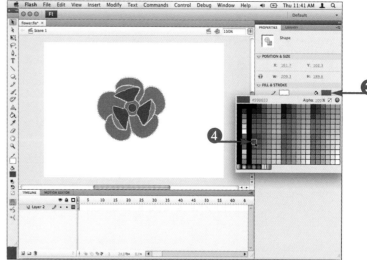

5 Click the Stroke Color swatch in the Properties inspector and select a new color.

6 Click a new color from the swatches.

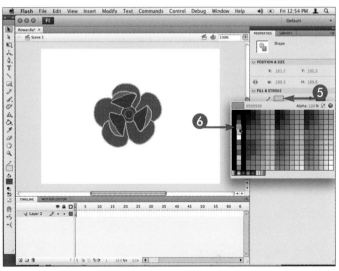

7 Your selected strokes change to the new color.

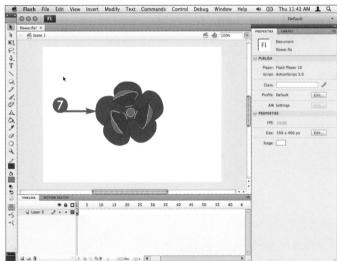

TIPS

How can I choose a more precise color that doesn't appear in the swatches?

There are many ways to use custom colors. One way is to click and drag in the rainbow gradient in the Color panel; another is to type RGB values into the panel; a third is to type a hexadecimal color value at the bottom of the Color panel or at the top of the swatches.

#CC99FF

How do I create colors that are translucent?

Click and drag the **Alpha** slider in the Color panel to adjust the percentage of transparency. You can also type an alpha value into the text field.

Customize Lines with the Ink Bottle Tool

You can change the appearance of lines in your illustration with the Ink Bottle tool. Basically, you choose a new set of properties that you want to apply to strokes in your artwork. Then you apply new properties to already drawn strokes.

① Select the **Ink Bottle** tool (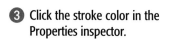) by clicking and holding the **Paint Bucket** tool button in the Tools panel.

② Open the Properties inspector.

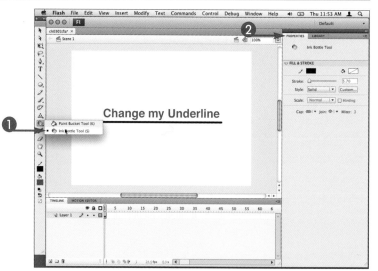

③ Click the stroke color in the Properties inspector.

④ Select a new stroke color from the swatches.

⑤ Click and drag the Stroke slider to adjust the stroke size.

⑥ Click a stroke style from the Style drop-down list.

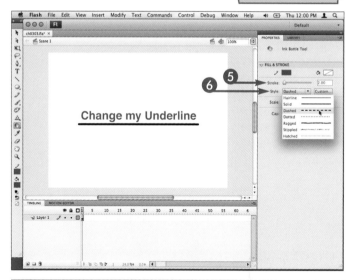

⑦ Click on any lines on the Stage to which you want the new properties applied.

The appearance of your lines change to reflect the new properties.

 TIPS

How can I quickly switch to a tool that is hidden behind another tool?

Each tool in Flash has a key on the keyboard that corresponds to it. You can press ⓢ to activate the Ink Bottle tool. To find the other shortcut keys, simply move your mouse over a tool in the Tools panel and a tool tip appears with the tool's name as well as the shortcut key in parentheses.

Reshape Lines and Shape Outlines

You can reshape any line or shape outline in different ways. You can use the Selection tool to modify lines by clicking and dragging when a special icon appears. You can also use the Subselection tool to modify anchor points and handles of lines and curves.

RESHAPE WITH THE SELECTION TOOL

① Click the **Selection** tool (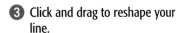).

② Move your cursor near a line or fill until the a curved line appears next to the cursor (▸).

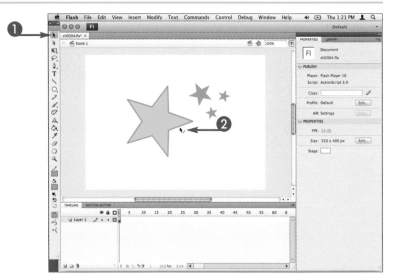

③ Click and drag to reshape your line.

Release the mouse button.

The curvature of your line is changed.

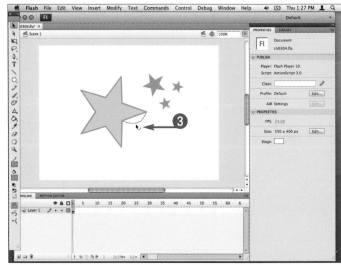

**RESHAPE WITH THE
SUBSELECTION TOOL**

1 Click the **Subselection** tool ( ).

2 Click on the line you want to
reshape.

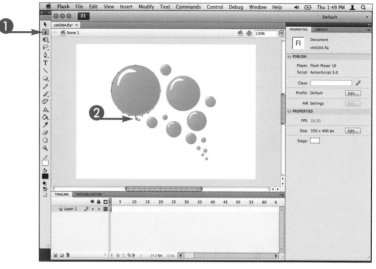

3 Click and drag anchor points and
handles to modify your lines.

You can click an empty area of
the Stage or work area to see
your edits completed.

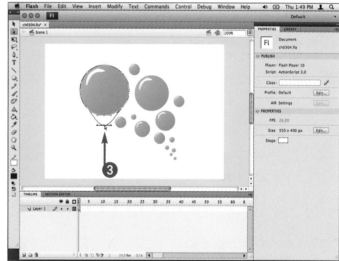

TIPS

How can I add or delete anchor points in my illustration?

If you click and hold the Pen tool, you see the additional Pen tools. They include
Add Anchor Point, Delete Anchor Point, and Convert Anchor Point. You can use
these tools to simplify or add complexity to your illustration.

Copy Attributes

You can use the Eyedropper tool to quickly copy attributes from one object to another. Copying attributes rather than reassigning them one at a time can save you time and effort. The Eyedropper tool copies fill and line attributes and enables you to apply the same formatting to other fills and lines.

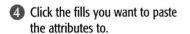
1 Click the **Eyedropper** tool (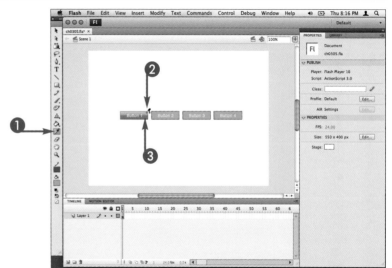).

2 Move the Eyedropper tool over the fill you want to copy.

3 Click the fill (✍ changes to ✍).

4 Click the fills you want to paste the attributes to.

Flash immediately applies the fills.

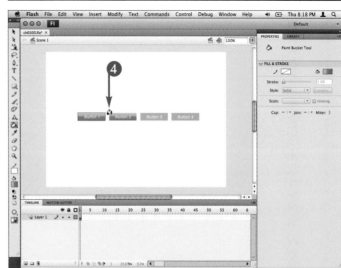

⑤ Click (🖊).

⑥ Move the cursor over the line from which you want to copy the attributes (🖊 changes to 🖊).

⑦ Click the line from which you want to copy the attributes (🖊 changes to 🖊).

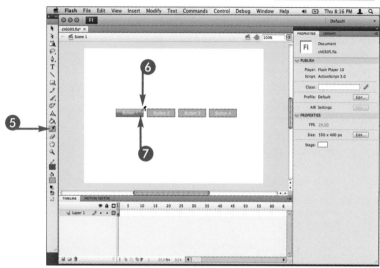

⑧ Click the lines you want to paste the attributes to.

Flash applies the copied line style.

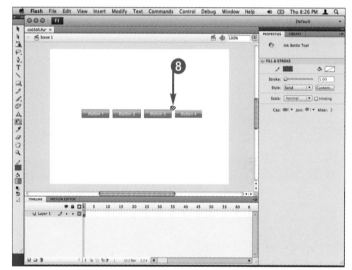

My Eyedropper tool does not work. Why?
When copying line attributes with the Eyedropper, you cannot paste those attributes with the Ink Bottle on grouped lines. Be sure to ungroup the lines first and then try copying and pasting the line attributes to each line.

Create Custom Color Swatches

You can add swatches to your Color panel to create a custom color set for your Flash project. Using custom swatches is a great way to keep your palette consistent. You can also save your favorite color sets to use in other Flash movies.

Create Custom Color Swatches

ADD A FILL

① Click **Window.**

② **Click Color.**

The Color panel appears.

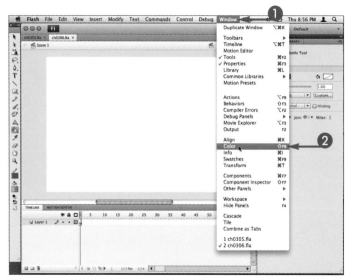

③ Click and drag in the color picker until you find the color you want.

④ Adjust the transparency of your color by clicking and dragging the **Alpha** slider.

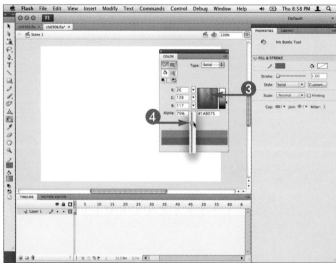

⑤ Click the Color panel drop-down ( ) in the upper-right corner of the panel.

⑥ Select **Add Swatch.**

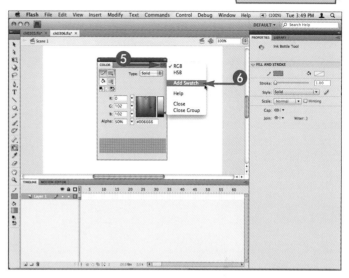

⑦ Click on the Fill color menu.

● Your new color appears in the palette.

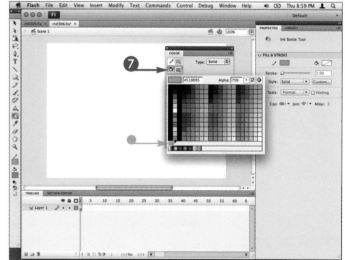

TIPS

How do I save and load my new colors?

Click **Window**, and then click **Swatches** to open the Swatches panel. In the upper-right corner of the Swatches panel, click and select **Save Colors**. This saves your colors as a CLR file. To load your colors, you can choose **Add Colors** or **Replace Colors** from the same drop-down menu and load your CLR file.

Can I add gradients to my color swatches?

Yes. You add a gradient to the palette the same way you add a solid color. Gradients, however, appear at the bottom of the panel.

Make a Custom Gradient Fill

Much like adding custom color swatches, you can add custom gradients to your Color panel. Designers use the swatches they create to maintain consistency across their designs. You can use your swatches to create a consistent look throughout your design or illustration.

① Click **Window**.

② **Click Color**.

The Colors panel opens.

③ Click the **Type** drop-down menu in the Color panel and select **Linear.**

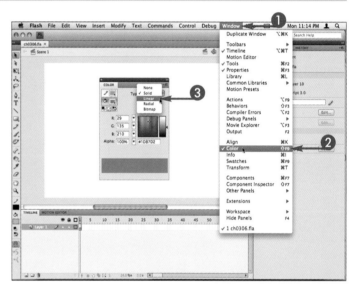

④ Click the left swatch of the gradient to select it.

⑤ Click and drag on the Rainbow Gradient in the Color panel to select a hue.

⑥ Click and drag the Brightness slider and adjust your color.

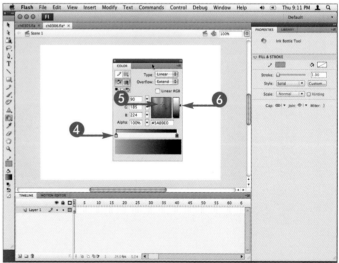

⑦ Click the right swatch of the gradient to select it.

⑧ Click and drag on the Rainbow Gradient in the Color panel to select another hue.

⑨ Click and drag the Brightness slider and adjust your color.

⑩ Click the Color panel drop-down menu (▾≡) in the upper-right corner of the panel and select **Add Swatch.**

Your new gradient is added to your swatches.

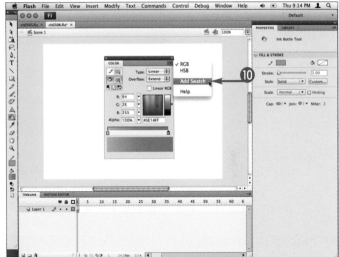

How do I create a gradient that transitions through multiple colors?

When you click between the two swatches of the gradient in the Color panel, your cursor will have a plus next to it (▸₊). Clicking when the plus is visible adds another color swatch to your gradient, and you can edit that color the same way you changed the other gradient colors.

How do I remove a color from my gradient?

You can click and drag any color swatch in the gradient and drag down to remove a swatch from the gradient. However, you must have more than two colors in your gradient to remove one.

Transform a Gradient Fill

You can change the way your gradient fill appears by using the Gradient Transform tool. It allows you to rotate and scale your fill. This tool is hidden behind the regular Transform tool in the Tools panel.

① Click the **Oval** tool (⬭).

② Click the **Fill Color** modifier (▣).

③ Click a gradient fill.

④ Click and drag on the stage with (⬭).

Flash draws an oval filled with a gradient.

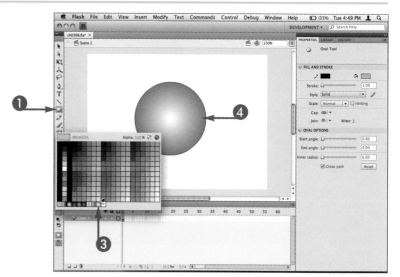

⑤ Click and hold the **Transform** tool in the Tools panel until the menu appears.

⑥ Select the **Gradient Transform** tool (▦).

⑦ Click on the gradient fill inside your shape.

The transform handles appear that allow you to rotate, scale, and move the center point of your fill.

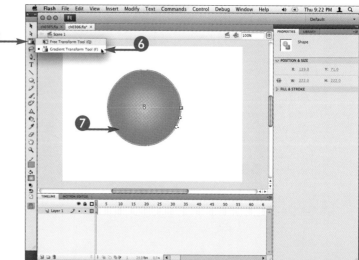

⑧ Click and drag the small white circle in the center of your fill to move the gradient's origin.

⑨ Click and drag the small white circle on the corner of your fill to rotate it.

⑩ Click and drag the small white square on the side of your fill to adjust the fill's scaling.

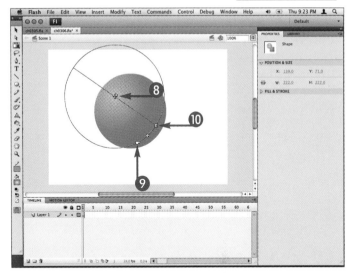

⑪ Click an empty part of the Stage to see your results.

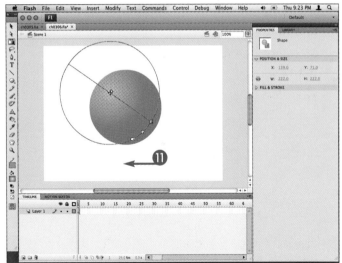

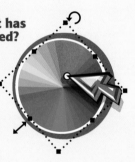

TIPS

Can I edit my gradient after it has been transformed?

Yes. If you select your gradient fill and edit its parameters in the Color panel, your changes are applied to the selected fill.

My fill takes up the entire Stage and I cannot see the fill's edit points. How do I view the edit points to transform the fill?

Click the **Zoom** tool (🔍). Then, click the **Zoom out** modifier (🔍), and click the Stage to zoom out. You can also click the **View** menu, click **Magnification**, then click a zoom level to zoom out and see more of the work area.

Scale and Rotate Objects with the Free Transform Tool

You can use the Free Transform tool in Flash to rotate, skew, scale, distort, and envelope objects. The default behavior of the Free Transform tool allows you to scale, rotate, and skew. There are modifiers at the bottom of the Tools panel that restrict the tool to one type of transformation.

Scale and Rotate Objects with the Free Transform Tool

① Click the **Free Transform** tool (▦).

② Click on the group or object you want to transform.

● A bounding box appears with handles for the transformation.

③ Move your cursor to one of the corners of the bounding box.

④ Click and drag on the corner of the object, and release the mouse button when you see your desired scale.

⑤ Move your cursor just outside the corner of the bounding box (⬉ changes to ↷).

⑥ Click and drag to rotate.

Your gradient fill rotates.

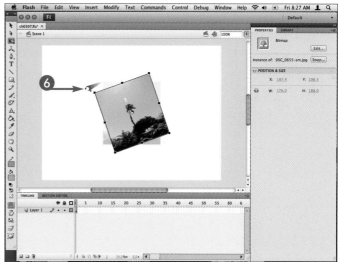

TIPS

How do I scale while maintaining the proportions of my group or object?

Press and hold the **Shift** key while scaling with the Free Transform tool to constrain to the proportions of your group or object.

How do I change the center point that my transform is based on?

You can click and drag the small white circle that appears in the middle of your transform to reposition the center point.

Create Groups of Lines, Fills, and Shapes

You can use groups to keep the elements of your artwork manageable. Groups are also very handy for drawing because they allow you to draw on top of another element without erasing what is behind it.

1 Click the **Selection** tool (￼).

2 While holding the ⇧Shift key, click one or more elements on the Stage.

● Flash highlights each item you select.

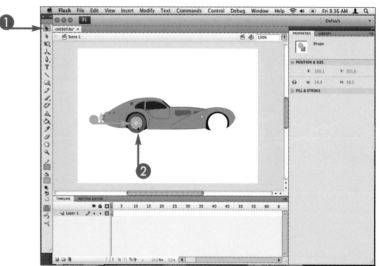

3 Click **Modify**.

4 Click **Group**.

You can also press Ctrl + G (⌘ + G).

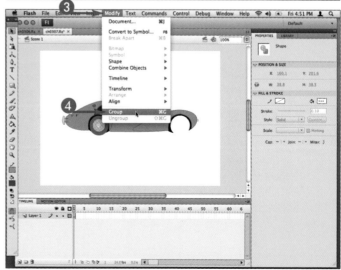

● A bounding box appears around your group.

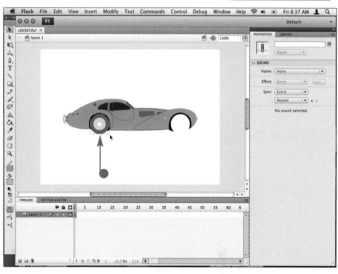

⑤ Click and drag your group to move all the elements of the group together.

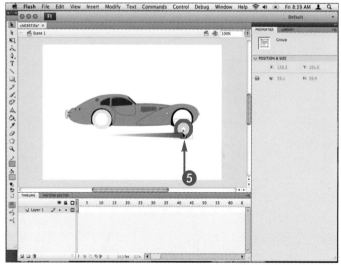

TIPS

How do I edit the elements inside my group?

You can double-click on your group to *go inside* your group. The individual elements are editable there. Double-click an empty area of the Stage to return to the normal editing mode.

How can I convert my group back to its raw elements?

You can do this in two ways. The first way is to select your group and click **Modify** and then **Break Apart**. Breaking your group apart removes all selected groups. You can also click **Modify,** and then **Ungroup**.

Send Groups Forward and Backward in Space

You can move lines, fills, and other objects behind or on top of each other using groups. By grouping items, you can then use the Arrange menu to adjust the depth of any group or symbol on the same layer.

Send Groups Forward and Backward in Space

① Click the **Rectangle** tool (▢).

② Click the **Object Drawing** modifier (▢) at the bottom of the Tools panel.

Note: *The Object Drawing modifier automatically draws your rectangle as a group.*

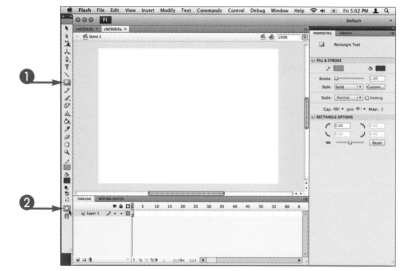

③ Draw a rectangle on the Stage.

④ Change your Fill color.

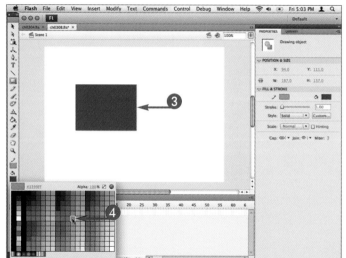

⑤ Draw a second rectangle that overlaps the one already on the Stage.

⑥ Click the **Selection** tool (▶).

⑦ Click the rectangle that is on top to select it.

You can choose a different fill color for the rectangle on top.

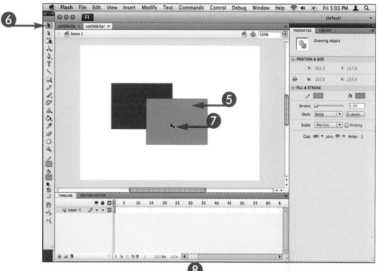

⑧ Click **Modify**.

⑨ Click **Arrange**.

⑩ To send the front rectangle back, click **Send to Back**.

The frontmost rectangle is now in the back.

⑪ To send the back rectangle forward, click the **Selection** tool (▶).

⑫ Click the rectangle that is on the bottom to select it.

⑬ Click **Modify**, **Arrange**, and **Bring to Front**.

The back-most rectangle is now in the front.

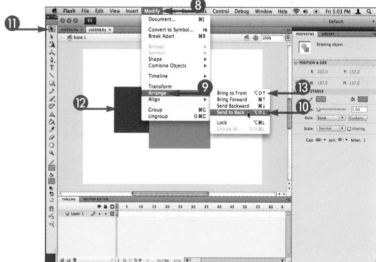

What are the other ways to arrange groups?

In addition to Send To Back, you can also use Bring to Front, Bring Forward, and Send Backward.

It didn't work. What happened?

Arranging objects and groups on the Stage only works when they are on the same layer. Make sure all the elements you want to arrange are not on different layers. See Chapter 6 for more information on layers.

Align Shapes

You can use the Align tool to make any shapes or objects on the Stage align to each other. This is especially useful when you design buttons or icons that you want perfectly aligned. You can also evenly space objects on the Stage using this tool.

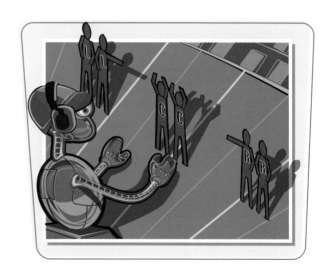

① Select several objects or groups with the **Selection** tool (▶).

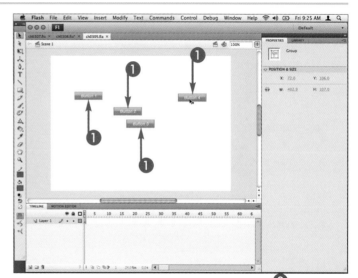

② Click **Window**.

③ Click **Align**.

You can also press Ctrl+K (⌘+K).

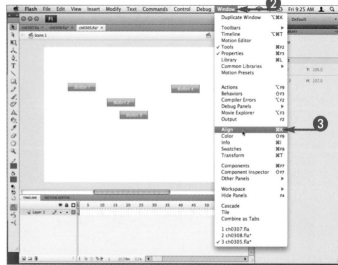

Modifying and Positioning Artwork

④ With the objects selected, click the **Align Vertical Center** button (🖼).

The objects and groups line up perfectly.

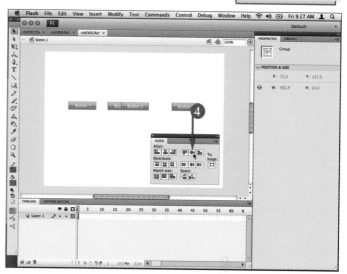

⑤ With the objects still selected, click the **Distribute Vertical Center** button (🖼).

The objects and groups are spaced evenly.

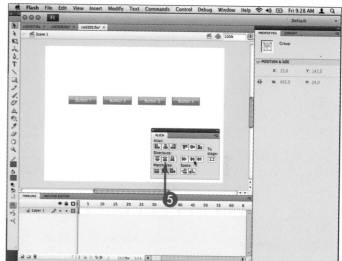

TIPS

What is the difference between Distribute and Space in the Align panel?

Distribute evenly spaced objects based on their centers or edges. When you have elements that are different sizes, sometimes the results appear irregular. To fix this, you can click the **Space** buttons on the Align panel, which create an even amount of space between each element.

Can I align objects relative to the Stage?

Yes. Click the **Align/Distribute to Stage** button on the Align panel and they no longer align relative to each other. They will align to the Stage.

Snap to Grid

You can keep elements aligned while you design your layout by using the grid and enabling Snap to Grid. Many interaction designers use a grid system to lay out their interfaces.

① Click **View**.

② Click **Grid**.

③ Click **Show Grid**.

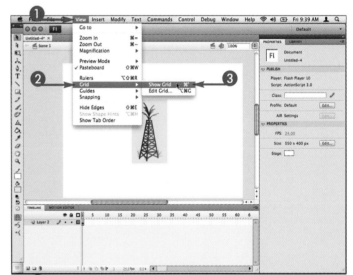

● A grid appears on the Stage.

④ Click **View**.

⑤ Click **Snapping**.

⑥ Click **Snap To Grid**.

An item that is clicked and dragged snaps to positions along the grid.

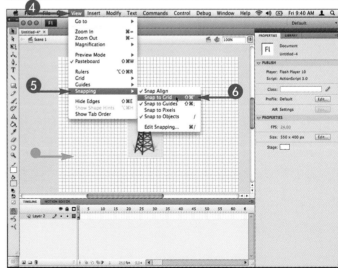

Snap to Objects

Much like Snap to Grid, you can use Snap to Objects to help you align elements on the Stage without having to use the Align tool.

Snap to Objects

① Click **View**.

② Click **Snapping**.

③ Click **Snap to Objects**.

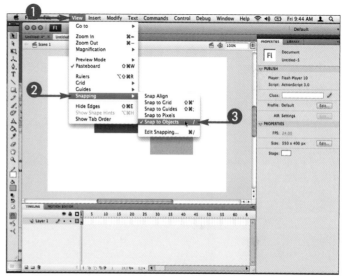

④ Click and drag any object or group.

⑤ Your dragged object or group snaps into place when it is near another object.

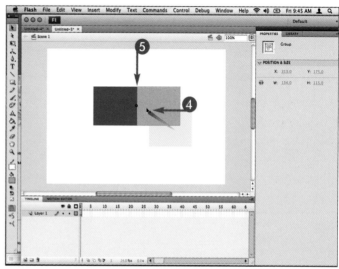

Working with Text

Do you need to add text to your Flash project? In this chapter, you learn how to add text to your illustrations and interactive projects.

Add Text with the Text Tool

You can add text to your Flash movie with the Text tool. In Flash, text fields have many properties, and can be formatted a number of ways. To start, you can create your text fields to be either fixed width or dynamic width. You can make further adjustments in the Properties inspector to get your desired look.

Dynamic width text fields expand in width as you type, whereas fixed width text fields wrap your text to a new line, but maintain their width.

Add Text with the Text Tool

CREATE A TEXT BOX WITH A DYNAMIC WIDTH

1. Click the **Text** tool (T) or press T.

2. Move the mouse pointer over the Stage area (arrow changes to cross).

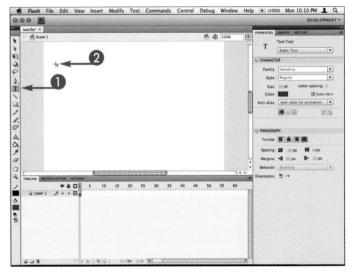

3. Click on the Stage.

● A text box appears on the Stage.

4. Type your text.

Your text appears on the Stage as you type.

● A circle in the upper-right corner of the text box indicates that it has a dynamic width.

To edit your text, you can click on the text with the **Text** tool (T) or double-click with the **Selection** tool (arrow).

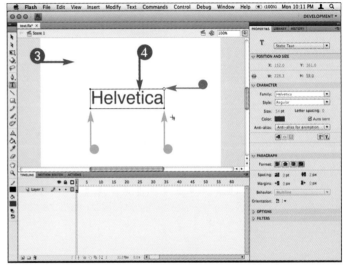

CREATE A TEXT BOX WITH A FIXED WIDTH

1 Click T or press T.

2 Click and drag from left to right on the Stage.

● A box appears on the Stage showing you how wide your text box will be.

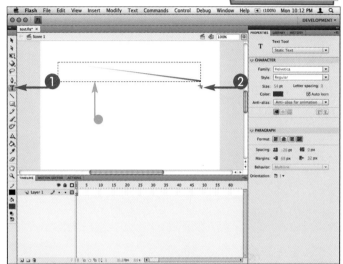

Release the mouse.

4 Type your text.

● A square in the upper-right corner of the text box indicates that it has a fixed width.

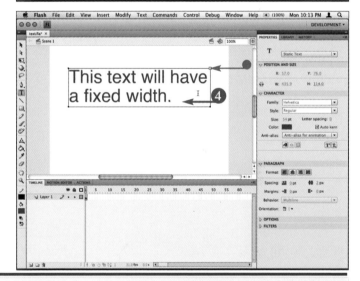

This text will have a fixed width.

TIPS

How can I turn a fixed-width text box into a dynamic-width text box, or vice versa?

Select the text box by clicking on it with the **Text** tool (T) or double-clicking with the **Selection tool** (↖). To switch from dynamic width to fixed, click and drag any corner of the text box to your desired width. To switch from fixed width to dynamic, simply double-click the square in the upper-right corner of the text box. Your text box automatically resizes and becomes dynamic width again.

How can I change the orientation of the text?

You can use the paragraph options in the Properties inspector to change text orientation. Click the **Orientation** button (📑▾), and select the orientation you want. If anything other than the default is selected, a button (📑) appears that allows you to change the orientation of the text in the box.

Format a Paragraph

You can format your text as a paragraph using the Properties inspector. You can align your text left, center, right, or justify. There are also options to set margins, line spacing, and indentation.

SET THE TEXT BOX ALIGNMENT

1. Click the **Selection** tool ( ) or press .

2. Click your text box to select it.

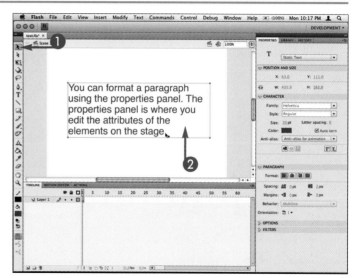

3. Open the Properties inspector.

4. Open the Paragraph options.

5. Click one of the Format buttons to choose basic alignment — left, center, right, or justify — for your paragraph.

   Flash formats your paragraph to the desired alignment.

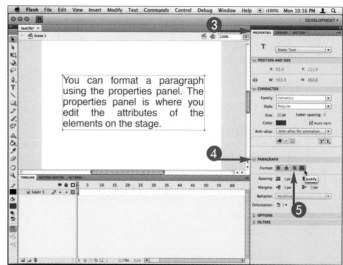

SET INDENTS AND MARGINS

1 Click 🔲 or press Ⓥ.

2 Click your text box to select it.

3 Open the Properties inspector.

4 Adjust spacing by clicking and dragging on the blue-colored values next to Spacing in the Properties inspector.

● This value sets indentation.

● This value sets line spacing.

5 Adjust margins by clicking and dragging on the blue-colored values next to Margins in the Properties inspector.

● This value sets the left margin.

● This value sets the right margin.

TIPS

How can I change the units of measurement for margins and indentation?

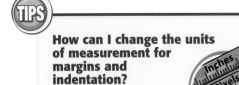

By default, Flash assumes you want to work with pixels as your unit of measure. You can, however, change it to inches, inches (decimal), points, centimeters, millimeters, or pixels. Click **Modify**, and then click **Document**.

How do I get my pixel font to render cleanly?

Pixel fonts can be tricky in Flash because Flash is based on vectors rather than pixels. To get clean pixel fonts, make sure your text box is located on a whole pixel. You can set the position to a whole pixel by entering non-decimal numbers to the X and Y values of the Properties inspector. If your pixel font is still not crisp, make sure your letter spacing, or kerning, is set to zero. You can also turn off anti-aliasing in the Properties inspector by setting the **Anti-alias** property to Bitmap Text in the Properties inspector.

Change Text Colors and Fonts

You can use the Properties inspector to customize the appearance of your text. This includes options for changing color, font, size, and more.

CHANGE FONT AND STYLE

1. Open the Properties inspector.

2. Select the text you want to modify.

   To change the entire text box, you can select it with the **Selection** tool ( ). To format only some of the characters, select them with the **Text** tool (T).

3. Choose a font by clicking the **Family** drop-down list and clicking your desired font.

   Your font changes on the Stage as soon as you choose a font family or style.

CHANGE TEXT COLOR, SIZE, AND SPACING

1 Open the Properties inspector.

2 Select the text you want to modify.

3 Click and drag on the blue number next to Size in the Properties inspector.

(🔍 changes to ↔).

Drag to the left to decrease the point size; drag to the right to make the text larger.

4 Click and drag the blue number next to Letter spacing in the Properties inspector.

(🔍 changes to ↔).

Drag to the left to make the characters closer together; drag to the right to space them farther apart.

5 Click the color swatch next to **Color** in the Properties inspector.

6 Click one of the swatches to choose a new color for your text.

Your text changes to the new color.

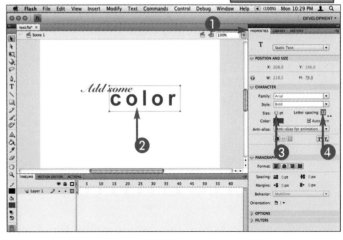

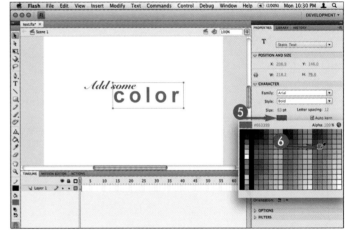

TIPS

Is there a faster way to change my font than to use the menu in the Properties inspector?

Yes. If you click the name of the font in the Properties inspector, you can delete it and start typing the name of the font you want to use. Flash automatically completes the font name after typing just a few characters. When you see the name of the font you want, press Enter and your font changes.

What are the anti-aliasing options for?

Use Device Fonts specifies that your Flash movie does not include font outline information and relies on the fonts installed on the end user's computer.

Bitmap Text (No Anti-Alias) exports font information only at the size of your text field. It results in very crisp type unless it is scaled or rotated.

Anti-Alias For Animation makes your text ignore kerning and spacing information, but renders well at any size.

Anti-Alias For Readability uses the Flash Text Rendering engine to improve legibility. This option is not recommended if you plan to animate your text.

Custom Anti-Alias lets you modify the font's sharpness, smoothness, and thickness.

Copy Text Attributes

After you formatted text box properties the way you want, there is an easy way to make subsequent text boxes share the same properties. You can use the Eyedropper tool with text boxes to automatically copy all properties from a text box and create new text boxes with the same properties.

Copy Text Attributes

① Click the **Eyedropper** tool (✐).

② Move the pointer over a text box (✐ changes to ✐).

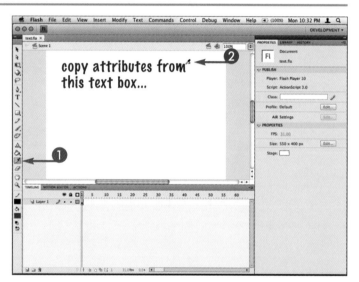

③ Click the text box and move your mouse to a place you want to add text (✐ changes to ⊹).

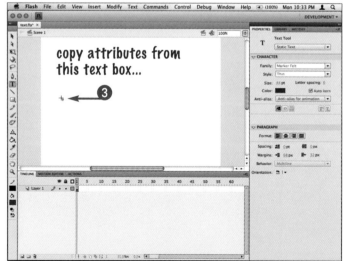

④ Click and drag to create a new text box.

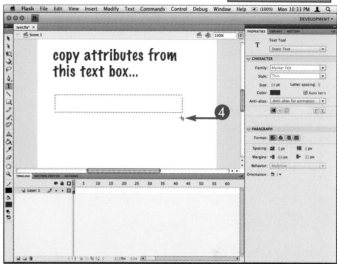

⑤ Begin typing your new text.

By creating a new text box after using the Eyedropper tool, your text will have the same formatting.

TIPS

Can I copy the attributes of elements other than text?

Yes, you can copy attributes from lines and fills as well. The Eyedropper tool changes its icon depending on what you roll the tool over. Moving your mouse over a fill displays a small paint bucket next to the Eyedropper. Strokes show a miniature ink bottle, and text displays a small letter A. Chapter 3 demonstrates how to copy attributes of lines, strokes, and fills.

How do I copy a fill color to my text without changing its formatting?

You can copy a fill color from any other fill and apply it to your text using the Eyedropper tool. Click on your text box with the **Selection** tool ( ) and then click the **Eyedropper** tool ( ) or press . Then click on any fill on the Stage to apply a copy of that color to your text.

Adjust Text Kerning and Leading

You can modify your type setting on a very granular level in Flash. Leading and kerning can be adjusted for an entire text box, you can kern a single word, or you can set each letter's kerning individually for the most precise type treatment.

KERN AND CHANGE LEADING FOR AN ENTIRE TEXT BOX

1. Click on a text box with the **Selection** tool ( ).

2. Open the Properties inspector.

3. Click and drag the blue number next to Letter spacing.

   Drag to the left to make your letters closer together; drag to the right to space them farther apart.

4. Click and drag the blue number next to the **Line Spacing** ( ) on the Spacing line of the Paragraph options.

   Drag to the left to decrease the space between lines; drag to the right to increase the space between lines.

KERN ONE WORD IN A PARAGRAPH

1 Click the **Text** tool (T) on the Tools panel.

2 Click and drag the **Text** tool over the word you want to kern.

You can also choose to kern a single letter.

3 Open the Properties inspector.

4 Click and drag the blue **Letter spacing** setting.

Drag to the left to make your letters closer together; drag to the right to space them farther apart.

● Your word now displays with different kerning than the rest of the paragraph.

Repeat these steps to hand kern each letter of a type treatment.

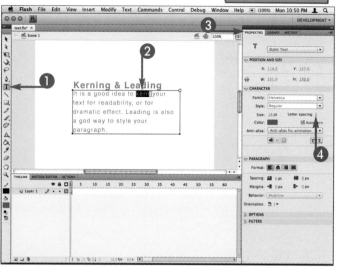

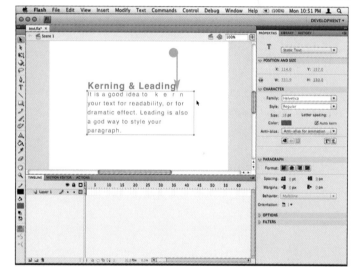

TIPS

How can I select a single word in a paragraph more easily than clicking and dragging?

Much like most word-processing applications, you can double-click on a word with the **Text** tool (T) to select a whole word. You can also press and hold down Shift and click the starting and ending points of the text you want to select.

How can I create superscript and subscript text?

There are two buttons in the Character portion of the text properties panel. Click T¹ for superscript, and click T₁ for subscript.

Move and Resize Text Areas

You can move your text areas around with the Selection tool. You can also resize your text boxes without affecting your formatting properties. This is very useful when you need to change your layout but don't want your font to grow and shrink as you make changes.

If you want to change the size of your text as you make changes, you'll want to use the Free Transform tool. For more on this, see Chapter 3.

MOVE A TEXT AREA

① Click the **Selection** tool (▶).

② Move your mouse over a text box

   (▶ changes to ▶).

③ Click and drag the text box to move it to a new location, and release the mouse button.

   Your text area is positioned in the new location.

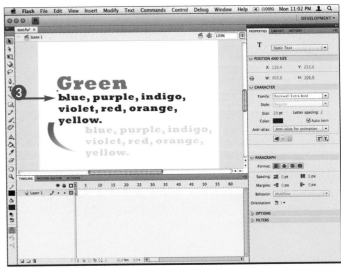

RESIZE A TEXT AREA

1 Click the text box you want to resize with ▶.

● A bounding box appears around the text.

2 Move the mouse pointer over one of the corners of the bounding box (▶ changes to ↔).

3 Click and drag to resize the text box.

Release the mouse button.

The text box is resized.

How can I rotate or skew a text box?

Select the text box with the **Selection** tool. Then click the **Free Transform** tool (⬚). Move the mouse pointer over the corner until the **Rotate** icon appears (↻). Click and drag to rotate. To skew your text area, move (⬚) over the top or bottom of the text box until the **Skew** button (⇌) appears. Click and drag to the left or right to skew your text. You can find out more about transforms in Chapter 3.

What does the Gap Size modifier do?

When you select the **Paintbucket** tool (◇), the Gap Size modifier appears at the bottom of the Tools panel. Click the Gap Size modifier to display a menu list of four settings. These settings determine how the **Paintbucket** tool treats any gaps that appear in the shape you are trying to fill. For very large gaps, you may need to close the gaps yourself before applying the fill color.

Break Apart Text

You can use the Break Apart command to convert your text into graphics and then manipulate the text with the Flash drawing and editing tools. Flash uses two stages of breaking apart. The first time you use the command, your text is split into editable, single character blocks. The second time, your text becomes filled shapes.

After you fully break apart text, you can no longer edit it with the Text tool, change the font, or modify the formatting. Flash considers broken-apart text as nothing more than a series of fills.

Break Apart Text

ADD A FILL

① Select the text you want to break apart.

② Click **Modify**.

③ Click **Break Apart**.

● Flash breaks the text into individual characters.

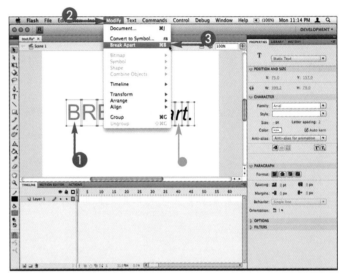

④ Click **Modify**.

⑤ Click **Break Apart**.

● Flash breaks the text into graphics.

● In this example, the insides of characters are filled with another color.

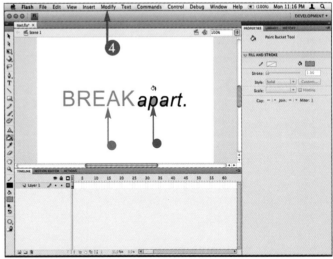

Transform Text

You can use the Envelope and Distort functions to transform the shape of your text. Use these to create dynamic-looking text like waves, exaggerated scaling, and other cool effects.

Transform Text

1 Select your text area.

2 Break apart your text area twice by pressing **Ctrl**+**B** (**⌘**+**B**).

See the section "Break Apart Text" to learn how to use the **Break Apart** command.

3 Click **Modify**.

4 Click **Transform**.

5 Click **Envelope**.

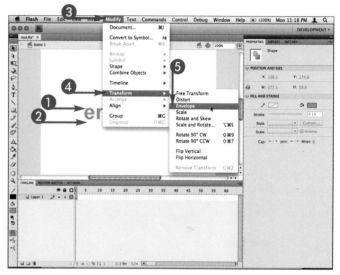

● Anchor points and handles appear on the bounding box.

6 Click and drag the anchor points and handles.

The shape of your text is modified.

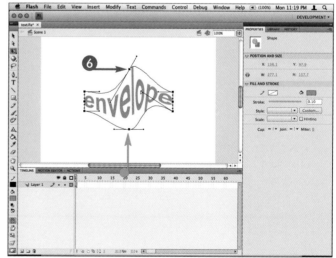

Importing Artwork

You don't need to create all of your graphics within Flash. Flash allows you to import bitmaps and vector graphics from many other applications, including Adobe Photoshop and Illustrator. In this chapter, you learn about vector art and bitmaps, and how to use them within your Flash projects.

Understanding Vector Art and Bitmaps

Originally, Flash was created as a tool to bring vector graphics and animation to the Internet. In many instances, vector graphics have smaller file sizes, and can be ideal for delivery over networks. Now, with broadband being practically ubiquitous, Flash can deliver a combination of many types of media, including video, audio, and bitmap images.

What Is a Bitmap?

Most images you see on a computer are bitmaps, such as pictures from a digital camera or images on a Web site. Essentially, a bitmap file stores the color information of each pixel. A 10-pixel by 10-pixel image file stores color values for 100 individual pixels as GIF, JPEG, or other image formats.

What Is a Vector?

A vector graphic uses the geometric equation for a line, curve, or shape in combination with additional attributes to describe that shape. For example, a line segment, in vector graphics, consists of two endpoints, and perhaps a color, thickness, and style.

Benefits of Vector Graphics

There are two major benefits to using vectors in Flash, especially for the Web. First, their file size is smaller (in many cases). The second is scalability. If you scale up a piece of vector art, there is no *pixellation*, or loss in edge quality. Scaling up a bitmap can result in odd artifacts because there isn't any information your computer can use to increase the image size.

Benefits of Bitmaps

In certain situations, bitmaps can be substantially smaller in file size than vector graphics. Photographs and very complex illustrations are generally smaller files as bitmaps than vectors. There are occasions where a complex illustration is better suited as a bitmap, and times when a bitmap should be traced into vectors. But, a general rule of thumb for Flash is to use bitmaps for photographs and vector graphics for everything else.

Creating Vector Graphics

When you use the Flash drawing tools, you are creating vector graphics. You can also create vector graphics that Flash can import using a more complex illustration program, like Adobe Illustrator. Flash can import many different types of vector graphics formats, including SWF, Illustrator, Freehand, and AutoCAD DXF files.

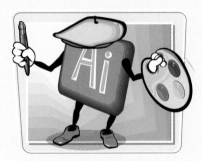

Creating Bitmaps

Most images on your computer are stored as some form of bitmap. You can create bitmaps in programs like Adobe Photoshop and Fireworks, and use those bitmaps in your Flash movies. Photographs from a digital camera are also bitmaps, usually stored in the JPEG or Camera RAW format. Flash cannot import Camera RAW, so if you want to use digital photographs in your Flash projects, you need to use the JPEG setting on your camera, or convert the RAW file to one of Flash's supported bitmap formats.

Import a Bitmap

You can import graphics, including vector or bitmap graphics, from other sources to use in Flash. You can then manipulate imported images with Flash commands. In addition to importing graphics, you can also use the Paste command to paste graphics you cut or copy from other programs.

IMPORT AN IMAGE

① Click **File**.

② Click **Import**.

③ Click **Import to Stage**.

● You can import a graphic directly to the file's Library to use later by clicking **Import to Library**.

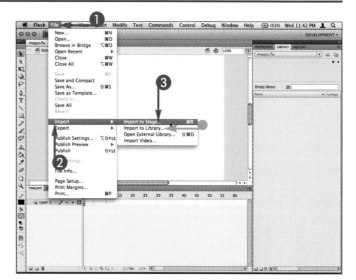

● The Import dialog box appears.

④ Navigate to the image file you want to import.

⑤ Click the filename.

⑥ Click **Import**.

Flash places the graphic on the Stage as a group. Flash also places the bitmap symbol in the Library.

COPY AND PASTE AN IMAGE

1. Open the program and file containing the graphic you want to copy.

2. Select the graphic, or a portion of the graphic.

3. Click **Edit**.

4. Click **Copy**.

Note: *In most programs, you can also press* Ctrl + C (⌘ + C) *to copy a selection.*

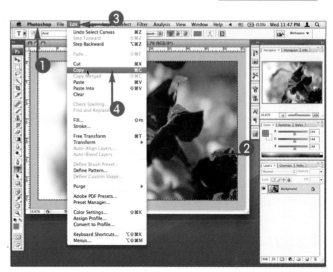

5. Change applications back to Flash.

6. Click **Edit**.

7. Click **Paste in Center**.

Note: *You can also press* Ctrl + V (⌘ + V) *to paste a selection.*

● Flash pastes the graphic into the center of the Stage.

● Flash also places a bitmap symbol in your Library.

TIPS

What graphic file types does Flash CS4 support?

Flash supports a wide variety of file types, including GIF, animated GIF, JPEG, PNG, BMP, DIB, TGA, TIFF, QTIF, WMF, EMF, PDF, PICT, PCT, PNTG, Freehand and Illustrator files, Flash Player files (SWF and SPL), QuickTime Movie (MOV), Photoshop files (PSD), and AutoCAD (DXF) file types.

Can I reuse the bitmap graphic?

When you import a bitmap graphic, Flash immediately adds it to the Flash Library for use in other frames in your movie. To view the Library, click **Window**, and then **Library**, or press Ctrl + L (⌘ + L). See Chapter 8 to learn more about using the Flash Library.

Break Apart a Bitmap

By default, a bitmap image is a group. You can use the Break Apart command to make your bitmap editable. The most common reason to break apart an image is to use the Eraser tool, Brush tool, and the Lasso Tool's Magic Wand modifier to clean up an image.

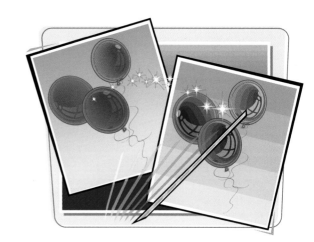

Break Apart a Bitmap

1 Select the bitmap image.

2 Click **Modify**.

3 Click **Break Apart**.

4 Click the **Eraser** tool ().

5 Erase unwanted portions of the image.

● Flash makes the erased portions transparent.

6 Click the **Lasso** tool (🔎).

7 Click the **Magic Wand** modifier (✨).

8 Click an area of your image that has a color you want to change.

9 Select a fill color.

● Flash applies the fill color.

How do I adjust the Magic Wand's settings?
Click the **Lasso Tool's Magic Wand Settings** modifier (✨) to open the Magic Wand Settings dialog box. The Threshold value indicates how similar a color must be to the color you clicked in order to be selected. A higher threshold usually selects a larger area; a smaller threshold, usually selects a more precise area. The Smoothing menu allows you to choose how Flash should make the selection. Pixels will have no smoothing at all. Rough, Normal, and Smooth settings create varying levels of curvature to your selection.

Create a Bitmap Fill

You can create a fill from a bitmap image that can be used the same way a gradient or a solid color fill would. Sometimes bitmap fills are used for patterns; other times you can use them to put photographs inside a nontraditional shape. Depending on the size of your bitmap, it may repeat in order to fill your shape completely.

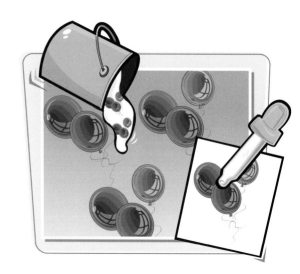

Create a Bitmap Fill

① Click **File.**

② Click **Import**.

③ Click **Import to Library**.

Note: See the section "Import a Bitmap" to learn how to import bitmaps.

● Your Bitmap appears in the Library.

④ Click the **Oval** tool, or press O.

⑤ Click the Fill Color button to select a fill color.

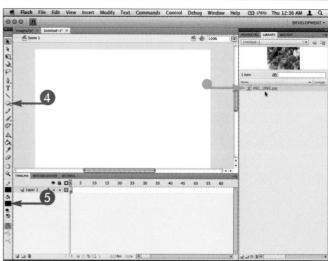

● Your image appears in the swatches.

⑥ Click on your image in the swatches to select it as your fill.

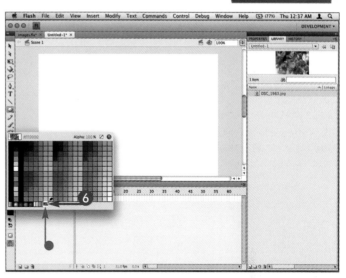

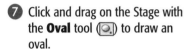

⑦ Click and drag on the Stage with the **Oval** tool () to draw an oval.

Your bitmap image fills the oval.

How can I modify my bitmap fill?

You can use the **Gradient Transform** tool (⊞) to transform your bitmap fill just like you would a gradient fill. To quickly edit your bitmap fill, select the fill and press F. The transformation handles appear as though you are working with a gradient. See Chapter 3 to learn about transforming fills.

Convert a Bitmap to Vector Art Using Trace Bitmap

You can use the Trace Bitmap command to convert a bitmap into a vector graphic. This command is usually applied to logos or simple art with a few colors, though you can also create some interesting painterly effects when using Trace Bitmap on photographs.

When you apply the Trace Bitmap command, you have an opportunity to adjust several parameters that define the rendering of the image, including how Flash handles the color variances, pixel size translation, and the smoothness of curves or sharpness of corners.

Convert a Bitmap to Vector Art Using Trace Bitmap

① Select the bitmap graphic you want to convert.

Note: See the section "Import a Bitmap" to learn how to import graphics. For more on selecting objects on the Stage, see Chapter 3.

② Click **Modify**.

③ Click **Bitmap**.

④ Click **Trace Bitmap**.

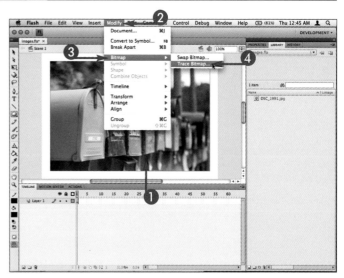

The Trace Bitmap dialog box appears.

⑤ Type a value that determines the amount of color variance between neighboring pixels.

A smaller value results in many vector shapes; a larger value results in fewer vectors.

⑥ Type a minimum pixel size for any vector shape.

This value determines the number of surrounding pixels that Flash considers when assigning the pixel color.

⑦ Click the Curve fit drop-down box and select how smoothly Flash traces outlines of the bitmap.

⑧ Click the Corner threshold drop-down box and select how sharply Flash traces corners.

⑨ Click **OK**.

● Flash traces the graphic, replacing the bitmap with vector shapes.

Can I preview my settings before I trace my bitmap?

Yes. Just click **Preview** in the Trace Bitmap dialog box, and you can adjust your settings before committing the trace.

How can I change the color of my traced bitmap?

There are two ways. One way is to adjust colors and saturation of your image in Photoshop and then import it and trace again. The other way — which can be tedious if your image is complex — is to use the **Paintbucket** tool (🪣) and fill each shape that your trace created.

Import Vector Graphics from Illustrator

You can import graphics from other drawing applications such as Adobe Illustrator. Illustrator is a great tool for drawing complex artwork and has many more options for drawing than Flash. Flash can import your Illustrator files entirely, or you can select specific parts of an illustration and build your Flash project with the pieces.

Import Vector Graphics from Illustrator

1. Click **File**.
2. Click **Import**.
3. Click **Import to Stage**.

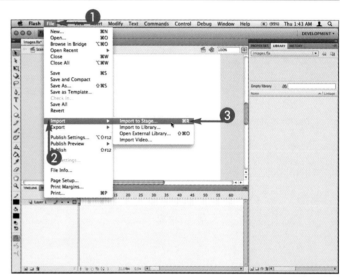

- The Import dialog box appears.
4. Click on an Illustrator file.
5. Click **Import**.

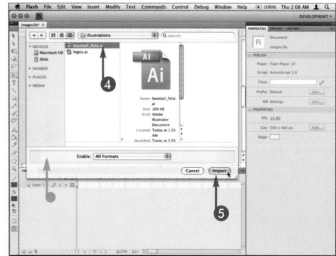

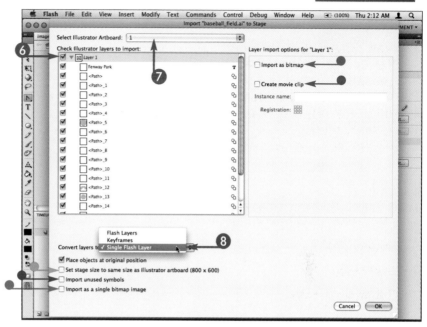

6 Select the check boxes to choose which paths or layers to import.

7 If your Illustrator file has multiple Artboards, click one from the **Select Illustrator Artboard** drop-down box.

● The **Import as bitmap** option converts your paths to bitmaps.

● The **Create movie clip** option automatically makes any path, layer, or group into a MovieClip symbol.

8 In the Convert layers to menu, click **Single Flash Layer**.

● Select the **Set stage size to same size as Illustrator artboard (800 x 600)** option to resize your Stage to the size of your Illustrator Artboard.

● Select the Import unused symbols option to import symbols that were turned off in Illustrator.

● Select the **Import as a single bitmap image** option to convert your entire illustration to a bitmap and discard all vector information.

TIPS

How can I set my preferences for importing Illustrator files?

You can click **Flash**, **Preferences**, and then click on **AI File Importer** to change Flash's default preferences for importing Illustrator files. You can then tell Flash how you normally prefer to import text, paths, images, groups and layers, as well as set general importing preferences.

My import window has an incompatibility warning. Why?

If your Illustrator file contains items not compatible with Flash, the **Incompatibility Report** button (⚠ Incompatibility Report) appears in the import window. Click this button to see a description of your possible incompatibilities and for information on how to modify your file for better compatibility with Flash.

continued

113

You can choose to import your
Illustrator text and paths so that
they can still be modified within
Flash. Or, you can have Flash
automatically raster your paths
and text as bitmaps.

Import Vector Graphics from Illustrator *(continued)*

9 Click on a text layer.

Note: *Text layers have the* $\boxed{\text{T}}$ *icon in the right column.*

- Select the **Editable text** option
  to convert your text to editable
  Flash text.

- Select the **Vector outlines**
  option to convert your text to
  path outlines.

- Select the **Bitmap** option to
  convert your text to a bitmap
  image.

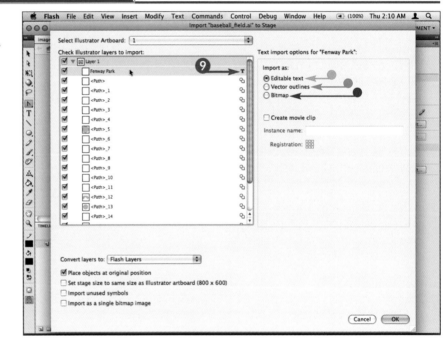

⑩ Click a path layer.

Note: Path layers have the ☒ icon in the right column.

● Select the **Editable path** option to maintain an editable vector path.

● Select the **Bitmap** option to convert your path to a bitmap.

⑪ Click **OK**.

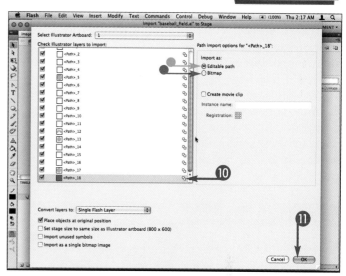

● Your illustration is imported as groups to the Stage.

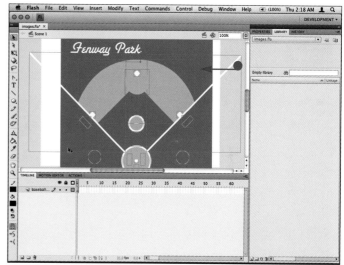

TIPS

Can I import my Illustrator assets to the Library?

Yes. If you click **File**, **Import**, and then **Import to Library**, your illustration appears as a graphic symbol in the Library. You can also drag and drop any imported artwork to the Library, and create a symbol for it. See Chapter 8 to learn about symbols.

Set Bitmap Properties

You can override your publish settings for individual bitmaps using the Bitmap Properties dialog box. Sometimes, you will have a Flash project where most of your images look great with a high level of compression. But there may be one or two images that you want to have less compression or no compression at all. You may also want to set individual bitmap properties to achieve the most optimized file size for your project.

Set Bitmap Properties

① Open the Library panel.

② Double-click on a bitmap symbol in the Library.

Note: Bitmap symbols have the 🖼 icon next to them in the Library.

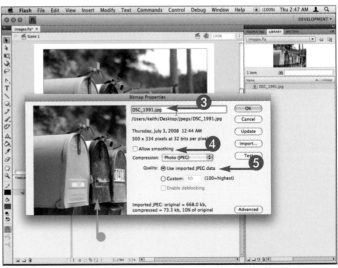

The Bitmap Properties dialog box appears.

● A preview of your image appears here.

③ Type a name for your bitmap here.

④ Select the **Allow smoothing** option to let the Flash Player smooth your image.

⑤ Select the **Use imported JPEG data** option so that Flash does not recompress your JPEG.

Note: If you are setting the compression of a non-JPEG bitmap, you have the option to use the default quality JPEG compression (Use publish setting).

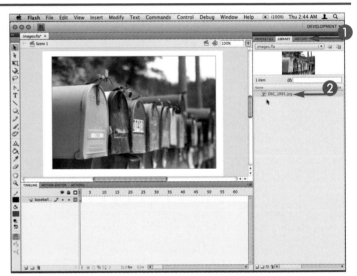

⑥ Click the **Compression** drop-down list and choose **Photo (JPEG)**.

Note: If you set properties of an image other than a JPEG, this option will be to use your current publish setting.

● You can click **Update** if you have edited your image in another program.

● You can click **Import** to import a new image to replace your current one.

● You can click **Test** to update the file size information after adjusting your settings.

● Your compression statistics appear here.

⑦ Click **OK**.

Flash stores your bitmap settings.

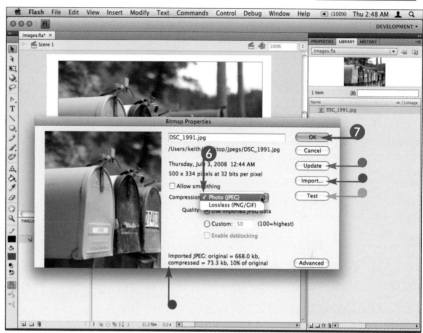

TIPS

What is the best way to compress my graphics?

If you are using another program, such as Photoshop, for example, to compress your image to a JPEG, it is usually best to use the imported data. If you import a TIFF or other format, you have a choice. You can set your compression to lossless, and have no additional compression, or you can let Flash convert you image to a JPEG. You can always change quality settings later, so the best course of action is to use your publish settings as a default and increase the quality of images that need it.

Is there a quick way to edit my image file in another program?

Yes. If you right-click on a bitmap in the Library, you can click **Edit With**. A dialog box appears that allows you to choose another program in which to edit. After making changes, you can right-click your bitmap in the Library again and click **Update** to bring your changes into Flash.

Import a PSD File

If you choose to design your Flash project in Photoshop, you can easily import your layers into Flash to add interactivity and animation. You also have the option of importing your text layers as editable text, vector outlines, or as a flattened bitmap image. If your Photoshop layers are designed as steps in an animation, you can also have Flash import them as keyframes, placing your animation right on the Timeline.

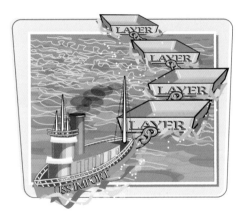

When you import layers from Photoshop, Flash gives you several additional options. You can override publish settings for individual layers and create movie clips from layers. You can also merge layers so that several of your Photoshop layers import as a single flattened bitmap.

Import a PSD File

IMPORT PSD LAYERS AS BITMAPS

1 Click **File**.

2 **Click Import**.

3 Click **Import to Stage**.

You can also press `Ctrl`+`R` (`⌘`+`R`).

The Import dialog box appears.

4 Select your PSD file from the Import dialog box.

5 Click **Open** (**Import**).

The Import to Stage dialog box appears.

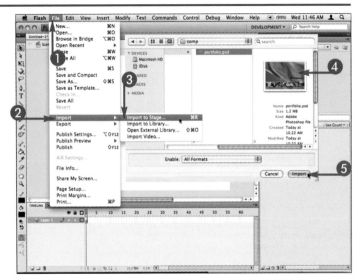

6 Click the check boxes to select and deselect which layers to import.

7 Click a layer you want to import as a bitmap.

Note: You can modify the import settings of multiple layers by clicking on two or more layers while pressing and holding `Ctrl` (`⌘`).

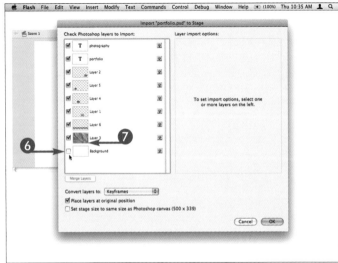

The options for the selected layer appear.

- Select the **Bitmap image with editable layer styles** option to allow you to use blend modes. Flash automatically creates a movie clip of the layer.

- Select the **Flatten bitmap image** option to create a flattened bitmap image.

- Select the **Create movie clip for this layer** option to create a movie clip of your layer.

- Click the text box next to **Instance name** and type a name if you want to give your movie clip an instance name for ActionScript.

- Registration determines where the center point of your movie clip will be.

- You can use the settings in the **Publish settings** section to override the publish settings of your bitmaps.

⑧ Click the **Convert layers to** drop-down list and choose **Flash Layers**.

⑨ Click **OK.**

- Your layers appear on the Stage, and in the Timeline as Flash layers.

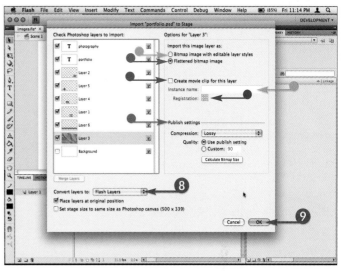

TIPS

How can I set my preferences for importing Photoshop files?
You can click **Flash**, **Preferences**, and then click on **PSD File Importer** to change Flash's default preferences for importing Photoshop files. You can then tell Flash how you normally prefer to import image layers, text layers, shape layers, and land layer groups. You can also adjust the compression publish settings for your imported bitmaps.

You can import your Photoshop text layers as editable text in Flash. Then, if you need to change the color, size, font, or other text properties, you can make your changes in Flash rather than making the changes in Photoshop and importing to Flash again.

IMPORT TEXT LAYERS FROM A PSD

1 Click **File**.

2 Click **Open** (**Import**).

3 Click **Import to Stage**. You can also press Ctrl+R (⌘+R), and then select the file you want, and click **Open** (**Import**).

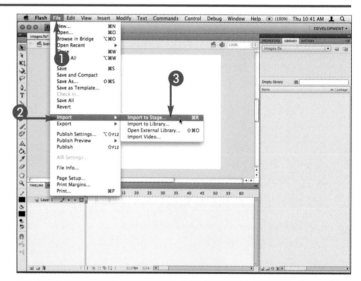

The Import to Stage dialog box appears.

4 Click the layer check boxes to select and deselect which layers to import.

5 Click a text layer.

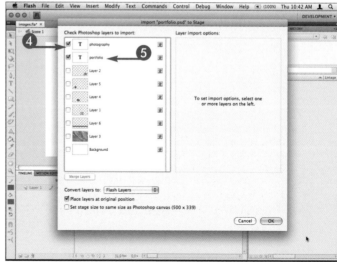

The options for the selected layer appear.

● Select the **Editable text** option to import your text layer as Flash text.

● Select the **Vector outlines** option to import your text as vector graphics.

● Select the **Flattened bitmap image** option to convert your text to a bitmap image.

● If you want to give your movie clip an instance name for ActionScript, click the text box next to **Instance name** and type it.

● Registration determines where the center point of your movie clip will be.

● You can use the settings in the **Publish settings** section to override the publish settings of your bitmaps.

⑥ Click the **Convert layers to** drop-down list and choose **Flash Layers**.

⑦ Click **OK**.

Your layers appear on the stage as Flash layers.

Note: See Chapter 6 to learn about working with layers.

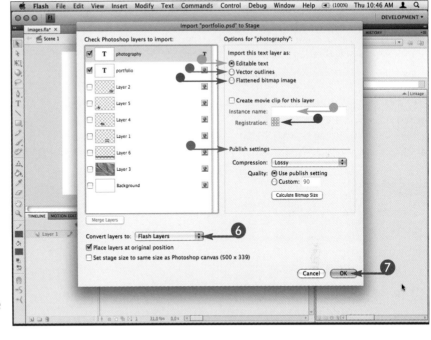

The colors of my imported PSD file don't match the colors in Photoshop. Why?
Flash only supports the RGB color space. If your Photoshop file is using the CMYK color space, Flash may not convert the colors to your liking. It is best to convert your Photoshop document to the RGB color space before importing it into Flash.

Can I import Photoshop smart objects?
Yes. But, Flash will rasterize your smart object as a bitmap when you import it. Flash does not support importing smart objects as editable objects.

Working with Layers

As your Flash project becomes more complex, you can use layers to keep organized. This chapter shows you how to work with layers in Flash.

Add and Delete Layers

When you create a new movie or scene, Flash starts with a single layer and a Timeline. You can add layers to the Timeline or delete layers you no longer need. Additional layers do not affect the file size, so you can add and delete as many layers as your project requires.

Layers are a great way to stay organized. You can put buttons and navigation on one layer, background art on another, and use individual layers for animation and dynamic content.

Add and Delete Layers

ADD A LAYER

1. Click the layer in the Timeline that you want to appear below the new layer.

2. Click **Insert**.

3. Click **Timeline**.

4. Click **Layer**.

● You can also click the **Insert Layer** button (⬜).

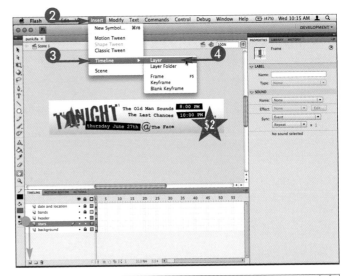

● A new layer appears.

Flash adds the same amount of frames to the new layer to match the layer with the longest frame sequence.

Note: See Chapter 7 to learn more about frames.

DELETE A LAYER

① Click the layer you want to delete.

② Click the **Delete Layer** button (🗑).

You can delete more than one layer by clicking the first layer you want to remove, and then pressing Ctrl (Windows) or ⌘ (Mac) while clicking other layers and then clicking 🗑.

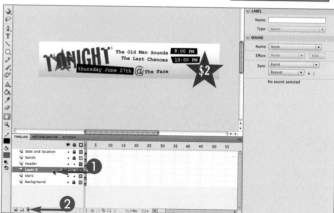

● The layer disappears from the Timeline.

Note: If you accidentally delete the wrong layer, you can click **Edit** and then **Undo Delete Layer**.

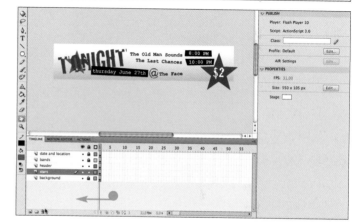

Why would I use layers?

Layers for Organization
The bigger your project, the more elements it is likely to contain. Rather than placing all of these elements in a single layer, which make them more difficult to locate and edit, you can insert them into separate layers. Then you can show and hide your layers to make it easier to find the element you want to edit.

For Animation
When you animate a movie clip or other symbol using tweens, your symbol is placed on a tween layer all by itself. See Chapter 9 to learn about tweens and Timeline animation.

Create Guides and Masks
Guide layers can assist you with the layout and positioning of objects on other layers. Mask layers enable you to hide elements in underlying layers. You create a transparent area in the mask layer that lets you view layers below.

Set Layer Properties

You can define the aspects of any given layer through the Layer Properties dialog box, a one-stop shop for controlling a layer's name, function, and appearance. The more you work with layers in Flash, the more necessary it is to change layer properties.

① Click the layer for which you want to set controls.

Note: *Flash automatically selects all objects associated with the selected layer.*

② Click **Modify**.

③ Click **Timeline**.

④ Click **Layer Properties**.

You can also right-click over the layer and click **Properties** to open the Layer Properties dialog box.

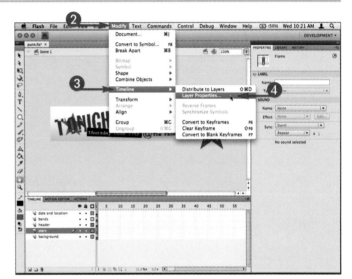

● The Layer Properties dialog box appears.

⑤ Type a distinctive name for the layer in the Name text box.

6 Change the desired layer properties. In this example, Type has been set to Guide and the Outline color has been changed to red.

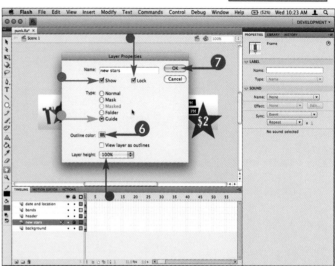

● To make the layer visible in the Timeline, leave the Show option selected.

● To lock the layer to prevent changes, select the Lock option (☐ changes to ☑).

● You can select one of the **Type** options to select a layer type.

● To increase the layer height in the Timeline, select a percentage from the Layer height drop-down list.

Note: Increasing layer height is useful for viewing sound waveforms in the layer.

7 Click **OK**.

● The layer properties change to your specifications.

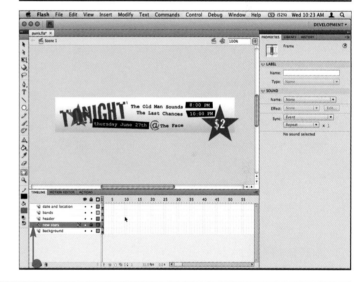

TIPS

What are layer types?
By default, all layers you add to the Timeline are *normal,* which means all the objects on the layer appear in the movie. Objects that you place on guide layers do not appear in the movie. A *guide* layer can be used for reference points and alignment. A *mask* layer hides any layers nested underneath it, which are *masked.* You can also place layers into folders to keep your movie organized. To change the layer type, select a type in the Layer Properties dialog box (○ changes to ⊙). Tween layers are layers that are automatically created when you create a motion tween.

Add a Guide Layer

You can place any elements you want to prevent from publishing on a guide layer. There are many reasons to do so. First, many illustrators place a photograph on a guide layer for reference and draw their asset on another layer. Guide layers are also useful when debugging your Flash movie. You can guide out layers, preventing them from exporting, and test your movie to isolate possible issues.

Older versions of Flash had another type of layer called a motion guide. Flash CS4 uses the motion editor and tween layers to animate objects along a path, making motion guide layers unnecessary.

Add a Guide Layer

① Open the **Timeline** panel, if it is not already present Ctrl + Alt + T (⌘ + Option + T).

② Click a layer where you want to insert your guide layer.

Note: Your new layer appears above the layer you select.

③ Click the **Insert Layer** button (🗒).

Flash adds a new layer to the Timeline.

④ Right-click the new layer name.

⑤ Click **Guide**.

- The layer becomes a guide layer, noted by its ✎ icon.

6 With your new guide layer selected, drag a symbol from the Library onto the Stage.

7 Click **Control**, **Test Movie**.

You can also press Ctrl + Enter (⌘ + Enter).

- Anything you placed on the guide layer does not appear in your exported file.

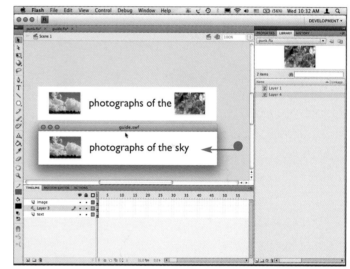

How can I lock my guide layer in place?

You will almost always want to lock your guide layers after your guide elements are positioned. That way, you won't move or delete something unintentionally. See the section "Lock Layers" to learn about locking.

How do I turn my guide layer back to a normal one?

Right-click on your guide layer. In the menu that appears, click **Guide**, which will have ✓ next to it. Your layer is now a normal layer.

Make a Layer Mask

You can use layer masks to only show or hide a portion of your layer. A mask is like a stencil or paper cutout, where you can see what is behind it through the holes. In Flash, you can have many layers *masked* by a single layer mask.

Make a Layer Mask

CREATE A MASK LAYER

1. Click the layer to which you want to add a mask.

2. Click ⬚.

● A new layer appears.

3. Right-click the new layer's name.

4. Click **Mask**.

The Stage appears blank because there is not yet any content in the mask layer. Flash marks the layer as a mask layer, locks it against any changes, and links it to the layer below.

DRAW THE MASK

1 Click 🔒 on your mask layer to unlock.

(🔒 changes to ⋅).

● The mask layer is denoted by the **Mask layer** icon (▣).

● Layers that are being masked are denoted by the **Masked layer** icon (▣).

2 Place some text on the mask layer.

Note: *See Chapter 4 to learn about working with text.*

3 Lock the mask layer by clicking ⋅ in the lock column.

(⋅ changes to 🔒).

● The masking effect is visible.

Note: *Anything appearing outside the fill shape is masked in the masked layer.*

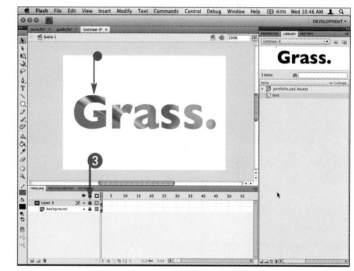

TIPS

I cannot see the mask effect. Why not?

If you cannot see the mask effect, you probably unlocked the layers. You must first lock the mask layer as well as the layers being masked to preview the effect. You can quickly make sure the correct layers are locked by right-clicking on the layer and clicking **Show Masking** in the pop-up menu.

Group Layers into Folders

You can organize your Flash layers into folders to keep your Timeline tidy. Placing background layers in their own folder, foreground layers in another, and guide layers in another is a good way to keep your Flash file uncluttered.

Group Layers into Folders

CREATE A FOLDER

① Click the **New Layer Folder** button (▣).

● You can also click **Insert**, **Timeline**, and then **Layer Folder**.

● Flash adds a layer folder to the Timeline.

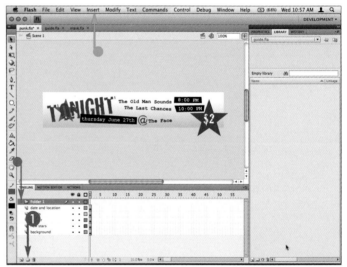

ADD A LAYER TO A FOLDER

① Click the layer you want to move into a folder.

② Drag the layer below the folder.

● A line appears indicating where your layer will be placed when you release the mouse button.

③ Release the mouse button.

The layer is moved to the layer folder and indented slightly in the list to indicate it appears in a folder.

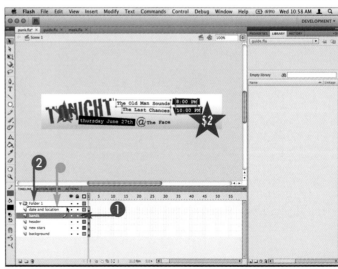

RENAME A FOLDER

1 Double-click the layer folder name you want to rename.

2 Type a new name.

3 Press [E].

The layer folder is renamed.

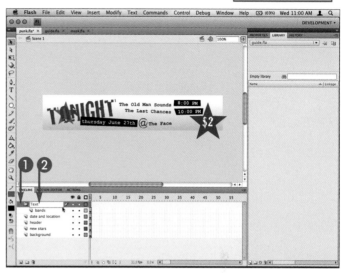

COLLAPSE A FOLDER

1 Click the layer folder's **Collapse/Expand** button ([▼] changes to [▶]).

Layers associated with the folder are now hidden.

You can click the layer folder's **Collapse/Expand** button ([▶]) to view the folder's contents again ([▶] changes to [▼]).

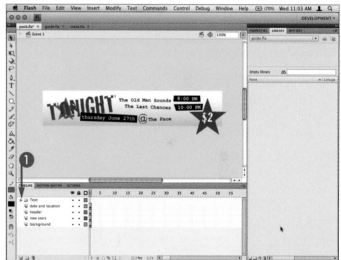

TIPS

How do I remove a layer from a folder?

Display the layer folder's contents, then click and drag the layer you want to remove from the folder and drop it elsewhere on the Timeline. To remove the layer completely from the Timeline, click the layer name and click [🗑].

Can I lock a layer folder?

Yes. You can lock and hide layer folders just as you can lock and hide layers. Locking a folder locks all the layers included within the folder. Click the folder layer's bullet ([•] changes to [🔒]). Flash locks the folder and any layers associated with the folder.

133

Show and Hide Layers and Layer Groups

When you have many layers in your Flash project, you can show the layers you are working on while hiding others, keeping the Stage and work area as tidy as possible.

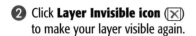

① Click the bullet (·) in the **Layer Visibility** column of the layer you want to hide.

· changes to ☒ and the entire layer becomes invisible.

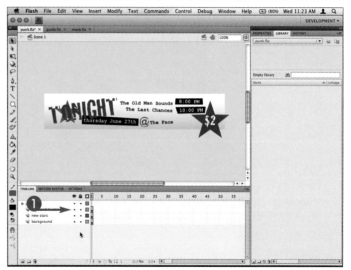

② Click **Layer Invisible icon** (☒) to make your layer visible again.

☒ changes to · and the entire layer becomes visible.

Show Layers as Outlines

You can view any of your layers as outlines to help with aligning elements by hand. Each layer has its own outline color assigned to it so you can easily distinguish between them as you work.

Show Layers as Outlines

① Click the **Layer Outline Color** icon (▣) in the **Show Layers as Outlines** column (▢).

● ▣ changes to ▢, and all of the contents of the layer are reduced to thin outlines.

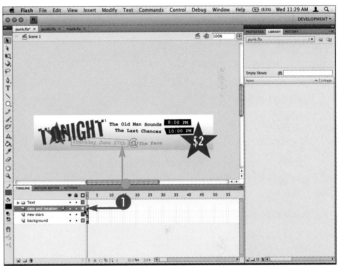

② Click **Show Layers as Outlines button** (▢) to make your layer fully visible again.

● ▢ changes to ▣, and all of the contents of the layer are restored to their original appearance.

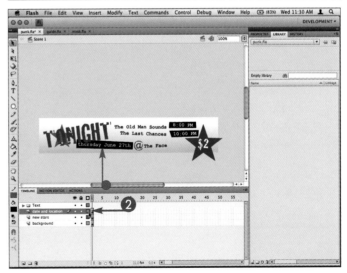

Lock Layers

Flash has an easy system in place for locking layers, helping you avoid moving or deleting elements by accident. While you can use the Layer Properties panel, it is much more useful to lock and unlock right in the Flash user interface.

① Click the bullet (•) below the **Lock Layers** button (🔒) of a layer you want to lock.

  (• changes to 🔒).

  If you try to select or edit any elements on this layer, Flash does not respond. The layer is locked.

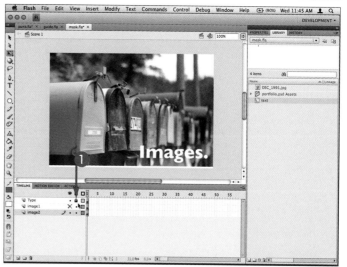

② To unlock the layer, click 🔒 on your layer.

  (🔒 changes back to •).

  You can now select and edit elements on the unlocked layer.

Rearrange Layers

To rearrange how objects appear in your Flash movie, you can stack layers. Layers act like sheets of transparent plastic. Depending on the placement of the layers, objects can appear in front of or behind objects on other layers.

① Click on the layer you want to move.

Flash selects all elements present on the selected layer.

② Drag the layer up or down in the list, depending on whether you want the layer to appear above or below its current location.

● An insertion bar appears to show where the layer will be placed when the mouse button is released.

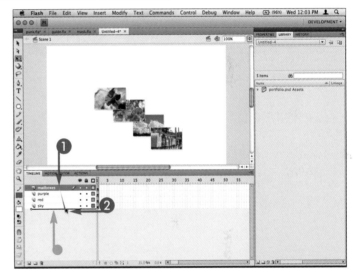

③ Release the mouse button.

● The layer is placed in its new location on the Timeline.

● The layer now appears behind the others.

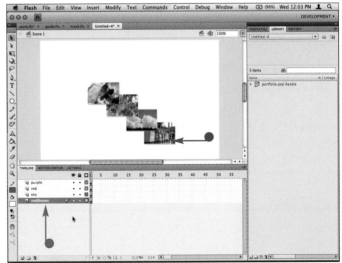

Working with the Timeline

The Flash Timeline is made up of layers and frames. Layers are a representation of depth in space, while frames are a representation of time. Frames can be used for building an animation over time. They can also be used for creating different states of your Flash project, much like interactive slides in a slide show.

Add and Remove Frames and Keyframes

You can add frames and keyframes to add time to your Flash movie. Keyframes are used for critical points in the Timeline where your content changes. Keyframes are also used to mark the beginning or end of an animation. You can add or remove frames to adjust timing between keyframes.

Add and Remove Frames and Keyframes

INSERT A KEYFRAME

① Click the Timeline tab.

*Note: if the Timeline is not open click **Window** and then **Timeline**.*

② Click a frame on the Timeline to select your keyframe's location.

③ Right-click on your selected frame and click **Insert Keyframe**.

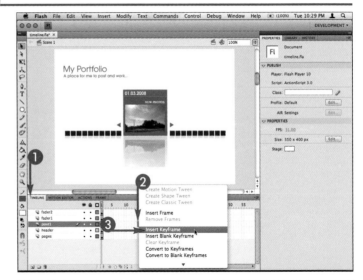

● Flash creates your keyframe.

● Flash also creates frames in between your keyframes.

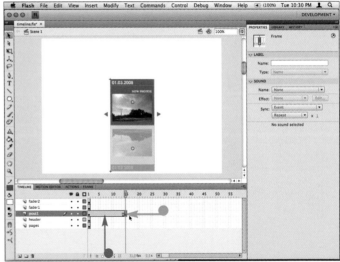

ADD AND REMOVE FRAMES

1 Right-click on the Timeline where you want to add frames and click **Insert Frame**.

● Flash inserts frames up to your inserted frame.

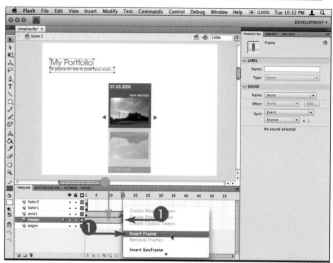

2 Click and drag over the frames you want to remove.

● Flash highlights the selected frames.

3 Right-click on any of the selected frames.

4 Click **Remove Frames**.

Flash removes the frames from the Timeline.

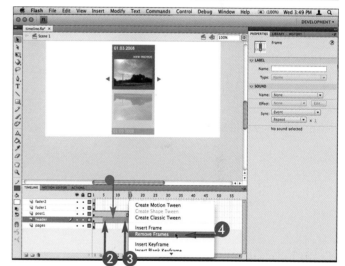

TIPS

How can I add and remove frames using keyboard shortcuts?

Flash has keyboard shortcuts for almost all of its functions. And as a general rule, Flash uses the Shift modifier for opposite commands.

To add frames, press F5.

To remove frames, press Shift + F5.

To add keyframes, press F6.

To remove keyframes, press Shift + F6.

When should I use Insert Blank Keyframe?

A blank keyframe is exactly the same as a regular keyframe. The only difference is that Flash automatically removes all of your content from the Stage at a blank keyframe. That way, if you want to start fresh at a certain point on the Timeline, you don't have to manually delete objects from the Stage.

Add Frame Labels

Frame Labels are a great way to keep the Timeline organized. You can add a label to any keyframe, although the general convention is to create a specific layer for all of your labels.

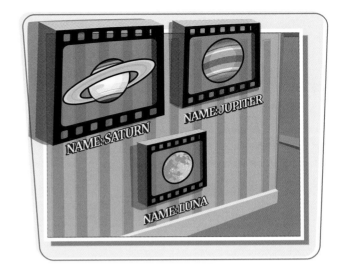

CREATE A NAME LABEL

1 Insert a keyframe on the Timeline.

Note: See the section "Add and Remove Keyframes" to learn how to insert a keyframe.

2 Click on your keyframe to select it.

Your keyframe is highlighted in blue.

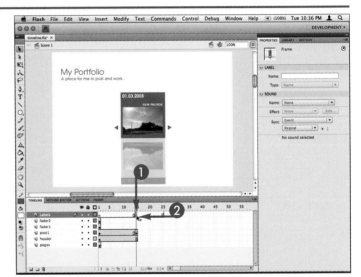

3 Open the Properties inspector.

4 In the Label section type a name for your label.

5 In the Type drop-down list, select **Name**.

● Your label appears on the Timeline.

● Name labels are identified by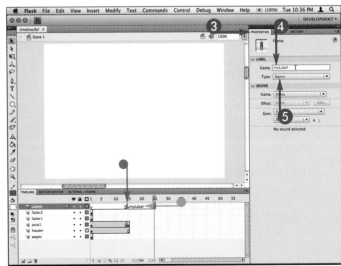

CREATE A COMMENT LABEL

① Insert a keyframe on the Timeline, and click on your keyframe to select it.

Note: *See the section "Add and Remove Keyframes" to learn how to insert a keyframe.*

② Open the Properties inspector.

③ In the Label section, type a name for your label.

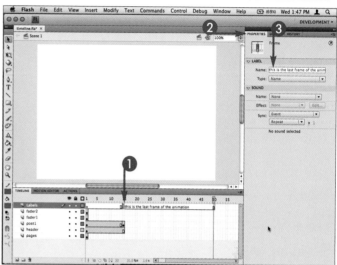

④ Click the **Type** drop-down list and select **Comment**.

● Comment labels are identified by the **Frame Label comment** icon (⬚).

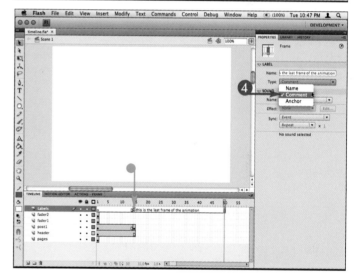

TIPS

Why use a Name label instead of a Comment label?

Comment labels are used to write notes for yourself or to other people working with your Flash document. They are not exported as part of your Flash movie. Name labels are not only good for organizing your Flash document, but they are also useful to ActionScript. See Chapter 10 to learn about adding interactivity with ActionScript.

What is the Anchor label type for?

Anchors are designed to enable users to bookmark specific sections of a Flash-based Web site and to enable usability features of the browser like the Back button. Unfortunately, getting anchors to work on multiple platforms and in multiple browsers can be quite difficult and is beyond the scope of this book.

Move Frames

You can move frames and keyframes around the Timeline, much like splicing a film together. You will want to move frames around often in order to keep your layers in sync with each other as you create animation.

Move Frames

1 Click and drag to select frames on the Timeline.

2 Move your mouse over the selected frames (changes to).

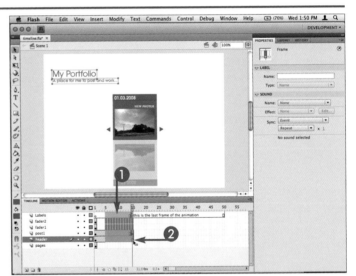

3 Click and drag the selected frames.

● Dragged frames display with a blue box around them to help you with placement.

4 Release the mouse button.

⑤ Flash moves your selected frames.

● Flash creates frames and keyframes, if necessary, where you insert your frames.

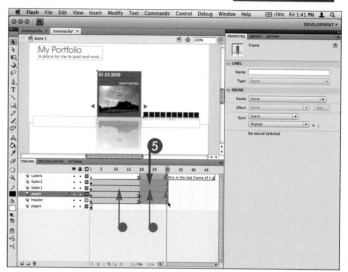

⑥ Select any frames that Flash added that you do not want.

⑦ Right-click on your selected frames and click **Remove Frames**.

Your unwanted frames are deleted.

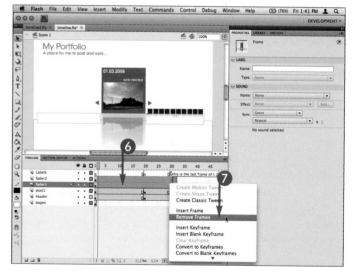

TIP

I accidentally dropped my frames in the wrong place. What should I do?

Like most well-designed applications, Flash has an Undo command. Any time you perform a task in Flash, you can reverse it. To undo your mistake, click **Edit** and then **Undo,** or press Ctrl+Z (⌘+Z). You can also open your History panel by pressing Ctrl+F1 (⌘+F1), and using the slider to step back through your history.

Cut, Copy, and Paste Frames

You can cut, copy, and paste elements in Flash just like you do in most other programs. Flash allows you not only to cut, copy, and paste elements on the Stage, but also allows you to use these commands to modify frames on the Timeline.

Cut, Copy, and Paste Frames

CUT FRAMES

① Click and drag to select frames on the Timeline.

② Move your mouse over the selected Frames (⬉ changes to ⬊).

③ Right-click on the selected frames and click **Cut Frames**.

The frames are cut from the Timeline, and Flash automatically adds blank keyframes where necessary.

COPY AND PASTE FRAMES

1 Click and drag to select frames on the Timeline.

2 Move your mouse over the selected frames (changes to).

3 Right-click on the selected frames and click **Copy Frames**.

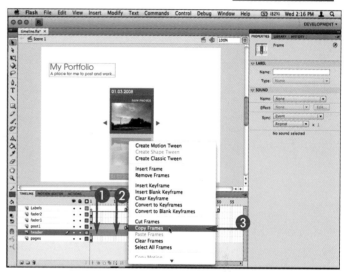

4 Click on the Timeline where you want to insert your pasted frames.

5 Right-click on the frames you have selected and click **Paste Frames**.

Your copied frames are inserted into the Timeline.

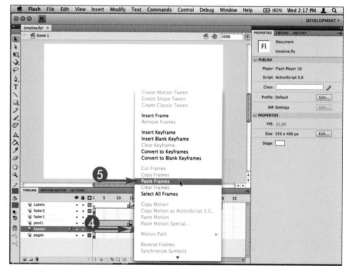

TIPS

How can I select frames without clicking and dragging?

You can select multiple frames by holding down the Shift key and clicking two points on the Timeline. You can also double-click any frame to select a section of the Timeline between keyframes. And you can right-click the Timeline and click **Select All Frames** to select every frame on the Timeline.

Is there a quick way to duplicate frames?

Yes. Select the frames you want to duplicate. Then, hold down the Alt (Option) key and drag your frames to a new location on the Timeline. Your frames are duplicated much like a copy-and-paste operation.

Reverse Frames

If you have something animate onto the Stage, many times you will want the same animation to play backwards as it animates off of the Stage. Reverse Frames is a great timesaver for achieving such an effect. Reversing frames is also a quick way to reorder a slide show.

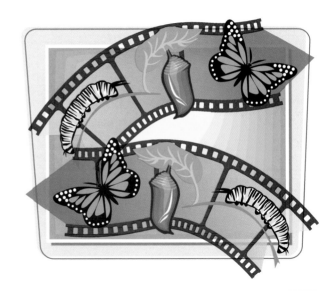

① Click and drag to select frames on the Timeline.

② Right-click on your selected frames.

③ Click **Reverse Frames**.

● Your frames are reversed on the Timeline.

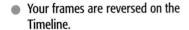

Preview Frames in the Timeline

You can view the Timeline in a way that is more like a filmstrip, where you can see the content of your keyframes on the Timeline itself.

Preview Frames in the Timeline

① Open the Timeline panel.

② Click the menu in the upper-right corner of the panel (⊟).

③ Click **Preview.**

● The Timeline shows thumbnail images of the contents of your frames.

Working with Symbols and Instances

Symbols are the building blocks of a Flash project. This chapter shows you how to create symbols, store them for reuse in the Library, and create instances of those symbols on the Stage to create a Flash movie.

Understanding Symbols and Instances

A symbol is basically the blueprint of an object in Flash. These blueprints are stored in the Library. When you drag a symbol from the Library to the Stage, you create an instance, which is the realization of that blueprint: An object is created.

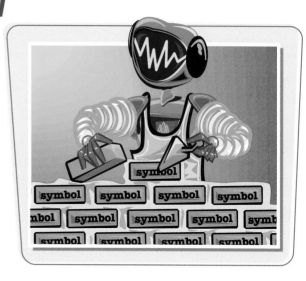

Symbols

A symbol can be a graphic, a movie clip, a button, a video, or a sound. Each of these unique objects is used for different purposes. You create these symbols so that they can be used in your Flash movie as instances.

Instances

An instance is the realization of a symbol. You can create many instances of the same symbol, each with its own set of properties. This way, you can have several instances of the same symbol, which can be different colors, different sizes, or instances that perform different actions, all while coming from the same blueprint.

Nesting

Placing one symbol inside another is called nesting. A good way of thinking about nesting is to think of a set of Russian dolls. You can have symbols inside of symbols inside of symbols, much like how the dolls are inside of each other. However, you can have more than one symbol at any level of nesting.

You can create symbols in Flash to make reusable graphics and animations. Flash has three main types of symbols: graphics, movie clips, and buttons.

Graphic Symbols

Graphic objects, which are the simplest symbols in Flash, are most commonly used as reusable graphical assets or are used for Timeline animation like tweens.

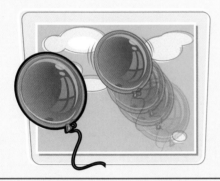

Movie Clips

Movie clip symbols are the foundation of Flash. In essence, they are their own Flash movies that can exist within your main Flash movie. Movie clips are also the base symbol type that can have an instance name, which allows ActionScript to reference your objects.

Button Symbols

Button symbols are a very specific object in Flash. They are similar to movie clips in that they can have an instance name for ActionScript. They also have a unique makeup that allows you to create simple rollovers with little effort.

Other Symbols

You can also create symbols for sound, video, and fonts. These symbols are used differently than graphics, buttons, and movie clips. See Chapter 12 to learn about sounds and Chapter 13 to learn about adding video.

Create a Graphic Symbol

You can create graphic symbols a couple different ways: directly on the Stage, and through the Library.

If you create a graphic symbol and decide later that you need another type, you can change it in the Library to the appropriate symbol type.

① Click and drag with the **Selection** tool (![pointer]) and select the artwork from which you want to create a symbol.

② Right-click on your selected elements and click **Convert to Symbol** from the menu.

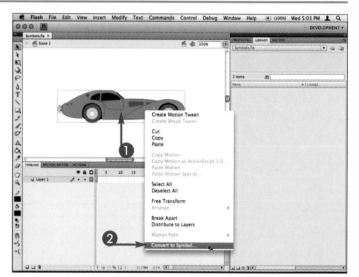

The Convert to Symbol dialog box appears.

③ Type a name for your Symbol.

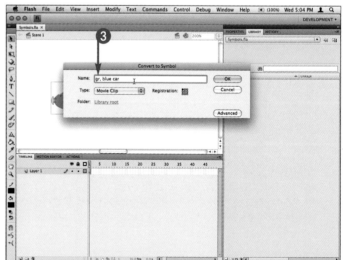

④ Choose **Graphic** from the Type drop-down menu.

● You click the icon next to Registration to select your symbol's registration point. Each of the little squares is clickable.

● You can place your symbol in a subfolder of your Library by clicking the blue text next to **Folder**.

● You can see the advanced symbol creation options by clicking the **Advanced** option.

Note: Advanced options are not available to graphic symbols.

⑤ Click **OK**.

● Your symbol appears in the Library and is ready to be used in your project.

● Graphic symbols are denoted by the **Graphic symbol** icon (🖾).

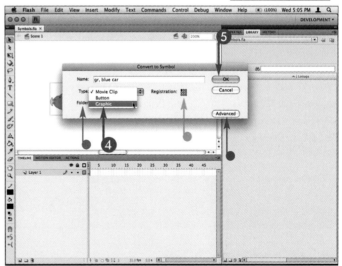

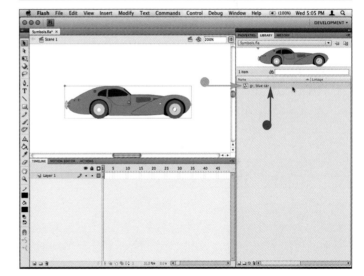

TIPS

How can I create a symbol and then add graphics to it?
You can add an empty symbol to the Library by clicking the **New Symbol** button (🖾) at the bottom of the Library panel. Then choose your symbol type, and click **OK**. Flash automatically resets the Stage for drawing that symbol. Click **Scene 1** at the top of the Stage to return to the main Timeline. You can also create a new symbol by clicking **Insert** and then **New Symbol**, or you can press Ctrl+F8 (⌘+F8).

Can I duplicate a Symbol?
Yes. Right-click on any symbol in the Library and click **Duplicate** from the menu that appears. Flash prompts you as though you were creating a new symbol, allowing you to rename, choose a new symbol type, and change other options available in the Duplicate Symbol dialog box.

Add an Instance of a Symbol to the Stage

After you have a symbol in your Library, you can add as many instances of that symbol to the Stage as you want without too much impact on the file size of your exported movie.

Normally, when you copy an object or a piece of artwork, you are copying all of the information for that object. With instances, you only copy a reference to an object in the Library.

Add an Instance of a Symbol to the Stage

① Click on the keyframe where you want to insert your instance.

② Open the Library panel.

③ Click and drag a symbol from the Library over the Stage (⬉ changes to ⬉).

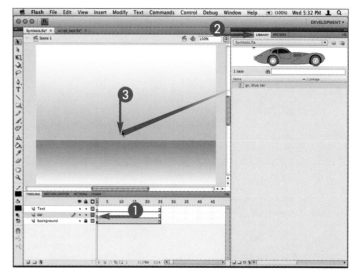

④ Release the mouse button where you want your instance to appear on the Stage.

Note: *Flash does not let you place an instance in a regular frame. You can only place instances in a keyframe in the Flash Timeline. Regular frames are reserved for tweened animation and the passage of time.*

Note: *Flash does not let you place an instance on the Stage on a locked layer. You need to make sure that you have an unlocked layer on which to place your instance. See Chapter 6 to learn about locking and unlocking Layers.*

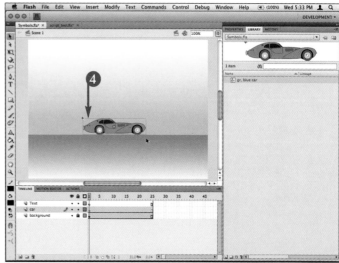

After you place an instance of a symbol on the Stage, you can change its properties without affecting the original symbol. For example, you can make your instance transparent, apply color effects, or scale and transform it.

You can also change the type of symbol from which your instance inherits properties. So, if you have a graphic symbol but want to use a blend mode, you can change the Instance to a movie clip in the Properties inspector.

Modify Instances

1 Click on an instance with the **Selection** tool ( ) to select it.

2 Open the Properties inspector.

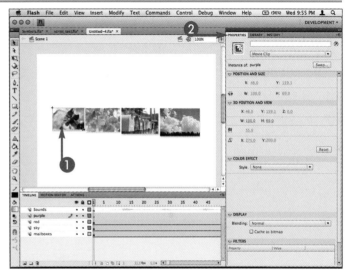

3 Click the **Style** drop-down list and select Alpha.

4 Drag the **Alpha** slider to affect your instance's transparency.

Drag the slider to the left to make your instance more transparent; drag the slider to the right to make it more opaque.

Note: *To modify multiple instances at the same time, select the objects by holding down the* **Shift** *key and clicking with the* **Selection** *tool ( ). Then you can adjust properties in the Properties inspector for all of the selected objects.*

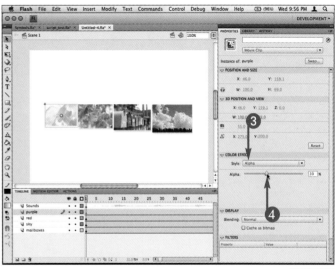

Swap Symbols

You can change what symbol your instances refer to. Many times, you will want to create placeholder buttons and simple graphics for your project in order to get things moving. Then you can simply swap them for symbols you create later with your polished design.

① Click on an Instance with the **Selection** tool (➤) to select it.

② Open the Properties inspector.

③ Click **Swap**.

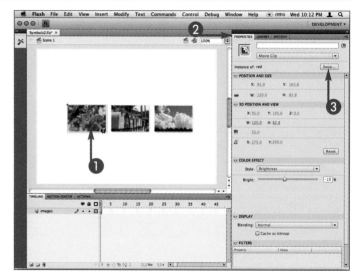

● The Swap Symbol dialog box appears.

● You can duplicate the selected symbol by clicking the **Duplicate Symbol** button (🗔).

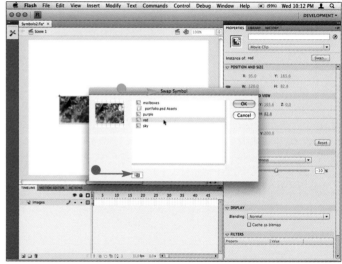

④ Click the symbol you want to swap for the current symbol.

● A preview of the selected symbol appears here.

⑤ Click **OK**.

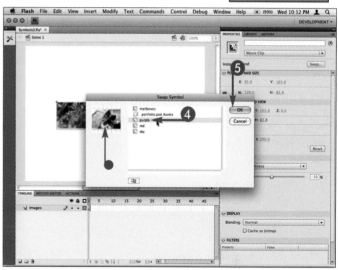

● The symbol is swapped.

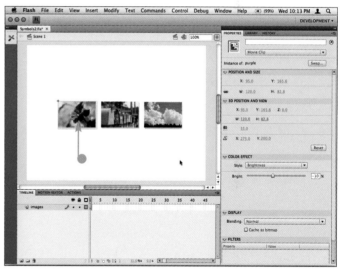

TIPS

Will I lose my color effects and filters if I swap symbols?

No. Changing your instance to a new symbol only changes the Library item that your instance refers to. Any modifications you make to the properties of your instance remain. This includes blending, color effects, filters, position, and size.

Sometimes the Swap button is grayed out. Sometimes it isn't even there. Why?

The Swap button may be unavailable for a couple of reasons. You cannot swap shapes. Look at the top of the Properties inspector to make sure of the type of object you have selected. You also cannot swap multiple symbols at once. A quick way to check to see if you have multiple symbols selected is to look at the top of the Properties inspector. If you have more than one symbol selected, it will say "Instance of: ---."

Create a Button Symbol

You can create buttons in Flash to add interactivity to your projects. Your buttons can trigger events and ActionScript commands. Button symbols also have a special Timeline that contains specific frames for the *states* of the button: Up, Over, Down, and Hit.

Create a Button Symbol

1 Click and drag with the **Selection** tool ( ) and select the artwork from which you want to create a button.

2 Click **Modify**.

3 Click **Convert To Symbol**.

You can also press F8 .

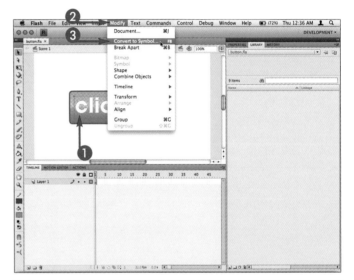

● The Convert to Symbol dialog box appears.

4 Click here and type a name for your button.

5 Click the Type drop-down list and choose **Button**.

6 Click **OK**.

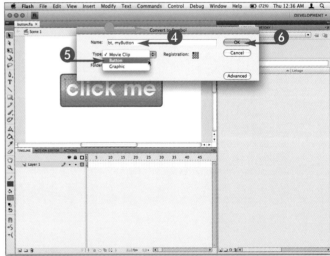

● Your symbol appears in the Library and is ready to be used in your project.

● Button symbols are denoted by the **Button Symbol** icon ().

⑦ Click **Control**.

⑧ Click **Enable Simple Buttons**.

You can also press Ctrl + Alt + B (⌘ + Option + B).

When you move your mouse pointer over your button, the cursor changes from � to the **Hand Cursor** (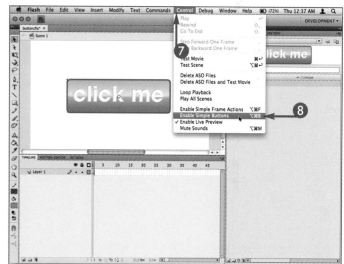).

I can't move or edit my button anymore. Why?
With Enable Simple Buttons turned on, your button is not selectable. Turn off this feature by clicking **Control** and then **Enable Simple Buttons**, or you can press Ctrl + Alt + B (⌘ + Option + B) a second time.

Edit the States of a Button

You can give your button a rollover effect and a clicked effect by editing the frames of your button symbol. Most of the time, you will want to have at least a rollover state so your users know your button is clickable. You also want a Hit state so Flash knows when the mouse is within the bounds of your button.

① Place an instance of a button symbol on the Stage.

Note: See the section "Create a Button Symbol" to learn how to create a button symbol.

② Double-click your instance to edit it in place.

● This area indicates that you are editing the button's Timeline.

③ Open the Timeline panel.

● The button Timeline appears here.

④ Select all frames of the button Timeline.

⑤ Right-click on the selected frames and click **Convert to Keyframes**.

● The selected frames are now keyframes.

⑥ Click the **Over** frame in the Timeline.

This frame becomes what is shown when a user moves the mouse pointer over the button.

⑦ Edit your button's elements with the Flash drawing tools.

See Chapter 3 to learn how to modify your artwork.

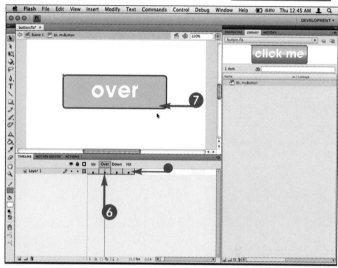

⑧ Click the **Down** frame in the Timeline.

This frame becomes what is shown when a user clicks the button.

⑨ Edit your button's elements with the Flash drawing tools.

See Chapter 3 to learn how to modify your artwork.

TIP

My button doesn't have Up, Over, Down, and Hit frames, but the Properties inspector says it is a button. Why?

If you place a graphic or movie clip symbol on the Stage and then cast it as a button in the Properties inspector, it will have simple numbered frames. Remember, when you edit a symbol you are editing the blueprint for your object and not just modifying an instance. In another symbol type cast as a button, frame 1 corresponds to Up, frame 2 to Over, frame 3 to Down, and frame 4 to Hit.

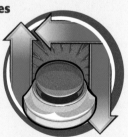

Your button will function
without editing the states.
However, rollover effects, and
down states make for a much
more rich interaction.

⑩ Click the **Hit** frame in the
Timeline.

This frame is not shown in Flash.
It simply denotes the Hit area of
your button.

⑪ Click the **Rectangle** tool (▢).

⑫ Click and drag to draw a rectangle
around your button.

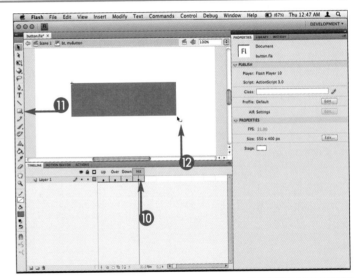

⑬ Click the **Scene 1** button.

● You are on the main Timeline
again.

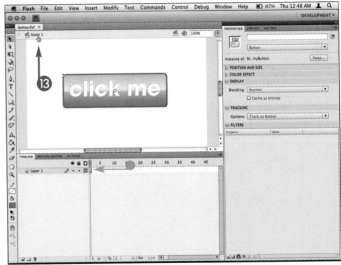

⑭ Click **Control**.

⑮ Click **Enable Simple Buttons**.

You can also press Ctrl + Alt + B
(⌘ + Option + B).

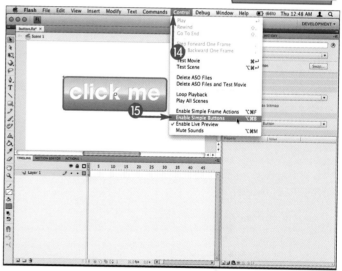

⑯ Move your mouse pointer over
the button.

You can see your rollover effect in
action.

You can also click your button to
preview the Down state.

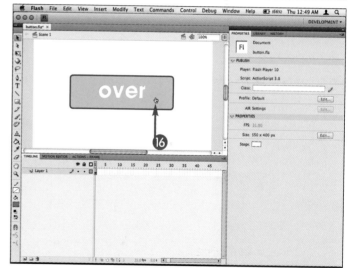

TIP

Why do I need to edit the Hit state?

As a general rule, it is good to always edit the Hit state of your buttons. A common
beginner's mistake in Flash is to create a button that is made up of text with no
background and not have a solid Hit state. By doing so, users must move their
mouse over the actual lines of the letters in order to click the button.

Add a Behavior to a Button

You can use the Behaviors panel to add simple actions to your button without the need to learn how to write ActionScript. Behaviors are a simplified way of adding interactivity to your Flash projects.

It is important to note that behaviors only work in Flash movies using ActionScript 2.0 or lower. You must adjust your publish settings accordingly in order to use behaviors. And, you must be careful to not use any ActionScript 3.0 commands or functionality.

Add a Behavior to a Button

1 Place an instance of a button symbol on the Stage.

Note: See the section "Add an Instance to the Stage" to learn how to place a button symbol on the Stage.

2 Click **Window**.

3 Click **Behaviors**.

You can also press Shift + F3.

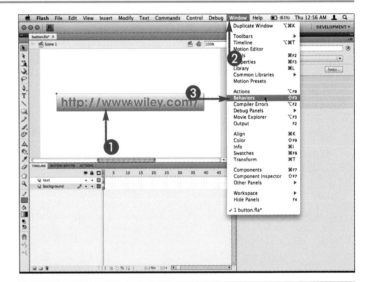

● The Behaviors panel appears.

4 Click the **Add menu icon** button (⊕).

5 Click **Web**.

6 Click **Web Page**.

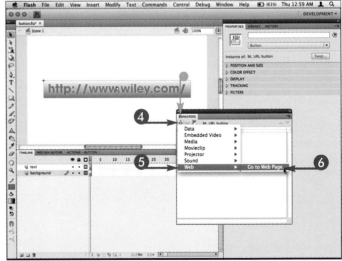

● The Go to URL dialog box appears.

⑦ Type a Web site URL.

This example uses http://www.wiley.com.

⑧ Click **OK**.

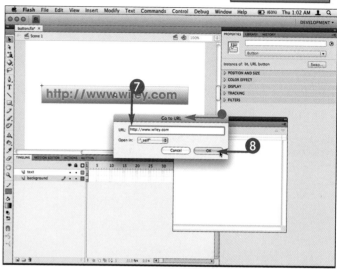

⑨ Press Ctrl + Enter (⌘ + Enter) to test your movie.

● The exported Flash movie appears.

⑩ Click your button.

● Flash opens a Web browser and displays the page you specified in your behavior.

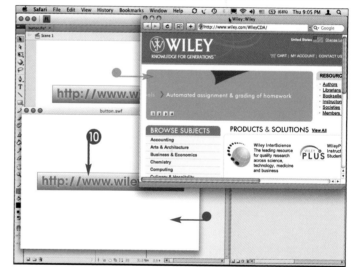

TIPS

How do I delete a behavior?

You can delete a behavior by opening the **Behaviors** panel, clicking on the behavior you want to remove, and then clicking the **Delete Behavior** button (⊟).

How do I edit a behavior?

Double-click on the name of the behavior you want to edit in the Action column of the Behaviors panel. Depending on the type of behavior you selected, a dialog box appears that allows you to adjust your settings.

Create a Movie Clip Symbol

You can create movie clips that contain graphics and animation. Movie clip symbols are more powerful than graphic symbols because you can give them instance names that allow them to be controlled by ActionScript.

Create a Movie Clip Symbol

1. Open the **Library** panel.

2. Click the **New Symbol** button (⬚).

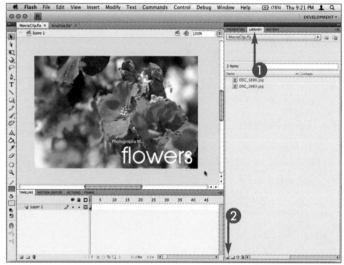

- The Create New Symbol dialog box appears.

3. Click here and type a name for your movie clip.

4. Click the **Type** drop-down list and select **Movie Clip**.

5. Click **OK**.

● Flash now shows the Timeline of your new movie clip, instead of the main Timeline.

⑥ Add elements to your movie clip with the Flash drawing tools.

See Chapter 2 to learn how to draw elements in Flash.

⑦ Click the **Scene 1** button to return to the main Timeline.

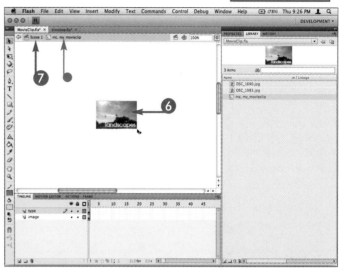

⑧ Click and drag an instance of your new movie clip from the Library onto the Stage.

Your new movie clip appears on the Stage.

TIPS

Can I create a symbol from elements already on the Stage?

Yes. There are two ways to create a symbol. One way is to use the New Symbol button in the Library, as described in this section. The other way is to use the **Convert to Symbol** menu item as described in the section "Create a Graphic Symbol."

Does using movie clips instead of graphics increase my file size?

Movie clips have a little more overhead than graphics do when exported in Flash Movies. Most of the time, however, the difference is negligible. If you are concerned about your file's size, it is more prudent to change your bitmap and sound compression settings. See Chapter 5 to learn how to set your bitmap properties, and Chapter 12 to learn how to edit audio settings for export.

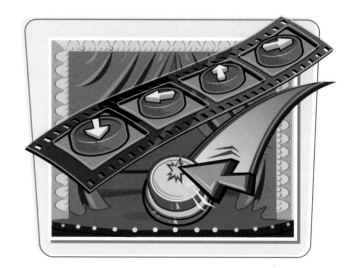

You can use the Library to play through your symbols so you can better identify them. Sometimes, symbols do not include any graphics on the first frame. For example, a picture that fades in is invisible on the Stage and does not show a preview in the Library. Or, you may have a sound symbol that does not have a very descriptive name.

Preview a Symbol

PREVIEW A SYMBOL IN THE LIBRARY

1 Open the **Library** panel.

2 Click the symbol you want to preview.

● Your symbol preview appears here.

● The **Play** (▶) and **Stop** (■) buttons appear here.

Note: If you do not have a symbol that has multiple frames, see Chapter 9 to learn about creating an animation.

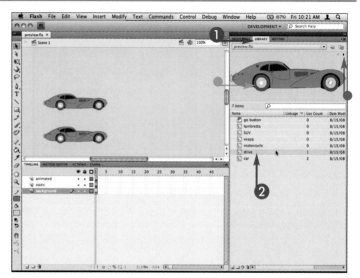

3 Click ▶.

Flash plays through all the frames of the symbol in the preview area.

4 Click ■ to stop the preview.

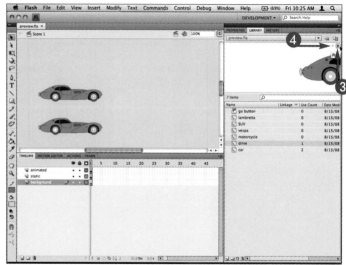

PREVIEW A SYMBOL ON THE STAGE

① Open the **Library** panel.

② Double-click the symbol you want to preview.

③ Open the **Timeline** panel.

④ Click frame 1 of your movie clip.

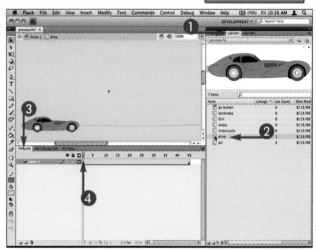

⑤ Click **Control**.

⑥ Click **Play**.

You can also press Enter.

Your symbol plays.

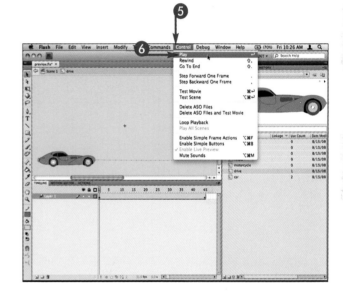

TIP

How do I stop the preview from playing on the Timeline?
You can simply press Enter again and the play head stops. You can also click **Window**, **Toolbars**, and then **Controller**, which displays a panel with DVD player-style controls for your Timeline.

Apply Filters to an Instance

You can add drop shadows, glows, blurs, and bevels to your button and movie clip instances. Using filters can be a good way to save file size by reducing the number of imported graphics you need.

ADD A DROP SHADOW FILTER

1. Click a movie clip or button symbol on the Stage with the **Selection** tool ( ).

2. Open the **Properties** inspector.

3. If it isn't already expanded, click **Filters** (changes to).

4. Click the **Add Filter** button ( ).

5. In the menu that appears, click **Drop Shadow**.

● The Drop Shadow options appear.

6. Click and drag the **Strength** setting until it has a value you like (changes to).

You can also adjust other values of the filter.

ADJUST COLOR

⑦ Click ().

⑧ In the menu that appears, click **Adjust Color**.

● The Adjust Color options appear.

⑨ Click **Hue** setting.

⑩ Type a value between -180 and 180.

Your instance changes hue on the Stage.

TIPS

How many filters can I have?

You can add as many filters as you want. In fact, you can have multiple versions of the same filter. For example, you can have a black drop shadow and a red drop shadow, or multiple gradient glows.

What does the Quality filter setting do?

Sometimes, depending on the power of your computer and graphics card, animation may stutter when using high-quality filters. If you plan on distributing your Flash project over the Web, consider using medium or low quality to accommodate those with less than optimal computers.

Apply a Blend Mode to an Instance

You can use blend modes that are very similar to those in Adobe Photoshop in Flash. Blend modes allow you to create transparency effects like darken, multiply, hard light, screen, overlay, and others.

Many times you will not know which blend mode you want until you see it. Try them all to get an understanding of the different effects they create.

① Click a movie clip or button instance on the Stage with the **Selection** tool ( ).

② Open the **Properties** inspector.

③ If it isn't already open, click **Display** in the Properties panel (changes to).

④ Click the **Blending** drop-down menu.

⑤ Click **Multiply**.

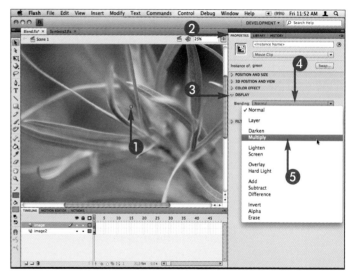

● Flash renders the blend mode on the Stage.

Normal

This mode indicates that no blending is applied.

Layer

This blend mode makes your symbol behave as though it is a single image, regardless of its subcomponents.

Darken

This blend mode shows the darkest color per pixel.

Multiply

This blend mode multiplies the color values. The result is usually darker.

Lighten

This blend mode replaces colors if they are lighter.

Screen

This blend mode multiplies the inverse of the blend and base colors.

Overlay

This blend mode darkens dark colors like multiply and lightens light colors.

Hard Light

This blend mode colors lighter than gray will screen, colors darker than gray will multiply.

Add

This blend mode adds the color values together, usually resulting in an increase in brightness.

Subtract

This blend mode subtracts color values from one another, usually resulting in a decrease in brightness.

Difference

This blend mode subtracts the less bright color from the brighter color.

Invert

This blend mode simply inverts the colors of anything underneath.

Alpha

This blend mode extracts the alpha (transparency) value and applies it to the objects underneath.

Erase

This blend mode inverts the alpha before applying it to the objects underneath.

Rotate and Translate MovieClip Instances with 3-D Tools

Flash CS4 has a new toolset for rotating and translating movie clip objects in three-dimensional space. To *translate* an object is simply to move it to a new set of coordinates. You can use these tools to create realistic-looking 3-D effects. Your publish settings must target ActionScript 3 to use the 3-D tools.

If you are familiar with other applications with 3-D capabilities, it is important to note that Flash does not do depth buffering. Basically, that means that objects that intersect in 3-D space do not follow the rules of 3-D, but follow the rules of layers and arrangement.

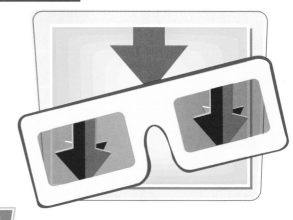

Rotate and Translate MovieClip Instances with 3D Tools

ROTATE IN 3-D

1 Click the **3D Rotation** tool ( ).

2 Click a MovieClip instance on the Stage.

Note: 3-D tools are only available to movie clip instances.

● The red line represents the X-axis.

● The green line represents the Y-axis.

● The blue circle represents the Z-axis.

● The orange circle is for free-form 3-D rotation.

3 Open the **Properties** inspector.

4 Click the blue number next to the **Camera** icon ( ) and set the perspective angle value to 140.

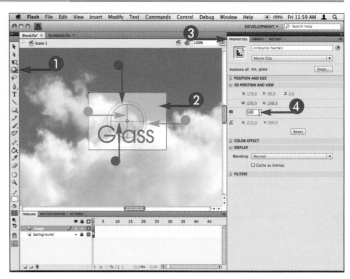

5 Click and drag the orange circle, which is the free-form 3-D rotation, and change the perspective of your movie clip.

TRANSLATE IN 3-D

1 Click .

2 Click a movie clip to select it.

● The red arrow represents the X-axis.

● The green arrow represents the Y-axis.

● The blue dot represents the Z-axis.

3 Click and drag the blue dot to move your movie clip backward and forward in 3-D space.

TIPS

I can't get my movie clip back to its original position and rotation. How can I?

A quick trick to reset your translation and 3-D rotation is to open the Properties inspector, and click the top-most drop-down menu, where Movie Clip is currently selected. Then click **Graphic** to cast your instance as a graphic. This resets your 3-D position and view because graphic instances cannot be moved in 3-D. Then, cast your Instance as a movie clip again to start over.

When I change my camera, it modifies every 3-D movie clip. Why?

You can only have one camera in Flash. So any time you modify the perspective angle it affects all of your 3-D objects.

Creating Timeline Animation in Flash

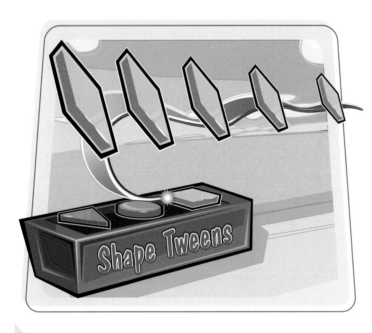

Flash was originally designed as an animation tool. Today, although many use Flash to create Web applications, AIR applications, and other interactive works, it is still an extremely powerful animation program. Adobe continues to improve Flash's animation capabilities. This chapter shows you how to create several different types of animation on the Flash Timeline.

Create a Frame-by-Frame Animation

You can create the illusion of movement in Flash by repositioning an object over the course of several keyframes. Any layer in Flash can be turned into an animation by adding keyframes and repositioning objects.

Create a Frame-by-Frame Animation

① Place a symbol on the Stage that you want to animate.

Note: For information on placing a symbol on the Stage, see Chapter 8.

② Right-click on frame 5.

③ Click **Insert Keyframe** (F6).

Flash inserts a keyframe that duplicates the previous keyframe's contents.

④ With your new keyframe selected, move or transform your symbol.

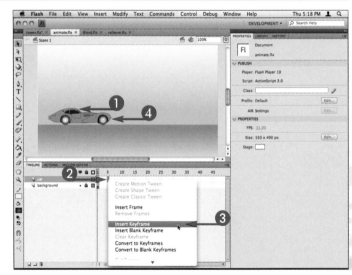

⑤ Insert another keyframe (F6) on the Timeline of the layer you are animating.

Flash inserts a keyframe that duplicates the previous keyframe's contents.

⑥ With your new keyframe selected, move or transform your symbol again.

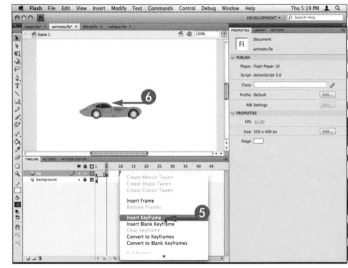

⑦ Repeat steps 5 and 6 until you have created several keyframes.

⑧ Add frames to any layers that you did not animate, but that you want to appear throughout your animation.

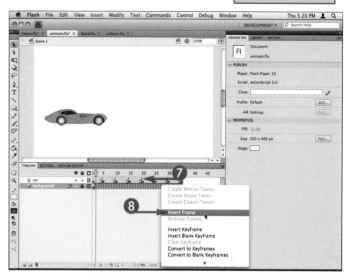

⑨ Click on Frame 1.

⑩ Press Enter.

Flash plays your animation.

Note: *You can also press* Ctrl + Enter *(*⌘ + Enter*) to preview your animation as an exported Flash movie.*

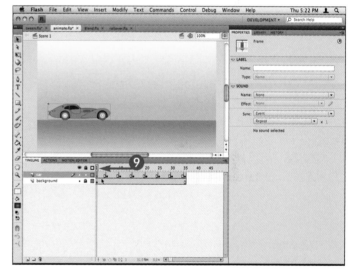

TIPS

How can I slow down my animation?

There are two ways to slow down an animation. You can adjust the frame rate of your Flash movie in the **Properties** panel, or you can add frames between your keyframes. You can add frames by right-clicking on the Timeline and clicking **Insert Frame** (F5).

When should I use frame-by-frame animation instead of tweening?

If you can accomplish the effect you want using a tween, you should. Frame-by-frame animation should be reserved for effects that require a lot of fine-tuning by hand and introducing or deleting elements on a prekeyframe basis.

Onion-Skinning an Animation

You can view your animation with onion-skinning turned on. This feature allows you to see the contents of multiple frames at once. By viewing the placement of objects in other frames, you can more clearly determine how you want to position the object in the frame in which you are working.

Onion-skinning offers two modes of display: dimmed content or outlined content.

① Click a frame.

② Click the **Onion Skin** button (🔲) at the bottom of the Flash Timeline.

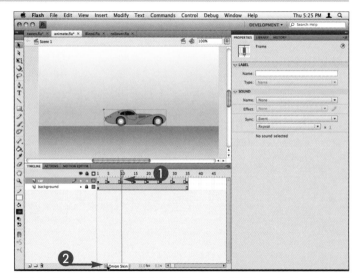

● Flash displays dimmed images from the surrounding frames and places onion-skin markers at the top of the Timeline.

● Flash creates handles for your onion-skin span on the Timeline.

③ Click and drag on the handles of the onion-skin marker to set the range.

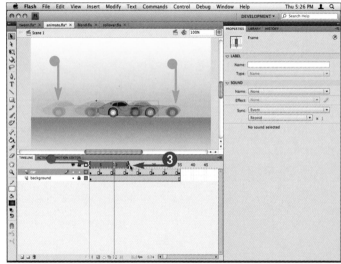

④ Click and drag the onion-skin marker group to move the selection.

⑤ Click the **Onion Skin Outlines** button ( ) at the bottom of the Flash Timeline.

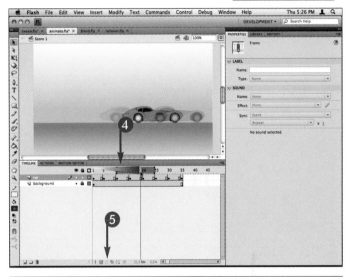

● Flash displays outlines of the objects from the surrounding frames and places onion-skin markers at the top of the Timeline.

To turn off onion-skinning, you can click or again.

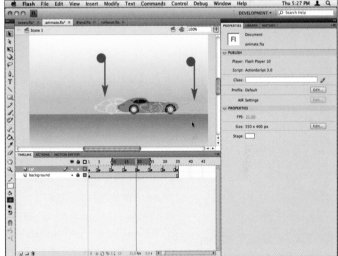

Can I edit the onion-skinned frames?

No. You can only edit the currently selected frame when using onion-skinning. See the section "Edit Multiple Frames" to learn how to edit multiple frames at once.

How can I modify the onion-skin markers?

Click the **Modify Onion Markers** button ( ). If you click **Always Show Markers**, the markers are visible on the Timeline even when onion-skinning is turned off. **Anchor Onion** locks the markers to the frames they are on. **Onion 2** automatically sets the markers to show two frames on either side of the selected frame, and **Onion 5** does the same for five frames. **Onion All** sets the markers from Frame 1 to the end of your Timeline.

Always Show Markers
Anchor Onion
Onion 2
Onion 5
Onion All

Edit Multiple Frames

You can reposition an entire animation sequence. Instead of selecting each frame and repositioning objects one at a time, you can move them all at once.

1. Click a frame.

2. Click the **Edit Multiple Frames** button (🖳) at the bottom of the Flash Timeline.

● Flash displays images from the surrounding frames on the Stage.

● Flash places markers at the top of the Timeline.

3. Click the **Modify Onion Markers** button (🔲).

4. Click **Onion All**.

● Flash sets the markers to span the entire Tiimeline.

⑤ Click **Edit**.

⑥ Click **Select All**.

You can also press Ctrl + A (⌘ + A).

● Flash selects all objects in the Timeline.

⑦ Move your animation by clicking and dragging it with the **Selection** tool ( ).

Note: For fine-tuning the position of your animation, you can use the arrow keys ↑, ↓, ←, and →. On Windows, Num Lock must be off to use the arrow keys in the numeric keypad.

 TIPS

How do I avoid editing other layers when I edit multiple frames?

The easiest way to avoid editing a layer is to lock it. See Chapter 6 to learn about locking layers. A second way to avoid editing elements is to select objects explicitly instead of using **Edit, Select All**.

Can I edit other properties of multiple frames besides position?

Yes. You can modify any properties in the Properties panel and the changes affect your selected multiple frames.

Understanding Tweening

A tween is a method of creating animation, where you tell Flash where to start and where to end, and Flash does all the work in the middle. There are three types of tweens: Classic, Shape, and Motion. Flash also has built-in methods to create more organic animation called Easing functions.

Classic Tweens

Classic tweens are the type of motion tween supported in Flash CS4 and earlier. If you plan to work on a project with others who do not have Flash CS4, you will need to use classic tweens.

Motion Tweens

Motion tweens are new in Flash CS4. With the new tweening system, you have access to more powerful animation tools, including complex easing methods, 3-D tweening, and a new system for animation along paths.

Shape Tweens

Shape tweens are essentially used for morphing from one shape to another. You can also use shape tweens to quickly morph from one color to another. Many times you may also need to use shape hints to tell Flash how you want your shape to change over time.

The Motion Editor

Flash CS4 introduces a new panel for fine-tuning your tweened animation called the motion editor. You can use the motion editor to add tweened effects like blurs and drop shadows. You can also use the motion editor to choose the types of easing you want.

Motion Keyframes

Flash needs keyframes to understand how you want your animation to appear. You essentially tell a symbol to go from one state to the next and let Flash do all the work between those keyframes.

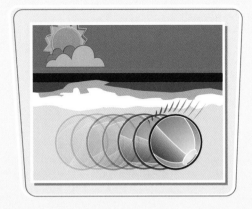

Motion Graph

The motion graph is a part of the motion editor that is designed to help you visualize tweens. It displays all the values and properties that are changing over time in the form of a series of line graphs. You can modify aspects of your tween directly in the graph.

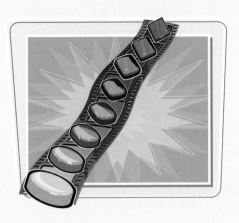

Easing

Flash has a built-in series of mathematical equations that create smooth and organic-looking movement. Usually, you want tweens to speed up or slow down over time — for which there are many options. There are also tweening options for bouncing, sine waves, and other smooth-looking effects.

Create a Classic Tween

You can use the classic tween to animate between two keyframes. If your animation does not require special *easing* or other features that the motion editor provides, a classic tween is all you need.

Classic tweens should always be used if you want to save your Flash files for Flash CS3. Otherwise, your tweens may be lost.

Create a Classic Tween

① Place a symbol on the Stage where you want your animation to begin.

② Right-click the frame where you want your tween to end and click **Insert Keyframe**.

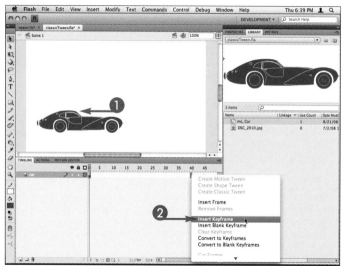

③ Click and drag your instance to a new location on the Stage with the **Selection** tool (⟍).

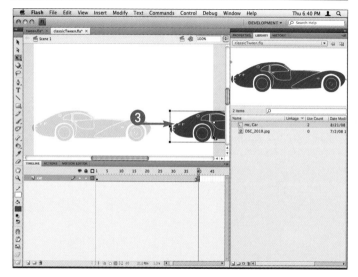

④ Right-click the frames between your keyframes and click **Create Classic Tween**.

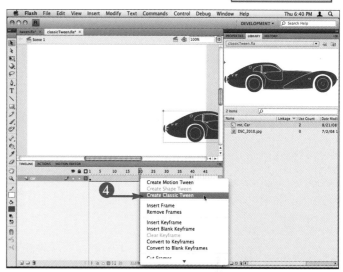

● Flash colors the tweened frames and draws an arrow through them.

⑤ Click and drag the play head (▯) to the left and right to preview the animation.

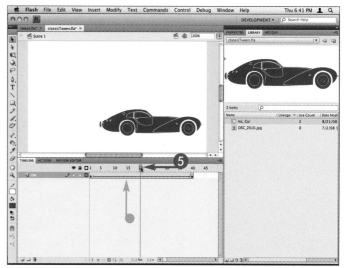

TIPS

How do I use Easing with a classic tween?

Click a frame of your classic tween and open the Properties panel. Under the Tweening header, you can set the value of your easing. Negative numbers create *"in" easing*, which means that your animation starts slowly and becomes faster. Positive numbers create *"out" easing*, which means your animation slows down.

Create a Motion Tween

You can use the motion editor to animate movement, filters, color effects, and apply complex easing to make your animation even more dynamic. The motion editor is a powerful tool with which you can create very complex animation on the Timeline.

① Place a symbol on the Stage where you want your animation to begin.

② Right-click on the Timeline where you want your tween to end and click **Insert Frame**.

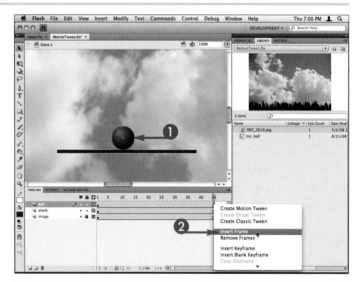

③ Right-click on the added frames on the Timeline and click **Create Motion Tween**.

● Flash colors your tween layer blue.

● Flash changes your layer icon to the **Tween Layer** icon ().

④ Click on the last blue frame in your tween layer.

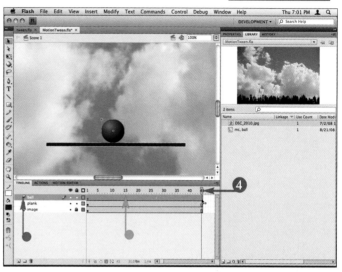

⑤ Click and drag your symbol with the **Selection** tool ( ).

Note: See Chapter 8 to learn how to modify your symbol's properties.

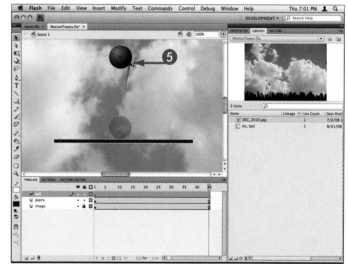

Can I customize the motion editor view?
There are three icons at the bottom of the motion editor panel that allow you to customize its appearance. You can change the motion editor's graph size by clicking the number next to 🔲 and entering a new value. The expanded graph size can be changed by changing the value next to 🔲. Click and change the value next to 🔲 to change how many frames the motion editor displays.

continued

The Motion Editor panel allows you to see all of the properties of your object that are being tweened in a two-dimensional graph. The lines on the graph are called *property curves*.

⑥ Click **Window**.

⑦ Click **Motion Editor**.

The **motion editor** opens.

⑧ Click the **Add** button (⊞).

⑨ Click **Bounce**.

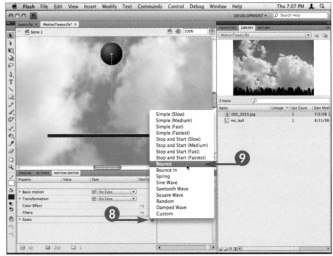

⑩ Click the **Selected Ease** drop-down menu.

⑪ Click **2-Bounce**.

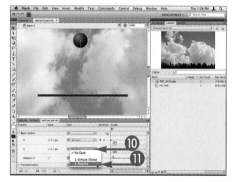

⑫ Click 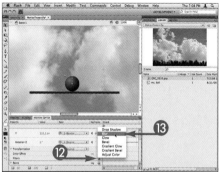.

⑬ Click **Blur**.

⑭ Click 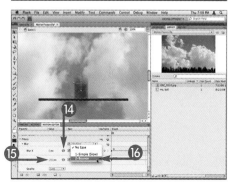 to unlink Blur X and Blur Y (ma078 changes to).

⑮ Click the **Blur Y** value and type a value of **100**.

⑯ Click the **Blur Y Selected Ease** drop-down menu and click **2-Bounce**.

Press **Enter** to watch your bouncing tween on the Stage.

Create a Motion Tween with 3-D Transformations

You can create visually stunning 3-D animation using motion tweens in combination with the Flash 3-D tools.

3-D transformations are only supported in the Flash 10 player or higher. This is also true of 3-D tweens. You also must make sure your publish settings target ActionScript 3.0.

1 Place a movie clip symbol on the Stage.

Note: Only movie clip symbols can be tweened in 3-D.

2 Right-click on the Timeline where you want your tween to end.

3 Click **Insert Frame**.

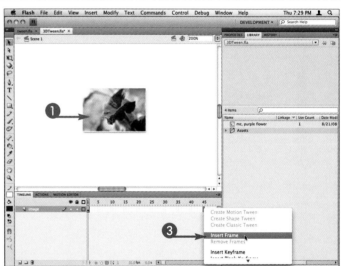

4 Right-click on the added frames on the timeline.

5 Click **Create Motion Tween**.

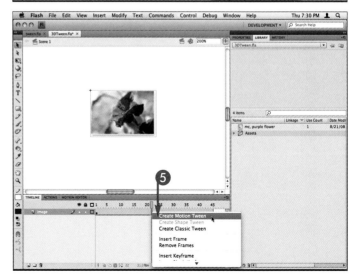

● Flash colors your tween layer blue.

● Flash changes your layer icon to .

6 Right-click the Timeline again and click **3D Tween**.

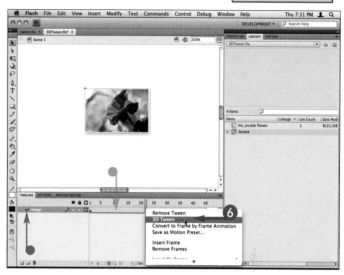

7 Click on the last blue frame in your tween layer.

8 Click the **3D Rotation** tool.

Note: See Chapter 8 to learn about the 3D Rotation tool.

9 Click and drag on the green line to rotate around the Y-axis.

Press Enter to preview your 3-D animation.

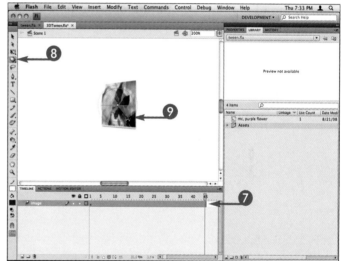

Are there Motion Tween presets that I can use in my animation?

Yes. Click **Window, Motion Presets** to open the **Motion Presets** panel. You can then browse the built-in animation presets. To apply a preset, select an object on the Stage with the **Selection** tool (🡒) click on a preset, and click **Apply**.

Can I save my tween settings to use with another object?

Yes. Click **Window, Motion Presets** to open the **Motion Presets** panel. Then, select your tweened object and click the **Save Selection as Preset** button 🔳.

You can add precision to your 3-D motion tween by entering specific values into the motion editor. You can also adjust the easing of your tween to achieve your desired effect.

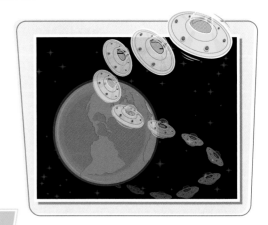

Create a Motion Tween with 3-D Transformations *(continued)*

⑩ Open the **Properties** panel.

⑪ Click the value next to the **Camera** icon (⬛) to set your Perspective Angle.

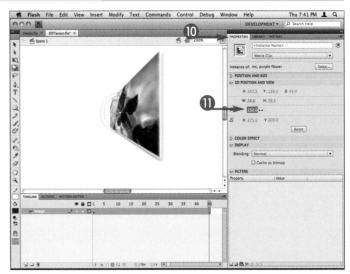

⑫ Open the **motion editor**.

⑬ Click the **Rotation Y** value to set it to a precise number.

This example uses a value of 180.

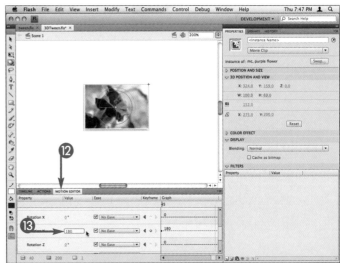

⑭ Click 🔁.

⑮ Click **Sine Wave**.

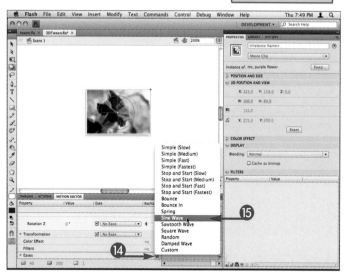

⑯ In the motion editor, in the **Rotation Y** row, click the **Ease** column drop-down menu.

⑰ Click **2-Sine Wave**.

Press Enter to watch your 3-D tween on the Stage.

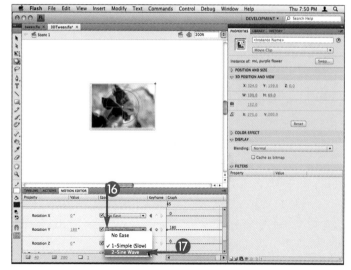

Can I remove my 3-D tween but keep the other aspects of the tweened animation?

Yes. Just right-click on your tween in the Timeline, and deselect the 3-D tween item in the pop-up menu. You can also use this trick to clear out your 3-D tween so that you can start from scratch with a new one.

I get prompted to change my publish settings in order to use a 3-D tween. Why?

You can only use the new Flash 3-D tools if you are publishing for Flash Player 10 or higher. Flash prompts you to change the target player whenever you choose a function that is only possible in a newer player than your current one.

Create a Shape Tween

You can use shape tweening to morph from one shape to another. For example, you can morph a circle into a square, or slowly change from the numeral 1 to the numeral 2.

Shape tweens can only be applied to shapes. So make sure you are either working with a shape or break apart any groups or symbols that might be part of your tween. You can animate any object you draw with the Drawing tools using the shape tween effect.

Create a Shape Tween

1. Select the frame in which you want to start a shape tween.

2. Draw the object you want to animate in frame 1.

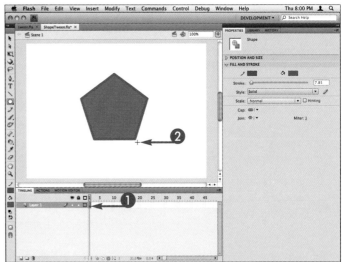

3. Right-click the frame where you want to end the shape tween.

4. Click **Insert Blank Keyframe**.

   You can also press F7 to quickly insert a blank keyframe.

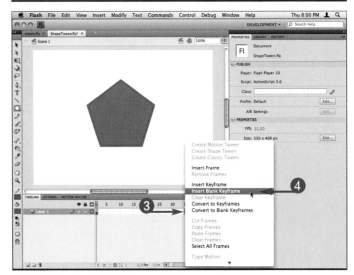

⑤ Draw the shape into which you want your image to morph.

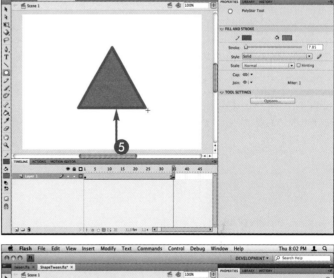

⑥ Right-click a frame in the middle of the tween sequence.

⑦ Click **Create Shape Tween**.

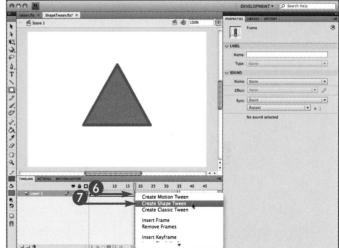

TIPS

Can my shape tween have multiple keyframes?
Yes. If your shape tween needs more keyframes in order to achieve your desired effect, you can add keyframes to the tween. Right-click on a frame of your tween, and click Insert Keyframe. Then, you can animate from one keyframe to the next. You will also have the opportunity to reposition shape hints on each keyframe to help with the desired effect. See the section "Add Shape Hints" to learn about shape hints.

continued

You can use shape tweens to morph shapes. You can also use them to tween a color, or to move a simple shape across the Stage.

● Flash colors the frames of your shape tween green.

⑧ Open the Properties panel.

⑨ Enter an **Ease** value of 100.

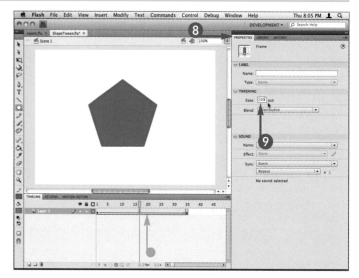

⑩ Click the **Blend** menu and click **Angular** to set your blending.

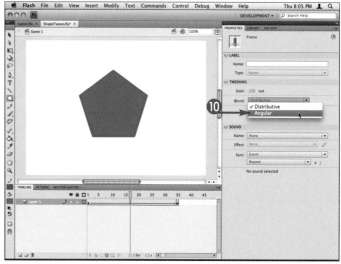

⑪ Click the first frame of your tween.

Press Enter to preview your tween on the Stage.

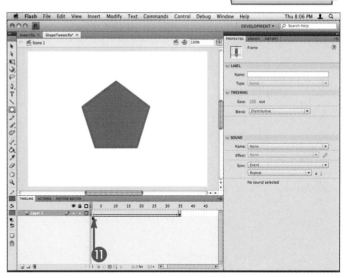

Flash plays the animation.

● Your shape morphs from the starting shape to the ending shape.

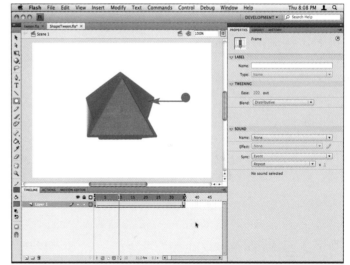

 TIPS

What is the difference between angular and distributive blending?

Angular blending attempts to keep your straight lines straight and corners sharp as the animation plays. Distributive blending attempts to smooth the transition of lines and angles into curves as the tween progresses.

What kinds of changes can I apply to shape tweens?

You can morph the shape, use the **Transform** tool, change colors, and change position of your shape. Shape tweens do not use the motion editor, so many of the controls you have access to with a motion tween are not possible with a shape tween.

Add Shape Hints

You can have more control over the morphing process during a shape tween by using shape hints. A shape hint is a marker that identifies areas on the original shape that match up with areas on the final shape and mark crucial points of change. Shape hints are labeled *a* through *z*, and you can use up to 26 shape hints in a shape tween.

Use shape hints when you are morphing a particularly complex shape. By assigning shape hints to the object you are morphing, you can help Flash figure out points of change.

① Create a shape tween animation.

Note: *See the section "Create a Shape Tween" for details.*

② Click the keyframe containing the original shape you want to morph.

③ Click **Modify**.

④ Click **Shape**.

⑤ Click **Add Shape Hint**.

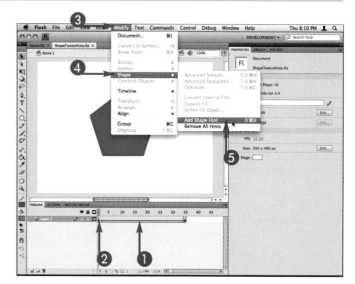

● Flash adds a **Shape Hint** labeled with the letter *a* (⊙) to the center of the shape.

⑥ Click and drag the shape hint to a crucial edge of the object Flash may need help with transforming.

Repeat steps 3 to 6 for any other parts of your shape that Flash needs help with.

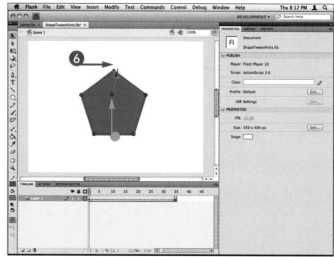

7 Click the last keyframe in the shape tween.

● In this example, shape hints have been added to the final shape.

Note: *Flash stacks all of your shape hints on top of each other in the middle of the stage. In the example, hints a through d are located underneath hint e.*

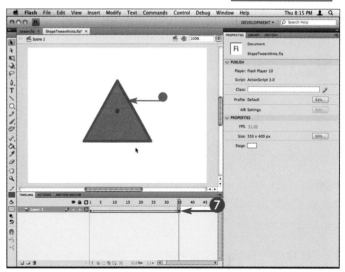

8 Click and drag each shape hint to where you want that point to finish the tween.

Preview your animation by pressing Enter.

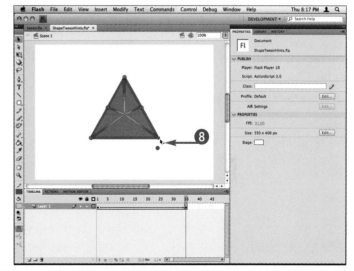

TIPS

What can I do if my shape hints vary their positions between the first keyframe and the last?

Seeing exactly where you place shape hints around an object is not always easy. To help you, make sure you have magnified your view so that you can see where you place the hints. Use the Magnification menu in the upper-right corner of the Stage to set a magnification. Next, turn on the onion-skin feature and move the onion-skin markers to show all the frames within the shape tween. Click 🔲 to turn on the outlining feature. See "Onion-Skinning an Animation" to learn more about onion-skinning.

Can I place shape hints randomly on the object?

Shape hints work best when they are in order, allowing the Flash feature to analyze the difficult points on the object. You may need to arrange your shape hints by trial and error until you get your desired result.

Animate Along a Path

You can create curved paths for your objects to follow during a tween. Flash defaults to a straight line but you can modify it simply by dragging the anchor points along the path. You can also orient your tweened symbol to the direction of the path.

① Create a motion tween.

Note: *See the section "Create a Motion Tween" to learn how to create a motion tween.*

- Your tween's path appears in the color of your layer's outline color.

- Your tween's path contains predefined anchor points.

- The dots on the Stage represent the actual motion of your object per frame.

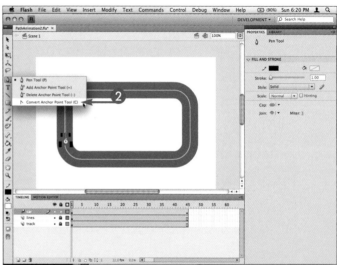

② Click the **Convert Anchor Point** tool ().

Note: *This tool may be hidden behind the Pen tool in the Tools palette. Click and hold the Pen tool to reveal the hidden tools.*

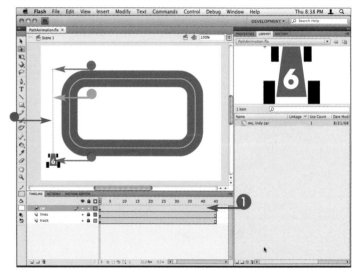

③ Click and drag your path's anchor points with the Convert Anchor Point tool ().

● Your path becomes curved.

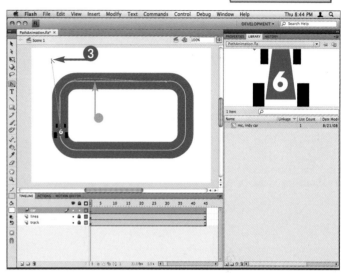

④ Open the Properties panel.

⑤ Click the first frame of your tween.

⑥ Click **Orient to path** in the Properties panel to make your symbol rotate in the direction of your curved path.

● Flash places keyframes for the rotation in your tween.

Press **Enter** to watch your object follow the path.

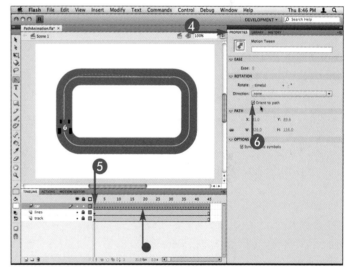

TIPS

How can I create a more complex curve?

You can add anchor points to your curve by adding keyframes in the Timeline during your tween. Right-click on a frame in the middle of your tween and click **Insert Keyframe**, and then click **Position** to add an anchor point to your curve.

Insert Keyframe, Position

My object is not following my path exactly. Why?

If you are using easing, you will notice that the dots on the Stage do not follow your path. Most commonly, this happens when you ease the X position but not the Y, and vice versa. To make your object follow your path exactly, be sure to use the same type of easing for both X and Y.

Create a Movie Clip of an Animation

You can save your animations as a movie clip so the movie clip can be reused in your Flash project. You can also create these movie clips to keep your main Timeline tidy as you add more and more elements and animation.

You can also save animations as graphic symbols for simple applications.

Create a Movie Clip of an Animation

① Select all of the frames of your animation.

② Click **Edit**.

③ Click **Timeline**.

④ Click **Cut Frames**.

You can also press Ctrl+Alt+X (⌘+Option+X).

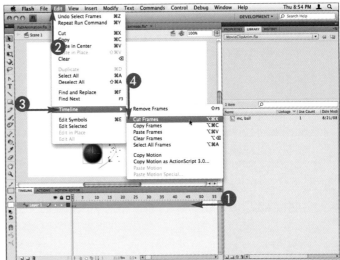

⑤ Open the Library panel.

⑥ Click the **New Symbol** button (🔲).

● The Create New Symbol dialog box appears.

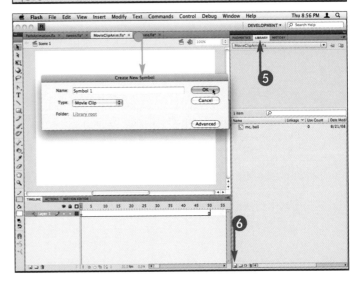

⑦ Click here and type a name for your symbol.

⑧ Click here and select **Movie Clip**.

⑨ Click **OK**.

Flash switches to Symbol Edit mode.

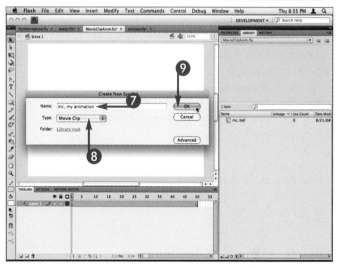

⑩ Click the first frame to select it.

⑪ Click **Edit**.

⑫ Click **Timeline**.

⑬ Click **Paste Frames**.

You can also press Ctrl+Alt+V (⌘+Option+V).

Your animation is now stored in the Library as a movie clip.

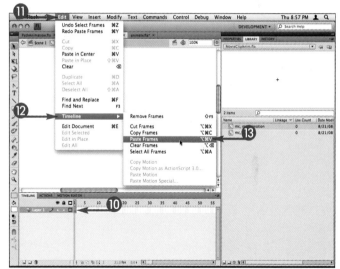

 TIPS

How do I place my animated movie clip into my Flash movie?
Click and drag your newly animated movie clip onto the Stage from the Library. Your animation loops by default. See Chapter 10 to learn how to assign frame actions to change the behavior of your movie clips.

Animate a Mask

You can create captivating movement sequences in Flash using animated masks. For example, you can use a mask to reveal an image in an interesting way or create a handwriting effect where your text appears to be hand-drawn onto the Stage.

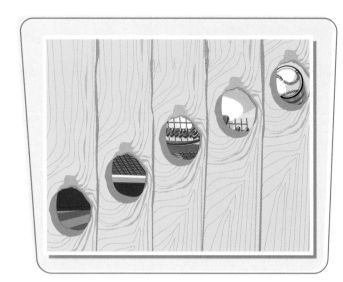

① Place an Image on the Stage.

② Click the **New Layer** button (□).

③ With your new layer selected, click and drag a graphic or movie clip symbol from the Library onto the Stage on top of your image.

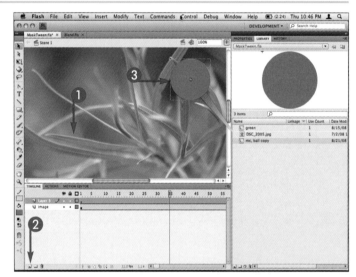

④ Right-click the new layer name.

⑤ Click **Mask**.

Flash locks your mask layer as well as the layer being masked.

⑥ Click the Lock icon (🔒) to unlock your mask layer.

(🔒 changes to ·).

⑦ Create a motion tween on your mask layer.

See the section "Create a Motion Tween" to learn how to create a motion tween.

⑧ Right-click on your mask layer.

⑨ Click **Show Masking**.

● Flash displays the masking effect.

Press Enter to watch your animated mask effect.

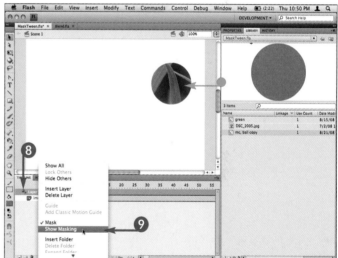

What types of animation can I use for my mask?

Masks can be animated using classic tweens, motion tweens, shape tweens, and frame-by-frame techniques.

Can I use transparency in my mask?

No. In Flash, masks can only be solid. An easy way to imagine a mask is to think of it like a piece of paper with a hole cut in it. The only part of the image you can see is what appears through the hole.

Add Animation to a Button

You can create professional looking rollover effects by adding animation to your buttons. For example, you can have a button fade in or pulse when rolled over. You can also use your imagination and create a rollover effect that does not appear to be a button at all.

① Create a button symbol.

Note: See Chapter 8 to learn how to create a button symbol.

② Open the Library panel.

③ Double-click your button symbol to edit it.

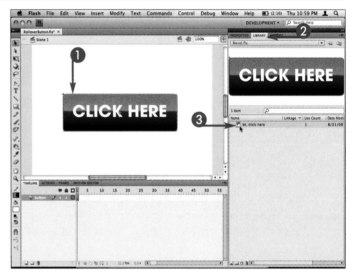

④ Open the Timeline.

⑤ Click the **Over** frame.

The elements on the **Over** frame are selected on the Stage.

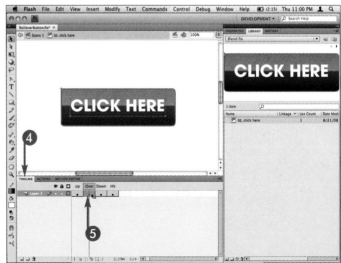

6 Right-click on a selected element on the Stage, and click **Convert to Symbol**.

See Chapter 8 to learn how to create a movie clip symbol.

7 Double-click your new movie clip symbol to edit it.

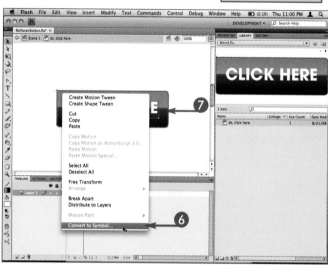

● You can see which symbol you are editing here.

8 Click **Insert**.

9 Click **Timeline**.

10 Click **Layer**.

Flash inserts a new layer.

11 Click on your button's fill with the **Selection** tool ( ).

12 Press Ctrl+X (⌘+X) to cut your fill.

13 Click on frame 1 of your new layer.

14 Press Ctrl+Shift+V (⌘+Shift+V) to paste your fill on the new layer.

15 Right-click frame 20 of your new layer.

16 Click **Insert Keyframe**.

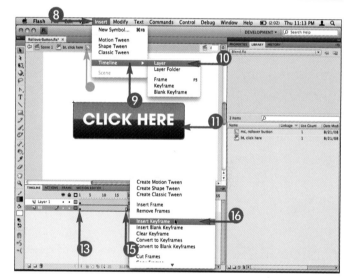

Can I add sounds to my animated button?
Yes. You can place sound symbols on your button's Timeline. Click **Window, Common Libraries, Sounds** to open a panel that includes several sound clips that come with Flash. Drag and drop a sound symbol onto the Stage to add these sounds to your button. To learn how to import and use your own sounds, see Chapter 12.

You can use shape tweens, classic tweens, and motion tweens to add animation to your button. You can also place other types of symbols like movie clips and graphics into the Timeline of your button.

⑰ Right-click on the Timeline between your keyframes.

⑱ Click **Create Shape Tween**.

⑲ Add a keyframe at frame 40.

　To learn how to add a keyframe, see Chapter 7.

⑳ Right-click on the Timeline between frame 20 and 40.

㉑ Click **Create Shape Tween**.

㉒ Click on frame 20 to select it.

㉓ Click on a fill on the Stage with ▸.

㉔ Change the fill color in the Properties panel.

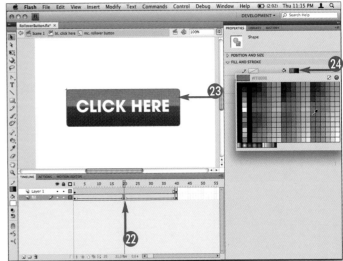

㉕ Press Ctrl + Enter (⌘ + Enter) to test your movie.

㉖ Move your mouse over your button to see the animated rollover effect.

 TIPS

Can I use a motion tween for my rollover animation?

You can. However, you need to create another symbol inside your rollover movie clip to do so. Remember, motion tweens can only be applied to symbols.

Can I also animate the other states of the button?

While it is not commonly done, you can animate the up and down states of your button. It is not a good idea to animate the Hit state because your button may behave unreliably.

Adding Interactivity with ActionScript

You can use ActionScript to ask your Flash movie for information, and to tell your Flash movie what to do.

Introducing ActionScript

You can create interactive projects from simple animations to full-fledged applications with ActionScript.

ActionScript is the programming language used in Flash to make rich interactive experiences and applications. It is based on the ECMAScript specification, much like JavaScript.

Frame Actions

In Flash, you can create actions that are triggered when the play head reaches a particular keyframe of your movie. Most of the time, frame actions are used to tell movie clips to stop or play, or go to a particular frame. You can also use frame actions to set up buttons, handle events (like mouse clicks), and create other functions that your movie can use.

Variables

A variable is a place for your script to store a piece of information. In Flash, you use the *var* keyword to declare a variable. It is also a best practice to add the variable *type* to your declaration. To declare any variable, you should use the syntax:

```
var <variable_name>:<variable_type> = value;
```

For example, to have Flash remember you have 100 tomatoes, you could write the statement:

```
var numberOfTomatoes:Number = 100;
```

Statements

Statements are the instructions of your ActionScript. Declaration statements set aside memory for a value that is assigned later. Assignment statements set a value to a variable. Conditional statements are formed with a premise and a conclusion: if A, then B. Loop statements cause a series of statements to execute continuously, as long as the test condition remains true.

```
var variableName:variableType;      // A declaration statement
variableName = value;                 // An assignment statement

// A conditional statement
if (condition) {
    // statements inside execute if the condition is true
}
// A loop statement
while (condition) {
    // statements inside execute repeatedly while the condition is true
}
```

Functions

A function is a piece of ActionScript that performs a task. To create a function in ActionScript, you use the following syntax:

```
function <function_name> (<parameters>):<return type> {
    // statements go inside the curly braces
}
```

For example, to write a function that doubles the number of tomatoes, you could write the function:

```
function doubleIt(aNumber):Number {
    return aNumber * 2;
}
```

To use this function, you can call it like this:

```
var newNumberOfTomoatoes:Number = doubleIt(numberOfTomatoes);
```

Classes and Instances

A *class* is a blueprint for an object or the concept of an object. Symbols and components in the Library are classes. And, like symbols in the Library, you can create instances in ActionScript. An *instance* is the realization of a class. For example, you could have a class called "Cat" but an instance of Cat would be "Murray." Similarly, in Flash you have a class called Button and could have an instance of that class called homeButton. To create an instance in ActionScript, you use the new keyword. For example:

```
var murray:Cat = new Cat();
```

You can create your own classes in Flash, but this chapter deals primarily with using the classes that Flash has already provided in ActionScript.

Using the Actions Panel

The Actions panel has many features that allow you to write ActionScript more easily, including a toolbox that contains all of the built-in objects and functions that you can use in your projects.

● The Toolbox

Allows you to select your ActionScript version and displays a menu of all of the commands available to you.

● ActionScript Editor

You can type your scripts here, or you can use the **Toolbox** or **Add new item to the script** (⊞) button to create scripts.

● Pin Active Script

Click the **pin** button to make the current script appear in the Actions panel regardless of what frame of the Timeline you have selected.

● Script Assist

You can click this button with ActionScript selected to get useful input fields that may help you in writing your script.

● Help

Click here for help with Adobe Flash. This button links to a Help page on the Adobe Web site.

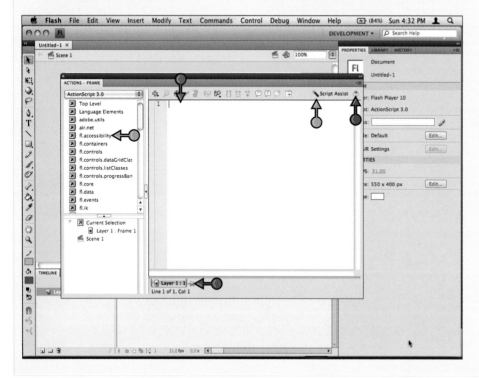

● **Add a New Item to the Script**

Click this button to add a new item to your script. The menu behind this button contains everything available to you in your chosen ActionScript version.

● **Find**

This button allows you to find and replace text in your script panel, much like you would in a word-processing application or other text editor.

● **Insert a Target Path**

You do not need to memorize the instance names and nesting of the movie clips in your movie. Click the Target button to see a dialog box that shows your instances in outline form. Clicking an instance places its path in your script.

● **Check Syntax**

Click this button to make sure your script is written properly. If you have any errors, Flash opens the Output panel and gives you a description of the issue.

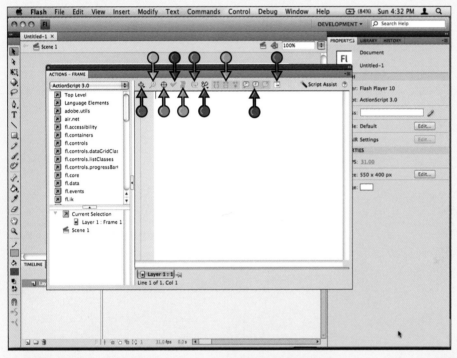

● **Auto Format**

This button automatically sets the indentation of your script to make it easier to read.

● **Show Code Hint**

Click this button when you type ActionScript and Flash offers suggestions of keywords that you can click to complete your script more easily.

● **Debug Options**

This button controls the use of breakpoints in your script.

● **Collapse and Expand Controls**

This set of buttons allows you to collapse and expand portions of script to help make it easier to manage longer scripts.

● **Commenting Controls**

This set of buttons allows you to quickly create and remove comments.

● **Show/Hide Toolbox**

You can click here to show and hide the Toolbox on the left of the Actions panel.

Assign Frame Actions

You can use frame actions to control the main Timeline or to control a movie clip. Frame actions must be placed on a keyframe. For clarity, it is a best practice to reserve a layer in the Timeline only for actions and to place other elements on other layers.

Assign Frame Actions

① Open the Timeline.

② Right-click on frame 20 and click **Insert Keyframe**.

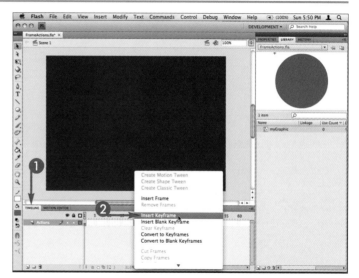

③ Right-click your new keyframe and click **Actions**.

The Actions panel opens.

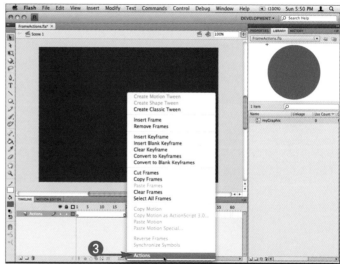

④ In the Actions window type **trace("Stopping at frame 20");**.

⑤ On a new line, type **stop();**.

● An icon (⊞) appears in your keyframe to show that it has actions in it.

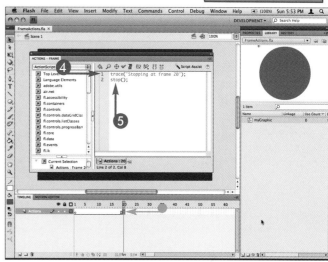

⑥ Click **Control**.

⑦ Click **Test Movie**.

Your movie plays and prints Stopping at frame 20 in the Output window and then stops.

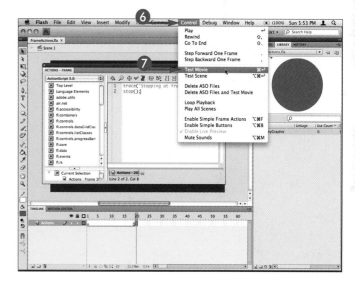

How can I edit my frame actions when the play head is on a different frame?

You can click the **Pin Active Script** button (📌) in the Actions panel. Doing so creates a tab in the Actions panel for the current script, which is accessible no matter what frame of the Timeline the play head is on.

Add a gotoAndPlay() Action to the Timeline

You can add actions to a movie clip's Timeline to control how it plays. You can make a movie clip animation play repeatedly using the gotoAndPlay() action, creating a looping effect.

Add a gotoAndPlay() Action to the Timeline

1 Open the Timeline panel.

2 Create a 20 frame motion tween on the main Timeline.

Note: *See Chapter 9 to learn how to create a tween.*

3 Click the **New Layer** button (■).

● A new layer appears on the Timeline.

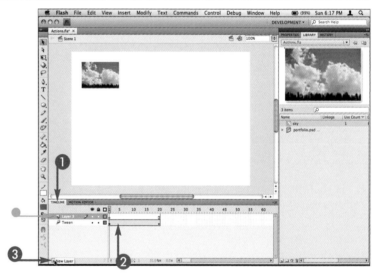

4 Right-click on frame 20 of your new layer, and click **Insert Keyframe**.

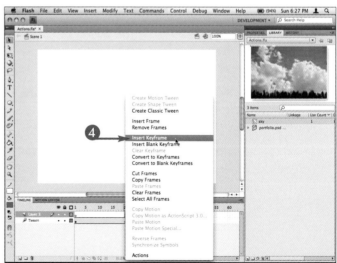

⑤ Right-click on your new keyframe and click **Actions**.

The Actions panel opens.

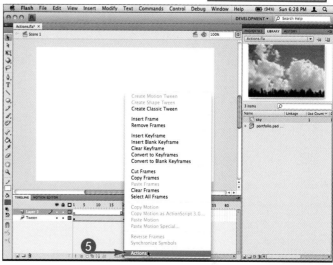

⑥ In the **Actions** panel, type **this.gotoAndPlay(1);**.

Press Ctrl + Enter (⌘ + Enter) to test your movie and watch your animation continuously loop.

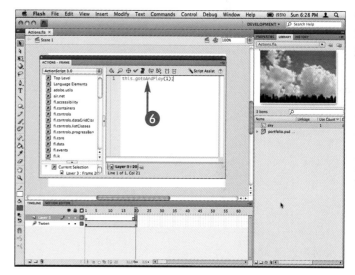

TIP

Can I preview my movie's frame actions without publishing or exporting?
Yes. Click **Control**, and then **Enable Simple Frame Actions**. Flash allows certain actions like play(), stop(), and gotoAndPlay() to work when you play through the Timeline.

Preview
Frame
Actions

Work with Instances in ActionScript

Any instance of a button, movie clip, or other object with an instance name can have properties. These properties can be read and modified. Instances can also have functions that can be called that affect their behavior.

Instance Names and Target Paths

Any instance that you want to be able to talk to through ActionScript needs an instance name. This name allows you to *target* the instance you want. You need to use the full *target path* to talk to an instance that is nested inside other objects. For example, from the main Timeline, to target a movie clip with the instance name "ball" on the main Timeline, you would use the following:

```
this.ball
```

To target a movie clip named ball that is inside an object named field that is inside an object named stadium, you would use the path:

```
this.stadium.field.ball
```

Relative Target Paths in Flash

Flash reserves three keywords to make it easier to access your movie clips and objects in ActionScript 3: this, parent, and root. The keyword refers to the Timeline you are currently working on. The parent keyword refers to the object that your current object is inside. For example, if you are writing a script on the Timeline of ball in the previous example, and you want to reference field, your target path would be the following:

```
this.parent
```

The root keyword always refers to the main Timeline of your Flash movie. So, to reference field another way from the Timeline of ball, you could use the following path:

```
root.stadium.field
```

Getting Instance Properties

You can ask an object what the values of certain properties are in ActionScript. To find the x position of the ball movie clip from the previous example, you could use the following syntax:

```
var x_position =
this.stadium.field.ball.x;
trace(x_position);
```

Setting Instance Properties

You can also set instance properties through ActionScript. To set the alpha of the ball movie clip to 50 percent, you can assign the value of the alpha property to 0.5, as shown in the following:

```
this.stadium.field.ball.alpha = 0.5;
```

Calling Instance Methods

An instance method is a function that specifies a behavior that your object can have. Movie clip objects have instance methods like play(), stop(), gotoAndPlay(), gotoAndStop(), nextFrame(), and prevFrame(). To call an instance method, you first type the target path to your object, add a dot (.), and then the method name. For example, to tell a movie clip with the instance name ball to go to its next frame, you would use the following script:

```
this.ball.nextFrame();
```

Move a Movie Clip with ActionScript

You can animate movie clip instances by listening for an ENTER_FRAME event. Every time Flash renders a frame, it broadcasts a message to every object that is listening. At 31 frames per second (fps), you can reposition a movie clip 31 times a second, creating a smooth animation.

The steps in this section assume you are using ActionScript 3.0. If you are using an earlier version of ActionScript, both your AddScript menu and the list in the Actions panel will differ.

Move a Movie Clip with ActionScript

① Press Ctrl+L (⌘+L).

The Library panel opens.

② Drag a MovieClip symbol from the Library to the Stage.

Note: See Chapter 8 to learn about creating movie clips.

③ Click the movie clip you want to animate with the Selection tool ( ).

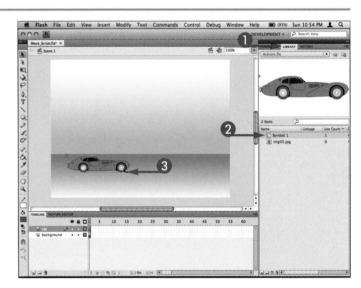

④ Open the Properties panel.

⑤ Click here and type an instance name for your movie clip.

This example uses a movie clip with the instance name mc_car.

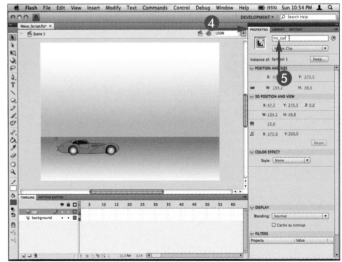

6 Press F9.

The Actions panel opens.

7 Click the **Target** icon (⊕).

Note: If your Actions panel says that the current selection cannot have actions applied to it, click on a frame in the Timeline to create your frame actions.

8 Click your movie clip to select it.

9 Click **OK**.

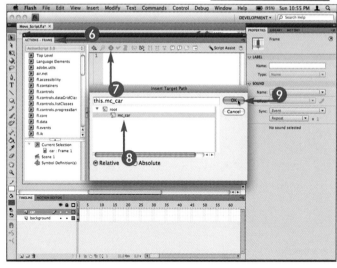

10 Click the **Add new item to the script** button (⊕).

11 Click **flash.events**.

12 Click **EventDispatcher**.

13 Click **Methods**.

14 Click **addEventListener**.

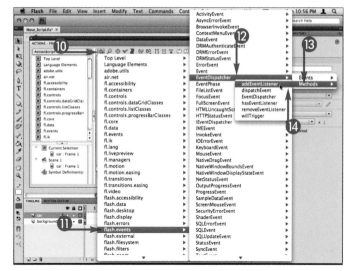

How can I set my font and color preferences for the ActionScript window?
Click **Flash**, **Preferences**, and then click on **ActionScript** in the left column. The Preference panel has options to change your font and syntax colors. There are also preferences that you can set for code hints, import and export file types, and language settings.

continued ▶

To move your movie clip, you can simply change its x and/or y properties. These property values are in pixels, so make sure you do not set their values to a number larger than the Stage size (or to a negative number), unless you want your movie clip to disappear.

Move a Movie Clip with ActionScript *(continued)*

⑮ Click 🔧.

⑯ Click **flash.events**.

⑰ Click **Event**.

⑱ Click **Properties**.

⑲ Click **ENTER_FRAME**.

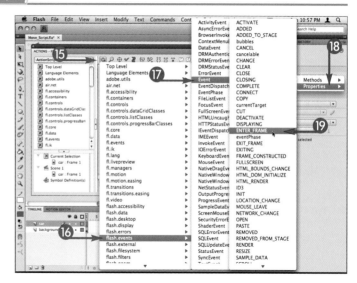

⑳ Type a comma, and then the second parameter, which references a function name.

In this example, the function name is **animate**.

Note: *"animate" is just the name that you will use for your animation function. You can use any name you want, as long as the term is not a reserved ActionScript keyword.*

㉑ Type a semicolon at the end of the line of script.

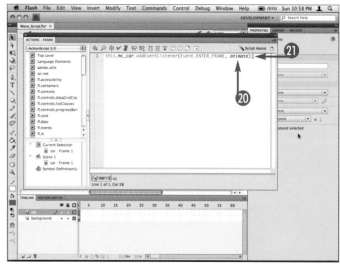

22 Declare a variable to store the final position of your movie clip by typing:

var destination:Number = 325;.

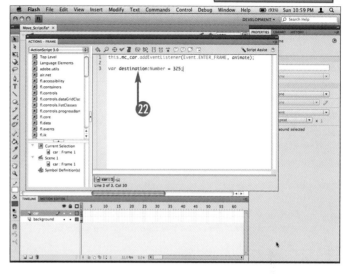

23 Type the animate function:

function animate(evt:Event){
evt.currentTarget.x -=
(evt.currentTarget.x -
destination) / 10;

}

24 Click **Control**, and then **Test Movie** to test your animation.

You can also press Ctrl + Enter (⌘ + Enter).

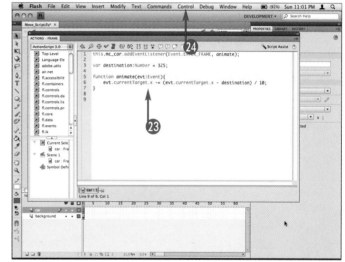

What other properties can I animate using ActionScript?

You can animate any property of a movie clip or object using ActionScript. To view a list of DisplayObject properties, click the **flash.display** category in the Actions window. Inside **flash.display**, click **DisplayObject**. Inside **DisplayObject**, click **Properties**. All display properties are listed inside.

With this example, you can easily change the script to move your movie clip along the y-axis. Change `evt.currentTarget.x` to `evt.currentTarget.y`. Test the move again, and watch your movie clip move vertically rather than horizontally.

How do I check my script for errors?

If you click the **Check Syntax** button (✓), Flash displays the Compiler Errors panel with your errors. The Compiler Errors panel also appears when you test your movie if your script contains errors.

Fade Out a Movie Clip with ActionScript

You can use the ENTER_FRAME event to perform other tasks over time in Flash. The following demonstrates how to gradually change the alpha property of a movie clip, creating a fade effect.

Fade Out a Movie Clip with ActionScript

① Open the Library panel.

② Drag an Instance of a movie clip on to the Stage.

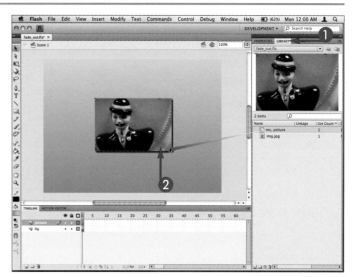

③ Open the Properties panel.

④ Click here and type an instance name for your movie clip.

This example uses a movie clip with the instance name mc_picture.

5 Press **F9**.

The Actions panel appears.

6 Type **this.mc_picture.addEventListener (Event.ENTER_FRAME, fade);** to add an event listener.

Note: If your Actions panel says that the current selection cannot have actions applied to it, click on a frame in the Timeline to create your frame actions.

● `this.mc_picture` is the target movie clip's instance name.

● `Event.ENTER_FRAME` is the event that the target is listening for.

● `fade` is the name of the function that is called when the event is triggered.

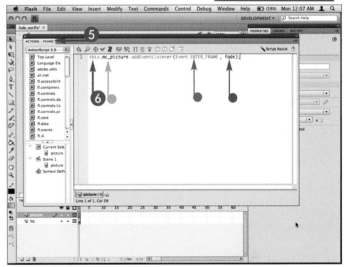

7 Type **function fade(evt:Event):void { }** to create a function named fade.

● Because the `fade` function is an event handler, it takes an event as a parameter.

● Because the `fade` function does not return a value, its return type is void.

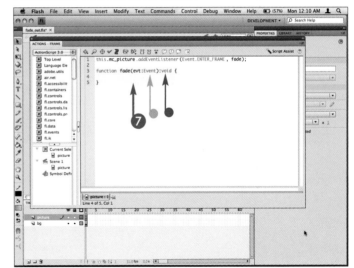

TIP

How can I change the appearance of my scripts in the Actions panel?
You can click **Flash, Preferences**, and then click on the ActionScript category to customize the Actions panel. Then, you can change your indentation preference, code hint timing, font, style, and syntax colors.

continued

By creating your animation in ActionScript, you can create scripts that can be used by multiple objects. This both saves you development time and gives your project a consistent animation style.

Fade Out a Movie Clip with ActionScript (continued)

8 Create an expression that subtracts 0.01 from the alpha property of the target object by typing the following between the curly braces of the fade function: **evt.currentTarget.alpha -= 0.01;**

● `evt.curentTarget` is a reference to the object that is calling this fuction.

● `-=` sets the first value to its current value minus the second value.

Note: For more on operators, see Appendix C.

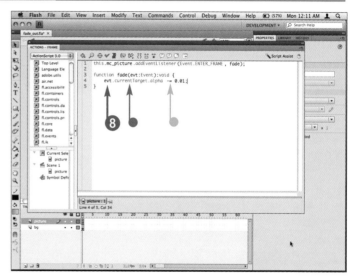

9 To test to see if your fade has completed, add an `if` statement to your fade function by typing:

if (evt.currentTarget.alpha <= 0) {

}

This statement checks to see if the **alpha** property is less than or equal to zero.

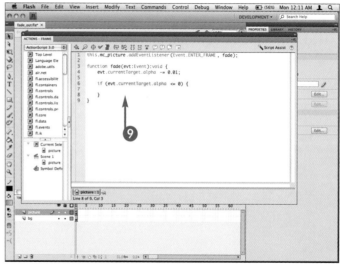

⑩ Inside the curly braces of your `if` statement, remove the event listener by typing:

evt.currentTarget.removeEventListener(Event.ENTER_FRAME, fade);

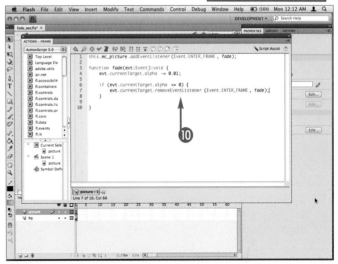

⑪ Click **Control**.

⑫ Click **Test Movie** to test your fade effect.

You can also press Ctrl + Enter (⌘ + Enter).

The movie clip fades out slowly.

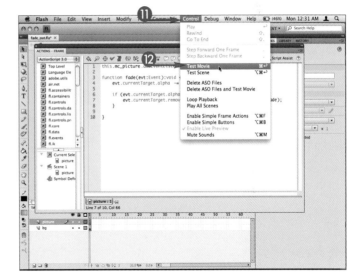

 TIP

How can I test to see that my `if` statement is working properly?

You can place a `trace()` statement inside your `if` statement to see if the condition is met. In this example, you might add:

```
trace("fade completed.");
```

between the curly braces of your `if` statement. If your condition is met, fade completed appears in the Output window when you test your movie.

Animate Using the Flash Transitions Package

You can create ActionScript transitions with tweens by using the Flash transitions package (fl.transitions). This package contains several classes that you can use for animation, such as Fade, Fly, Iris, Zoom, and more.

Animate Using the Flash Transitions Package

① Open the Library panel.

② Drag an instance of a movie clip onto the Stage.

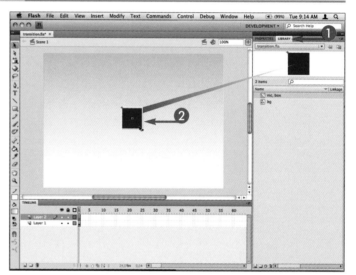

③ Open the Properties panel.

④ Click here and type an instance name for your movie clip.

This example uses a movie clip with the instance name box.

⑤ Click on the keyframe where your instance appears on the Stage.

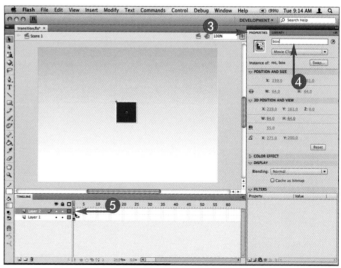

6 Press F9 (Option + F9).

The Actions panel appears.

7 Type **import fl.transitions.*;** to import the transitions package.

8 Type **import fl.transitions.easing.*;** to import the easing classes.

9 Type **TransitionManager.start(box, {type:Fly, direction:Transition.IN, duration:3, easing:Elastic.easeOut, startPoint:2});**

● This is the Instance name of the object the transition is applied to.

● These are the parameters of the transition.

10 Click **Control**.

11 **Test Movie**.

Flash plays your transition in the test movie window.

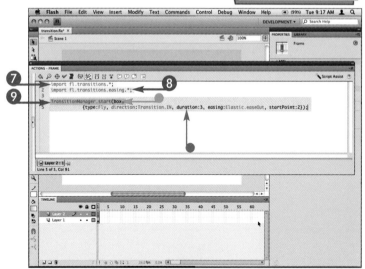

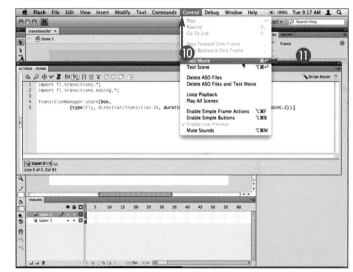

What are the different options for startPoint in my transition?

The startPoint property is a number that corresponds to a particular starting position relative to the stage. Top left = 1, top center = 2, top right = 3, left center = 4, center = 5, right center = 6, bottom left = 7, bottom center = 8, and bottom right = 9.

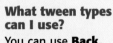

What tween types can I use?

You can use **Back, Bounce, Elastic, None, Regular,** and **Strong** easing. And, all of these can be eased in, out, or both in and out.

Understanding Events and Event Handlers

In Flash, an Event is any type of interaction, such as a mouse click, mouse move, rollover, or key press. Events can also be triggered by object instances in Flash. For example, MovieClip objects can broadcast events like ENTER_FRAME, and Loader objects can broadcast events like COMPLETE.

About Events and Event Handlers

A good way to think about events and event listeners is to think about the police responding to a crime, like a robbery. Any time there is a robbery, the police precinct dispatches officers to the crime scene. The officers *listen* for a *robbery* event, and *dispatch* whenever a robbery occurs. Then, the officers need to know how to respond to a robbery. For example, maybe they need to proceed on foot and draw their weapons. In ActionScript, your *event handler* is the function that performs actions when an event occurs.

Adding Event Listeners

In ActionScript 3.0, you can add events to objects by calling the addEventListener() function like this, where *officers* is the target, *ROBBERY,* is the event, and *dispatchToRobbery* is the event handler:

```
officers.addEventListener(ROBBERY,
dispatchToRobbery);
```

In practice, you will likely use a listener more like this:

```
myButton.addEventListener(MouseEvent.M
OUSE_DOWN, onMouseClick);
```

This statement tells Flash to listen for a mouse click on an instance called myButton. When that event occurs, the function onMouseClick is executed.

Creating Event Handlers

The *event handler* is the function that is executed when an event occurs. In ActionScript 3.0, event handlers take an object of type `Event` as a parameter. The following is an example of what the `dispatchToRobbery` handler might look like, taking the parameter named `evt`, of type `Event`:

```
function dispatchToRobbery(evt:Event):void {
// proceed on foot and draw weapons
}
```

A handler for the mouse click example might look like this:

```
function onMouseClick(evt:Event):void {
   trace("my button was clicked! ");
}
```

Event Targets

There are two places you use your event target in ActionScript. You provide the target when you create the listener, but you can also use the target in your event handler. For example, if you want the `myButton` object to disappear when clicked, your handler might look like this:

```
function onMouseClick(evt:Event):void {
   myButton.visible = false;
}
```

But, if you wanted *any* button to become invisible when clicked, you could add the same event listener to all of them, but change your handler to look like this:

```
 function onMouseClick(evt:Event):void {
   evt.currentTarget.visible = false;
}
```

In this case, `evt.currentTarget` is a reference to whichever listening button is clicked.

Removing Event Listeners

Sometimes, you want your objects to stop listening for events. To do so, you remove the listener by calling `removeEventListener`. Suppose in the police officer example the officers go on vacation, and they no longer need to respond to robberies. The script to remove their event listener looks like this:

```
officers.removeEventListener(ROBBERY,
dispatchToRobbery);
```

In the practical example, you would delete your mouse click listener like this:

```
myButton.removeEventListener(MouseEvent.MOUSE_DOWN,
onMouseClick);
```

Start and Stop an Animation with a Button

You can create interactivity in your Flash movies by combining animation with controls like buttons. Your buttons can listen for mouse events, and perform actions when those events occur.

Start and Stop an Animation with a Button

1 Open the Library panel.

2 Drag a movie clip animation onto the Stage.

Note: See Chapter 9 to learn how to make a movie clip of an animation.

3 Drag an instance of a button symbol onto the Stage.

Note: See Chapter 8 to learn how to make a button symbol.

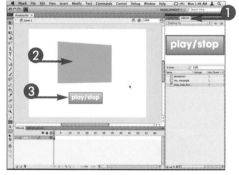

4 Open the Properties panel.

5 Click your movie clip to select it.

6 Click here and type an instance name.

In this example, it is named animation.

7 Click your button to select it.

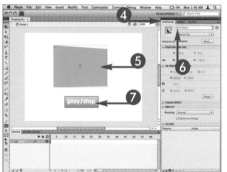

8 Type the instance name myButton.

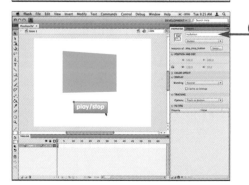

9 Click a keyframe and open the **Actions** panel.

You can also press **F9**.

The Actions panel opens.

10 Declare a variable called `isPlaying` and set its value to `false` by typing:
var isPlaying = false;.

11 Add an event listener to your button by typing:
this.myButton.addEventListener(MouseEvent.MOUSE_DOWN, onButtonClicked);

12 Type the event handler function:
**function onButtonClicked(evt:Event):void {
}**

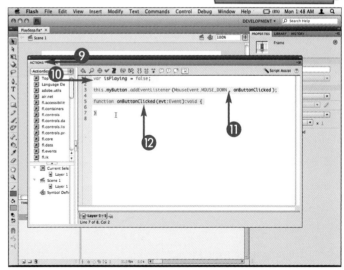

13 Inside the curly braces of the `onButton Clicked` function, type:
**if (isPlaying) {
    animation.stop();
    isPlaying = false;
} else {
    animation.play();
    isPlaying = true;
}**

Test your movie **Ctrl**+**Enter** (**⌘**+**Enter**) and click your button to see it start and stop your animation.

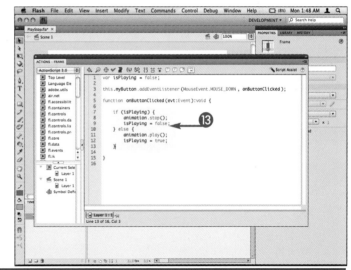

TIPS

How can I create comments to make my script more readable?

You can write comments in ActionScript to give yourself or someone else reading your code information that you want Flash to ignore. A single line comment is written with two backslashes like this:

`// this is a single-line comment`

You can write multiline comments like this:

`/* Multiline comments start with a slash followed by an asterisk. To end a multiline comment type an asterisk followed by a slash */.`

My ActionScript has odd indentation. Is there an easy way to format it properly?

You can click the **Auto Format script** (▤) button to have Flash automatically reset the indentation of each line of your script. However, if your script contains errors, the formatting will fail.

Create a Dynamic Text Counter

You can set the value of a dynamic text field to display information generated by ActionScript. Dynamic text fields are used to display things like game scores or results in an application like a calculator.

1. Click the **Text** tool (T).

2. Open the Properties panel.

3. Click the top drop-down list in the Properties panel and choose **Dynamic Text.**

4. Click and drag on the Stage to create a dynamic text field.

5. Click here and type an instance name for your text field.

   In this example, the text field has the instance name myField.

6. Create a button instance on the Stage.

Note: See Chapter 8 to learn about creating buttons.

7. Click here and type an instance name for your button.

   In this example, the button has the instance name myButton.

240

8 Right-click on the first frame of the Timeline and click **Actions**.

9 Add an event listener to your button by typing:
this.myButton.addEventListener(MouseEvent.MOUSE_DOWN, myButtonClicked);

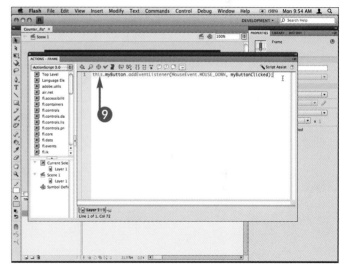

TIP

Can I use HTML in my text field?
You can. But instead of setting the .text property, you need to set the .htmlText property. Like this:

```
this.myField.htmlText = "<b>bold HTML text<b> ";
```

continued

Create a Dynamic Text Counter *(continued)*

Dynamic text fields can only display *strings* in ActionScript 3.0. If you want to display other types of information in your text field, such as numbers or objects, you can convert them to a string using the toString() method.

⑩ Declare a variable that will store the number of clicks and set it to 0 by typing:
var clicks = 0;

⑪ Type the event handler function:

**function
myButtonClicked(evt:Event):
void {
}**

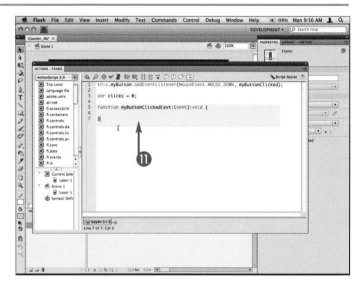

⑫ Inside the curly braces of the event handler, type:
this.myField.text = clicks++;

● myField is the instance name of the dynamic text field.

● The text property of a text field is the text that will be displayed.

● The ++ operator adds one to the value of the `clicks` variable.

Note: *See Appendix C to learn about other ActionScript operators.*

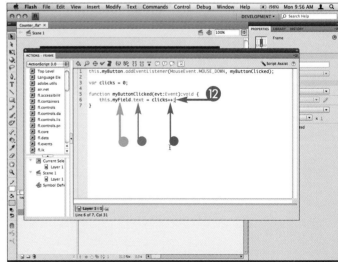

⑬ Click **Control**.

⑭ Click **Test Movie**.

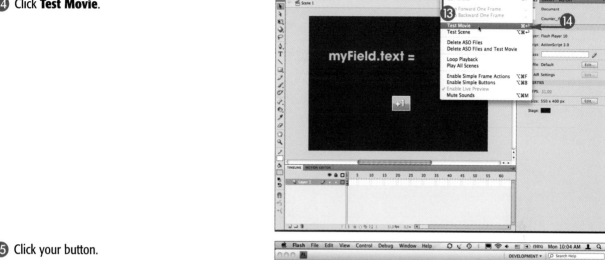

⑮ Click your button.

The value of the text field increases.

TIPS

How can I put letters inside my text field along with the number?

You can place more complex dynamic content into your text field using *concatenation.* In Flash, the **+** operator is used to concatenate. Try replacing this:

`this.myField.text = clicks++;`

with this:

`this.myField.text = "number of clicks: " + clicks++;`

My dynamic text gets cut off once the number reaches multiple digits. How can I fix this?

You can edit the text field on the Stage to make it wider. Or, you can set your text field to automatically resize to fit. In ActionScript, you can set the autoSize property of your text field to true, like this:

`this.myField.autoSize = true;`

Create and Include an External ActionScript File

You can compose your scripts in a separate ActionScript (.as) file and include them in your Flash movie. This is a great way to keep your Scripts organized, and it also makes them easy to reuse in other projects.

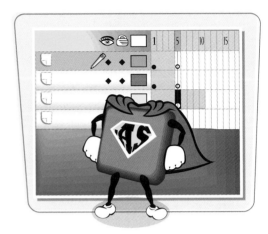

CREATE THE SCRIPT FILE

1 Click **File.**

2 Click **New.**

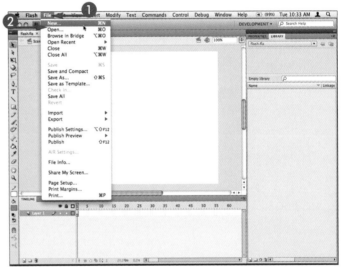

The New Document dialog box opens.

3 Click **ActionScript File**.

4 Click **OK**.

Flash creates a new file.

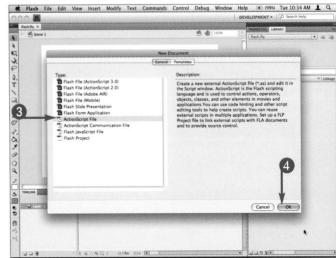

⑤ In your new ActionScript file, type: **trace("helo separate script file!");**

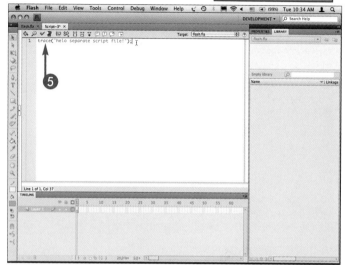

⑥ Press **Ctrl**+**S** (**⌘**+**S**).

The save dialog appears.

⑦ Name your ActionScript file test.as.

⑧ Click **Save.**

Flash saves the file.

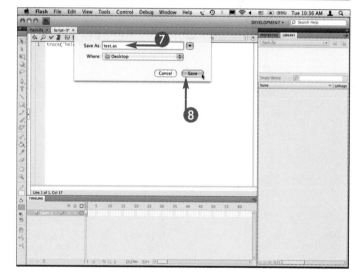

Your external scripts are executed on the frame where you include them, unless they only contain function and variable declarations.

Create and Include an External ActionScript File *(continued)*

INCLUDE THE SCRIPT IN YOUR MOVIE

① Click **File**.

② Click **New**.

③ Click **Flash File (ActionScript 3.0)**.

④ Click **OK**.

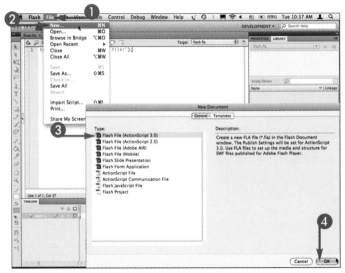

⑤ Right-click on the first frame of the Timeline.

⑥ Click **Actions**.

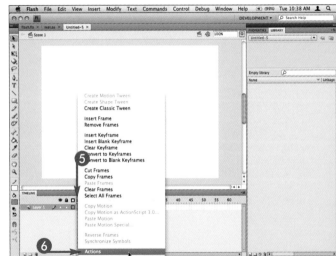

The Actions panel opens.

7 Type **include "test.as."**

Note: *Your script file must be in the same directory as your Flash movie for this* `include` *statement to work.*

Test your movie Ctrl + Enter
(⌘ + Enter).

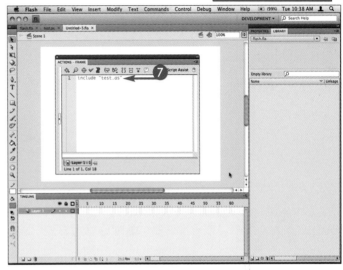

● Flash prints **helo separate script file!** to the Output window.

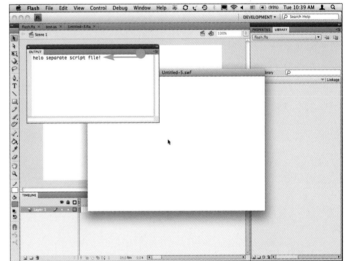

Can I create external ActionScript files with other programs?
Yes. Many developers prefer to use external editors to write their script, like TextMate, or Eclipse. You must make sure that whatever editor you use, that you save your file as *plain text*, to ensure that Flash can read it properly.

Adding Interactivity with User Interface Components

Components are special movie clip symbols that have extra functionality built in. You can use these components to create anything from a simple form to full-fledged, rich Internet applications.

Components are the building blocks for creating applications and rich interactive experiences in Flash. They allow you to quickly build projects that include user interface elements such as lists, combo boxes, and scrolling areas. Components also make it easy to have a consistent look and feel for all aspects of a user interface.

The Components Panel

This panel works very much like the Flash Library. It is prepopulated with all of the components that are on your system. You can drag and drop these components right onto the Stage to use them in your project.

The Component Inspector

Use this panel to set your component's parameters. The other two tabs, Bindings and Schema, can only be used with ActionScript 1.0 or 2.0.

Component Properties

Because a component is a movie clip, you can use the Properties panel to adjust its size, color effects, and blending.

Component Skins and Assets

The component skin is the look of the component. The skin is made up of several assets, which appear in your Library. However, the easiest way to change the look of your component is to place it on the Stage, double-click it, and edit the elements that appear inside.

9-Slice Scaling

Most if the UI components use 9-slice scaling. This type of scaling allows you to change the height and width of an object without distorting rounded corners or stretching sides in the usual way.

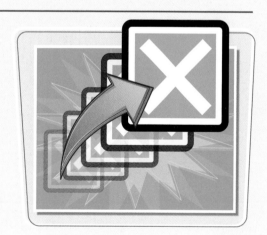

Add a Component

You can add a user interface component to your Flash movie as easily as you would a movie clip, graphic, or button symbol.

Add a Component

1 Click **Window**.

2 Click **Components**.

3 Click here to expand the User Interface components.

4 Click and drag a component onto the Stage.

● In this example, a button component is added.

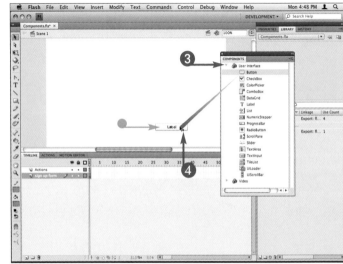

5 Click **Window**.

6 Click **Component Inspector**.

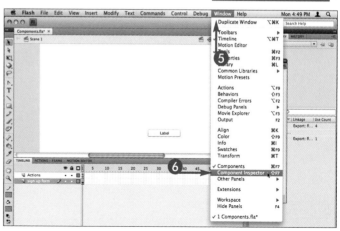

The Component Inspector appears.

7 Click the **Parameters** tab.

8 Click the Value column to edit the parameter values you want to change.

● In this example, the label parameter has been changed to Sign Up!

● The emphasized parameter has also been set to true.

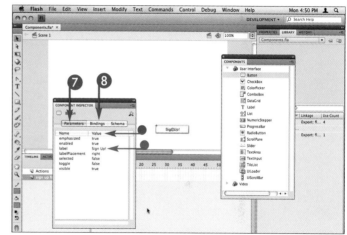

How do I make Flash react to clicking my button component?

You need to write some ActionScript to use the button component. First, give your component an instance name in the Properties panel. In this case, the button's instance name is myButton. Then click a the keyframe on the Timeline that contains your component and open the Actions panel. Type this script:

```
import fl.events.ComponentEvent;
myButton.addEventListener(ComponentEvent.BUTTON_DOWN, onClick);
function onClick (evt:Event) {
    trace("Sign Up!");
}
```

When you test your Flash movie, clicking the button prints Sign Up! to the output window. See Chapter 10 to learn more about Flash events and adding interactivity with ActionScript.

Delete a Component

You can delete a component from the Stage by clicking it with the Selection tool and pressing Delete. But there will be leftover assets in your Library that you can clean up as well. Here are two ways to keep your Library tidy when removing components.

COMPONENT DELETION
WASTE REMOVAL CORP.

Delete a Component

① Click a component that is on the Stage with the **Selection** tool (➤).

In this example, there is a Sign Up form on the Stage.

② Click **Edit**.

③ Click **Clear**.

You can also press Delete.

In this example, we deleted a check box component.

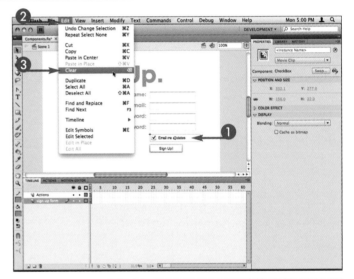

④ Open the Library panel.

● Your components appear in the Library.

● The Use Count column tells you how many instances of a symbol are used in your Flash movie.

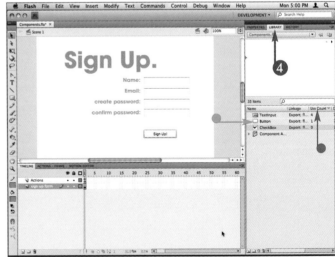

⑤ Click a component with a use count of 0.

⑥ Click the **Delete** button ().

You can also click `Delete`.

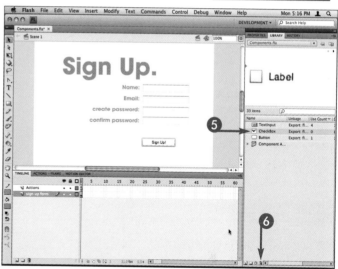

⑦ Expand the Component Assets folder in the Library.

Note: If you are using a version of ActionScript earlier than ActionScript 3, your component's assets are not added to the Library.

⑧ Click on the Skins folder that corresponds to the component you deleted.

⑨ Click .

Your component is deleted from both the Stage and the Library.

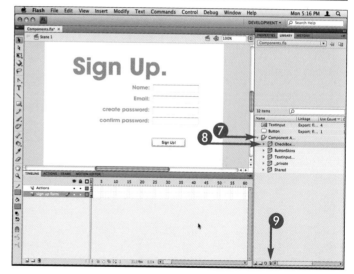

TIP

I clicked the Select Unused Items menu item in the Library, but it didn't select my unused component. Why?

Components, by default, are always exported with your Flash movie so that ActionScript can use them. So, even though you are not technically using a component, Flash needs to keep it in the Library in case your scripts call for it. You can see what symbols are being exported for ActionScript by looking at the Linkage column in the Library panel.

Modify a Component's Parameters

You can change a component's parameters using the Component Inspector. Depending on which component you are working with, you can add things like a prompt, a label, parameters that control the behavior of the component, additional data, or other parameters.

Modify a Component's Parameters

1 Add a ComboBox component to the Stage.

See the section "Add a Component" to learn how to add a component to the Stage.

2 Click **Window**.

3 Click **Component Inspector**.

The Component Inspector panel appears.

4 If your component is not selected, click your component with 🔦.

5 Click the **Value** column next to Prompt.

6 Type a prompt message in the text box that appears.

In this example, Select one... is typed.

7 Click the **Value** column next to DataProvider.

8 Click the magnifying glass icon (🔍).

The Values dialog box appears.

chapter **11**

⑨ Click the **Add** button (🖰).

⑩ Click the Value column for data and label and type your menu items in the text box that appears.

Repeat steps 9 and 10 to populate your ComboBox with menu items.

⑪ Click **OK**.

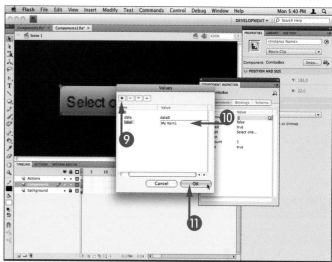

⑫ Click **Control**.

⑬ Click **Test Movie**.

You can use your ComboBox.

TIP

My Component doesn't appear properly on the Stage. Why?
Click **Control, Enable Live Preview** if it is not checked. Live Preview allows you to view components on the Stage with the look that they will have in your exported Flash movie.

Skin a Button Component

You can change the appearance of the Flash user interface components by creating a new skin. The easiest way to create a new skin is to simply edit the default skin to make it look the way you want.

Skin a Button Component

1. Add a button component to the Stage.

   See the section "Add a Component" to learn how to add a component.

2. Right-click on the button component and click **Edit**.

The component's assets appear on the Stage.

- Selected_up, selected_over, selected_disabled, and selected_down states appear when you press Tab to select the button in your exported movie.

- Down, over, and up are the standard states of a button.

- Emphasized and disabled states can be used through ActionScript or through the component's parameters.

- The focusRectSkin is shared by many components. Make sure when you edit this asset that it works with all components that use it.

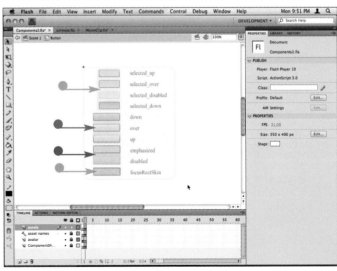

③ Right-click on one of the assets of the component and click **Edit**.

④ Using the Flash drawing tools, draw a new button background.

See Chapter 2 to learn how to use the Flash drawing tools.

⑤ Adjust the guides for 9-slice scailng.

⑥ Click here to return to your button component's assets.

Repeat steps **3** to **6** to edit all of the assets of your component that you use.

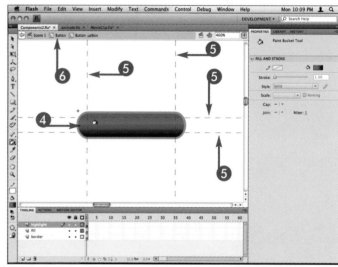

TIPS

Does my new button skin apply to all button components in my Flash movie?

Yes. The default for Flash is to use the same skin for all components of the same type. While it is possible to create unique skins for individual components, it is a fairly complicated process that isn't used very often.

Do I need to create skins for every element of my component?

No. Your component will function as expected whether you skin one element or all elements of the skin. However, once you change part of a component skin, you will usually want to change the remaining parts in order to create a unified look and feel for the whole component.

continued

259

The assets appear in your Library as movie clips when you add a component to your Flash movie. You can skin your components by editing these movie clips. If you make a mistake and want to go back to the original skin, you can delete the assets from the Library and drag a new component to the Stage.

Skin a Button Component *(continued)*

● The necessary component assets have been redesigned.

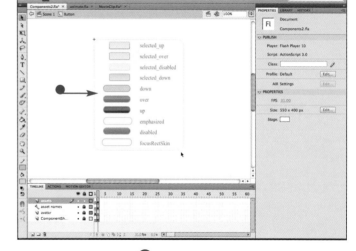

⑦ Click **Control**.

⑧ Click **Test Movie**.

Your movie appears in the Flash Player, showing the new up state of your button.

⑨ Move your cursor over the button to check the rollover state.

⑩ Click here to test the down state of your component.

How do I make my new button download an image?

First, give your component an instance name in the Properties panel. In this case, the button's instance name is myButton. Then click a frame on the main Timeline and open the Actions panel. Type this script:

```
import fl.events.ComponentEvent;
myButton.addEventListener(ComponentEvent.BUTTON_DOWN, onClick);
function onClick (evt:Event) {
    navigateToURL(new
URLRequest("http://www.google.com/intl/en_ALL/images/logo.gif"), '_blank');
}
```

When you click your button, it opens a Web browser and attempts to load an image from the Internet. See Chapter 10 to learn more about Flash events and adding interactivity with ActionScript.

Integrating Sound

Sound is a great way to make your Flash movies feel more alive. You can add music, audio loops, user interface sounds, and animation sounds to enhance your projects.

Flash does not have the ability to record sounds directly, but you can import various sound files for use in your project. After you import a sound, it becomes a symbol in your Library that can be reused wherever you need it in your project.

1 Click **File**.

2 Click **Import**.

3 Click **Import to Library**.

Note: *You can also use the Import to Stage command, which imports your file both to the Stage and to the Library.*

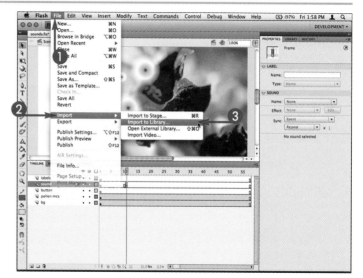

4 Click the sound file you want to import.

● If you want to import a particular file format, you can select it here.

5 Click **Import to Library**.

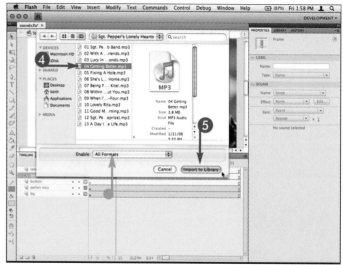

⑥ Press `Ctrl`+`L` (`⌘`+`L`) to open the Library panel if it is not already open.

You can also open the Library by clicking **Window**, and then **Library**.

⑦ Click on your sound file in the Library.

● Your sound waveform appears as a preview.

⑧ Click the **Play** button (▶).

Flash plays your sound.

TIPS

Will a sound file make my Flash movie's file size huge?

It depends. Short interface sounds are fairly lightweight, while long audio loops and MP3 song files can be very large. You can compress the audio in your project by right-clicking on your sound symbol and then clicking **Properties**. The Properties inspector has options for compressing your audio.

What kinds of audio files can Flash import?

Flash supports several sound formats, including MP3, AIFF, WAV, AU, Adobe Sound Document, and SDII.

Add Event Sounds to the Timeline

You can add event sounds when you have sounds that are dependent on animations or sounds that you want to trigger when you reach a particular frame of the Timeline.

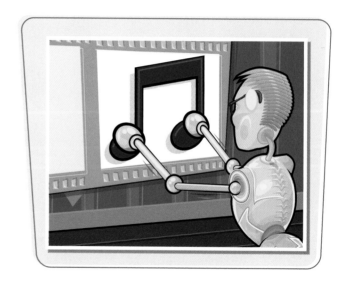

Add Event Sounds to the Timeline

① Insert a blank keyframe where you want your sound to begin.

See Chapter 7 to learn how to insert keyframes.

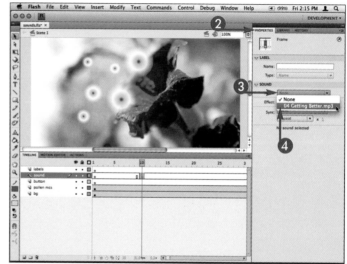

② Open the Properties inspector.

③ Under the Sound section, click the **Name** menu.

④ Click your sound to select it.

● A sound wave appears in the Timeline.

5 Click **Control**.

6 Click **Test Movie**.

You can also press Ctrl + Enter (⌘ + Enter).

Flash tests your movie.

TIP

What do the Sync options do?

Event always plays a sound in its entirety, independent of whether the Timeline stops or changes frames.

Start sync does almost exactly the same thing as an Event sound, but if your sound is already playing, another instance begins to play.

Stop sync stops a sound that is already playing.

Stream forces your Flash movie to keep up with the sound. Sometimes this causes Flash to skip frames in order to keep up with the sound and remain synchronized.

See the section "Add Streaming Sound to the Timeline" to learn how to add and test streaming sounds.

Add Sound to a Button

The most common user interface sounds are triggered when you mouse over or click on buttons. You can add these sounds easily using event sounds.

① Place an instance of a button symbol on the Stage.

See Chapter 8 to learn about placing an instance on the Stage.

② Right-click on your button and click **Edit in Place**.

Note: *You can also edit in place by double-clicking an object on the Stage.*

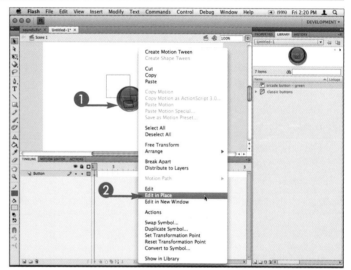

● The Timeline of the button appears with frames for button states.

③ Click a keyframe in the Down column.

Note: *If you do not have a keyframe in the down column, right-click the frame and click **Insert Keyframe**.*

④ Open the Properties inspector.

⑤ Choose a sound from the Name menu.

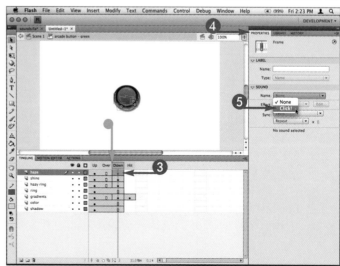

6 Make sure your sync is set to **Event**.

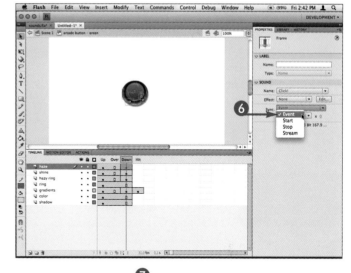

7 Click **Control**.

8 Click **Enable Simple Buttons**.

9 Click **Scene 1** to return to the main Timeline.

When you click your button, the sound plays.

TIPS

Which button frame should I assign my sound to?

Typically, you add sound to the Over frame, creating a rollover effect. You may also want to add sound to the Down frame to let your user know that the button has been clicked. Do not add sound to the Hit frame because Flash never reaches the Hit frame, so your sound will never play.

I don't have the option to add sound to a frame. Why not?

You can only add sounds to keyframes, and not to regular frames in the Timeline. Make sure to add a keyframe wherever you want to add sound.

Add Streaming Sound to the Timeline

You can use streaming sounds to ensure that your picture is in sync with your audio. Flash automatically skips over frames on the Timeline to ensure sync. On the Web, streaming sounds also do not need to be completely downloaded in order to begin playing.

Add Streaming Sound to the Timeline

① Right-click on the Timeline where you want your sound to begin and click **Insert Blank Keyframe**.

② Open the Properties inspector.

③ Under the Sound section, click the **Name** menu.

④ Click your sound to select it.

● A sound wave appears in the Timeline.

⑤ Click on the **Sync** menu and click **Stream**.

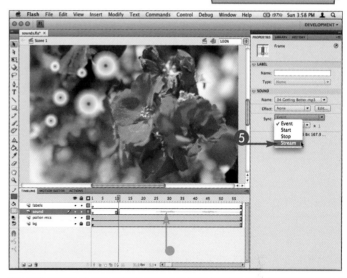

⑥ Click and drag the Timeline's play head (▯) across the sound wave.

You hear the sound associated with each frame you drag over.

TIP

My streaming sound doesn't play all the way through. Why?
When using streaming sounds, you need to make sure you have enough frames in your Flash movie. An easy way to make sure is to add frames to the Timeline until you no longer see the blue sound waveform (▭────▭).

Fade a Sound In and Out

Flash includes some very simple sound-editing tools. You can fade your sounds in and out, set a stereo fade, and set the number of loops. Using these types of fades can give your sound design more polish and enhance your animations.

Fade a Sound In and Out

1. Add a sound to the Timeline.

   To learn how to add sound to the Timeline, see the section "Add Event Sounds to the Timeline."

2. Open the Properties inspector.

3. In the Sound section, click **Edit**.

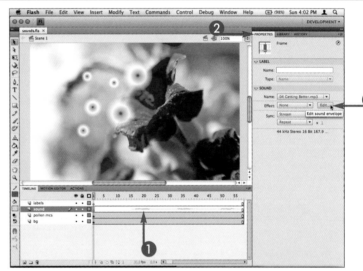

- The Edit Envelope dialog box appears.

4. Click the sound wave and drag the first cue point (⬜) to a volume of zero.

5. Click and drag the sound wave to create a second cue point, and position it at the top.

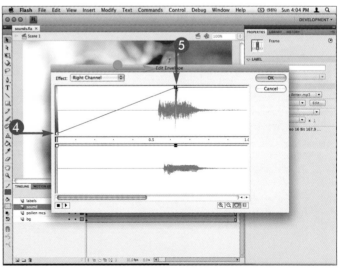

6 Click and drag to add another cue point, and return the volume to zero.

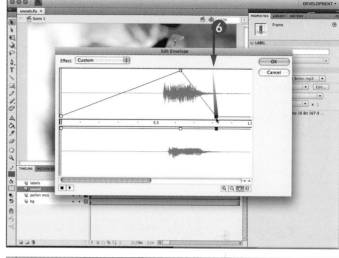

7 Repeat **steps 4 to 6** for the left channel if your sound file is stereo.

8 Click **OK**.

You can click **Control** and then **Test Movie** to test your movie.

Your sound fades in and out.

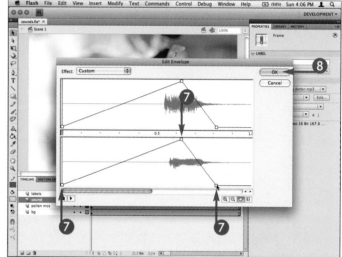

When I export my movie, it drops too many frames and looks choppy. What can I do?

You can solve this issue a few different ways. One way is to lower your Flash movie's overall frame rate. Another is to simplify your animation. You can also try setting your sound sync to Event or Start.

Create a Sound Loop

You can use looping to create background music or other ambient audio for your Flash project. Music loops require precise editing in an application other than Flash, while ambient loops can be achieved using Flash's built-in fading effects.

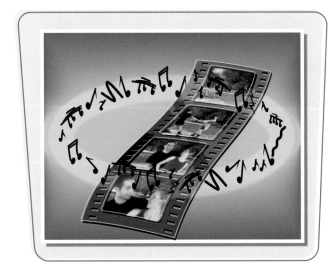

Create a Sound Loop

① Add a sound to the Timeline.

Note: *See the section "Add Event Sounds to the Timeline" to learn to add sounds to the Timeline.*

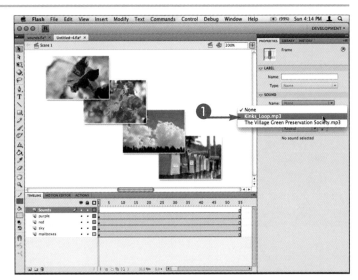

② Open the Properties inspector.

③ Click the **Sync** menu and click **Event**.

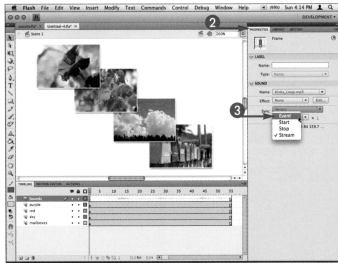

④ Click the second **Sync** menu and click **Loop**.

⑤ Click **Control**.

⑥ Click **Test Movie**.

Flash tests your movie and your sound loops continuously.

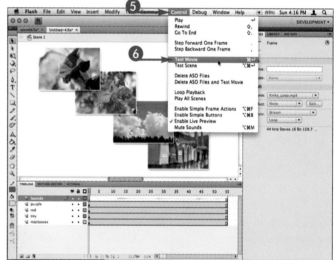

Can I have my sound loop a limited number of times?

Yes. Instead of setting your sync to Loop, you can set it to Repeat. Then, if you click on the blue number next to the Sync menus, you can type the number of times you want your sound to play.

I hear a popping sound between loops. Can I fix this in Flash?

Yes. If you place very short fade effects at the beginning and end of your sound, you can minimize pops and clicks between loops. See the section "Fade a Sound In and Out" to learn how.

Edit Audio Settings for Export

You can control how sounds are exported in your Flash files. Depending on where you are going to display your final movie, you may want to limit file size by using a lot of compression. Or you may want the best quality possible when downloading is not an issue. By default, Flash exports your sounds as 16Kbps MP3 files.

Edit Audio Settings for Export

① Click **File**.

② Click **Publish Settings**.

The Publish Settings dialog box appears.

③ Click the **Flash** tab.

④ Click **Set** next to the type of sound you want to modify.

Note: *In this example **Audio event** is being set.*

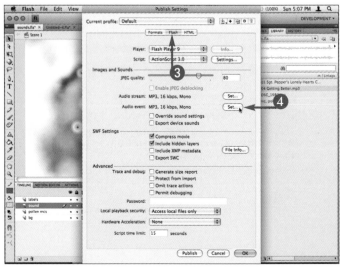

The **Sound Settings** dialog box appears.

⑤ Click the **Compression** menu drop-down box.

⑥ Click the compression format you want to use.

Depending on the format you select, the remaining options change.

⑦ Modify your sound options.

⑧ Click **OK**.

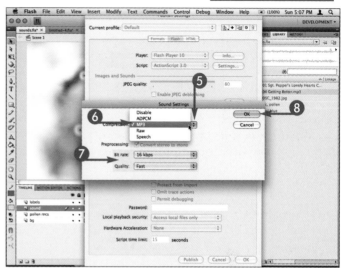

⑨ Click **OK**.

Flash saves your audio settings.

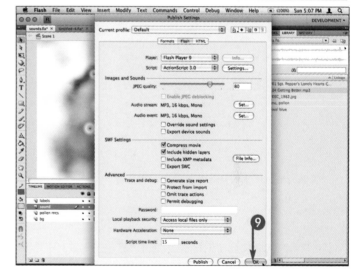

How can I use a different type of compression for a particular sound, leaving the default for all other sounds?

In the Library, you can right-click on a sound symbol and click **Properties**. This displays the Sound Properties dialog box, where you can change the export settings for a single sound. Many times, you can use a fairly low-quality default setting for user interface sounds and then set the quality individually for music and ambient loops.

Adding Video

You can use video in your Flash projects and create playback controls for them. This chapter demonstrates a few basic methods for including video in your Flash movies.

Understanding FLV and F4V Files

Adobe uses its own video formats for use with Flash: FLV and F4V. If you want to convert a movie from another format use Flash Media Encoder, or a similar application, to encode your file.

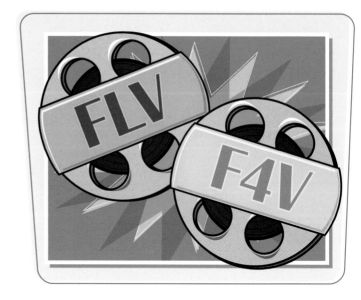

FLV

FLV files can be played in Flash Player 6 and higher. About 80 percent of the video content online right now is encoded in the FLV format. You can work with FLV files as external resources. Or you can use FLV files by importing them directly into the Library for use in the Timeline.

F4V

Beginning with Flash Player 9 Update 3, Flash Player can play F4V files. F4V allows for higher quality than the older FLV. Flash Media Encoder has many presets for this new format, including many high-definition options, as well as options designed for delivery over the Web.

Flash Media Encoder

Flash Media Encoder is the tool that allows you to create your own FLV and F4V files. If you do not have it on your system, you can download it for free at www.adobe.com/cfusion/entitlement/index.cfm?e=fme.

Flash Media Encoder Presets

In most cases, you can use the menu of presets to find a compression level to suit your needs. The default presets include 1080p at various sizes, NTSC, PAL, and settings for the Web.

Flash Media Encoder Export Settings

You can use Flash Media Encoder to do things like remove the audio track, adjust audio encoding, add a blur effect, and adjust many other settings. You can also save your own special settings to add to the list of presets.

To learn more about Flash Media Encoder, look on the Adobe Web site at www.adobe.com.

Embed a Video

You can embed video directly into your Flash movie for playback on the Timeline. It is recommended that you only embed video this way when using short clips (10 seconds or less) and no audio. Flash uses a wizard to make it easy to import video files.

Embed a Video

① Click **File**.

② Click **Import**.

③ Click **Import Video**.

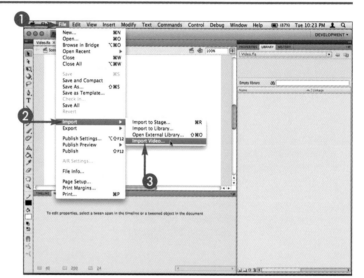

The Import Video Wizard appears.

④ Select the **On your computer** option for the location of your FLV file.

● Flash presents any warnings here.

⑤ Click **Browse** and choose an FLV file to open.

⑥ Select the **Embed FLV in SWF and play in timeline** option.

⑦ Click **Next (Continue)**.

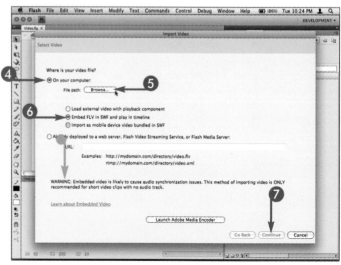

⑧ Click **Embedded video** from the Symbol type drop-down list.

⑨ Make sure the **Include Audio** option is deselected.

⑩ Click **Next (Continue)**.

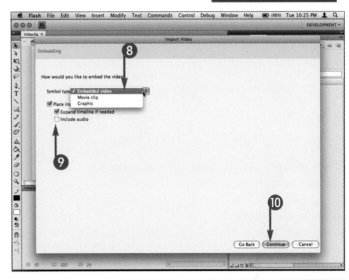

⑪ Review your video importing settings here.

⑫ Click **Finish**.

Flash places your video in the Library, as well as on the Stage.

You can test your movie Ctrl + Enter (⌘ + Enter) to see it play.

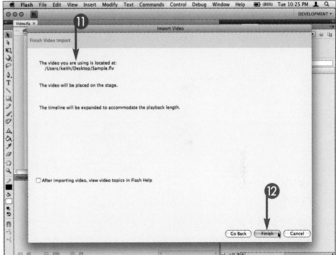

Can I import my video as a movie clip?

Yes. Sometimes you will want the small videos you embed in your Flash movie to have effects, blend modes, transforms, and other properties that movie clips can have. In the Import Wizard, just set the type to MovieClip and Flash creates a MovieClip symbol in the Library instead of a video symbol.

You can import video for playback using a video player component. Using this method, your video file and playback component are not a part of your exported SWF file. The video file and player component are external files that your main Flash movie loads dynamically at runtime.

If your FLV or F4V file is already on the Internet, you can stream that video into your Flash movie.

Import a Video

1. Click **File**.
2. Click **Import**.
3. Click **Import Video**.

The Import Video Wizard appears.

4. Select the **On your computer** option for the location of your FLV file.

- If you have a Web server or streaming service, you can select this option and type the URL of your video file.

5. Click **Browse** and choose an FLV file to open.

6. Select the **Load external video with playback component** option.

7. Click **Next (Continue)**.

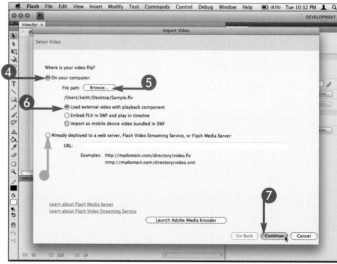

8 Click the **Skin** drop-down box, and choose **SkinUnderAll.swf**.

Note: If you want to limit the video controls, you can choose another skin.

9 Click here and select a color for your video player component.

10 Click **Next (Continue)**.

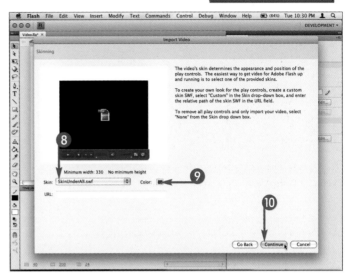

11 Review your video-importing settings here.

12 Click **Finish**.

Flash places a video placeholder on the Stage.

You can preview your movie by clicking **File**, **Publish Preview**, and then **Default**, or you can press `Ctrl`+`F12` (`⌘`+`F12`).

 TIP

How can I allow my video to be viewed at Full-Screen?
There are three things you need to do to make the Full-Screen option work in Flash. First, click **File** and then **Publish Settings**. Then click the HTML tab, and change your template to Flash Only – Allow Full Screen. Then click the Full Screen button to select a component when you import your video file. Finally, publish your movie and view it in a Web browser. You can test this quickly by clicking **File**, **Publish Preview**, and then **HTML**.

Skinning the Video Player Component

You can create your own component skin to create a unified look and feel to your project. Flash components are made up of movie clip assets that make up the *skin*. You can change the look of your components by editing these assets or by creating your own.

Skinning the Video Player Component

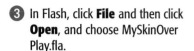

① In Windows Explorer (or Finder on a Mac), make a copy of Common/Configuration/FLVPlayback Skins/FLA/ActionScript 3.0/SkinOver Play.fla on your Desktop.

② Rename the file MySkinOverPlay.fla.

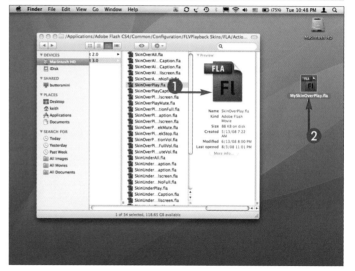

③ In Flash, click **File** and then click **Open**, and choose MySkinOver Play.fla.

④ Click **Open**.

The skin file opens.

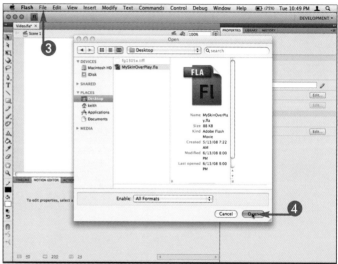

⑤ Click the **Edit Symbols** button ().

⑥ Click **Play Button**.

⑦ Click **Assets**.

⑧ Click **PlayIcon**.

⑨ Draw your own icon with the Flash drawing tools.

Note: *To learn how to draw in Flash, see Chapters 2 and 3.*

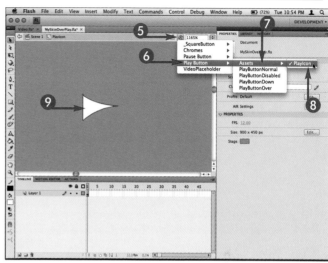

⑩ Click again.

⑪ Click **_SquareButton**.

⑫ Click **SquareBgNormal**.

● A square version of the button appears.

● Dashed guides for 9-slice Scaling appear.

   You can now edit the look of your component with the Flash drawing tools.

Note: *See Chapter 3 to learn about modifying artwork in Flash.*

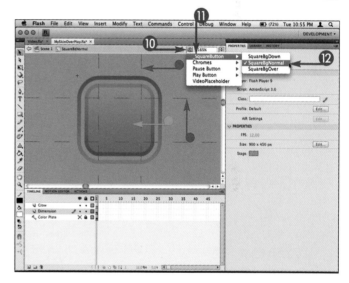

TIP

What is 9-slice Scaling?
9-slice Scaling allows a movie clip to scale without affecting the proportions of corners and edges. In Flash, when you edit a movie clip with 9-slice Scaling enabled, a set of dashed guides appears denoting the slices. When the movie clip is scaled or transformed, the outer slices remain the same size, while the center slice changes scale. This method of scaling is very useful when you have many buttons or pop-up windows of various sizes and you want them all to have the same graphic style.

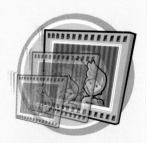

Once you create your own video player skin, you can use it in as many projects as you want. You can also use your own component skin as the basis for creating a new one.

Skinning the Video Player Component *(continued)*

⑬ Click **Scene 1**.

Repeat steps **5** to **9** for the remaining elements of the skin.

⑭ Look at the **Sample Controls Layers** and see if you need to edit other button states, and edit them as you did in steps **4** to **12**

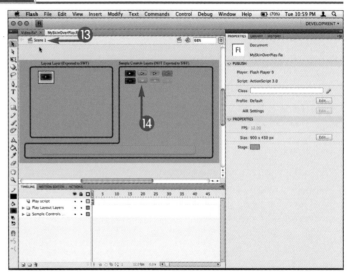

⑮ Click **File**.

⑯ Click **Export**.

⑰ Click **Export Movie**.

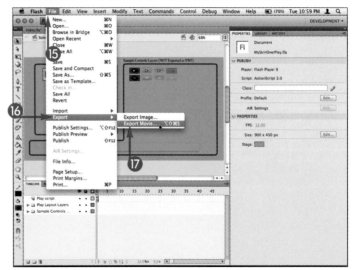

⓲ Place your exported SWF file in the Flash folder: Configuration/ FLVPlayback Skins/ActionScript 3.0.

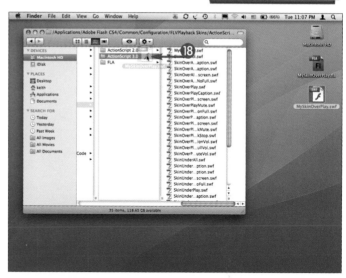

⓳ Your skin appears in the Skin menu of the Import Video Wizard.

Note: *See the section "Import a Video" to learn how to use your new skin.*

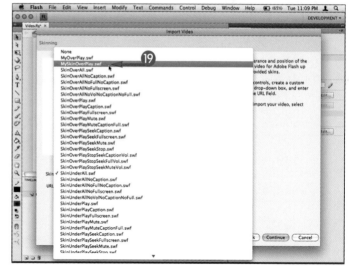

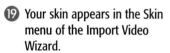

TIP

Can I modify my skin's look and behavior after importing a video with it?

Yes. Once you import a video with a video player skin, you can click **Window**, **Component Inspector** to open the inspector. You can then change the behavior and other properties of the video player the same way you would customize other components. There are options to set your video to auto-play, set the preview frame of the video, set the background color of the skin, adjust the way your video can scale, and several other options.

Loading External Elements Dynamically at Runtime

You do not need to put all of your images and text inside your Flash movie. You can load separate, external files that contain your content and use your Flash movie as a shell.

Understanding Dynamic Content in Flash

You can use dynamic content to keep your text, images, and other Flash movies externalized, so they may be edited without needing to republish your movie. Dynamic Flash content is content that is not a part of your Flash movie or exported SWF file. It is content that your Flash movie loads on demand, through ActionScript or through the UILoader component.

Use Dynamic Content for Flexibility

Sometimes, you will want to replace an image or change some text in your Flash movie. If all of that content is part of your published SWF file, you need to open Flash, make your changes, and republish. But, if you load your image and text dynamically, you can simply edit those assets and leave your Flash movie alone. Dynamic content also makes it easy for you to work on a Flash project with other people. You can separate your project into several sections and then bring together those sections by loading them as they are needed.

Managing Asset Loading

Suppose you want to build a 200-image photo gallery in Flash. If you put all those images in your Flash movie, it could take a very long time to load over the Internet. However, you can load your photos as needed and not include them in your Flash movie at all. This way, you can minimize the file size of your main movie and create a better, faster experience for your users.

XML

The preferred way to pass data into your Flash application is to load files written in Extensible Markup Language (XML). You can create XML files that contain text you want to display in your movie, paths to images and other Flash movies, numbers, color information, or any kind of data your Flash movie might need. Flash has built-in methods that allow you to easily get information from a loaded XML file.

The UILoader Component

You can use the UILoader component to dynamically load SWF, JPEG, PNG, and GIF files into your movie. You can also change the height and width of the UILoader component to fit your design. The UILoader also works seamlessly with the ProgressBar component, so you can create loading bars for content that may take time to load over the Internet.

Classes for Loading Content

You can use ActionScript classes to load content dynamically. The URLLoader class is used to download data from a URL like XML data, text files, or binary information. You can use the Loader class to load SWF files and images. Both of these classes broadcast events to let you know when a download has completed or changed status.

Load a JPEG File Dynamically with a Component

You can use the UILoader component to dynamically load an image into your Flash movie. There are two ways to use the UILoader component: through the Component Inspector and through ActionScript.

Load a JPEG File Dynamically with a Component

① Click **Window**.

② Click **Components**.

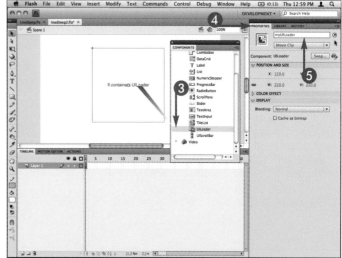

③ Click and drag an instance of the UILoader component onto the Stage.

④ Open the **Properties** panel.

⑤ Type an instance name and press **Enter**.

In this example, the instance name is myUILoader.

294

⑥ Click **Window**.

⑦ Click **Component Inspector**.

The Component Inspector opens.

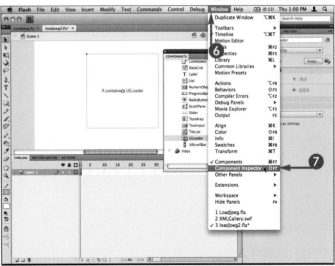

⑧ Type the URL of an image in the Value column next to source.

Test your movie Ctrl + Enter (⌘ + Enter) and your image loads into the component's area.

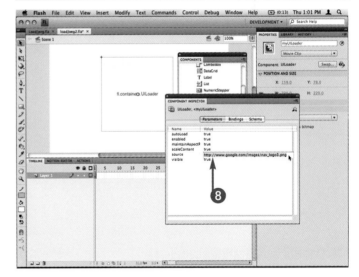

TIPS

How do I load an image from my hard drive?

You can place an image file in the same folder as your Flash movie and set the source value to the name of your image. You can also set the source value to the path of the image on your computer.

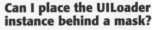

Can I place the UILoader instance behind a mask?

Yes. Very often you will want to constrain the height and width of your loaded image without setting it to stretch in the component. Placing the UILoader behind a mask is a great way to do that.

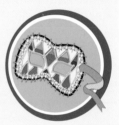

Load a SWF File Dynamically with ActionScript

You can load SWF files and images with the Loader class. The Loader class works in a similar way to the UILoader component, but it does not require a component — only ActionScript.

Load a SWF File Dynamically with ActionScript

LOAD THE SWF

① Click a keyframe on the Timeline.

② Click **Window**.

③ Click **Actions**.

The Actions panel opens.

You can also press **F9** (**Option** + **F9**).

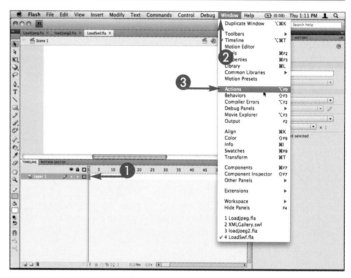

④ Type **var mySwfPath:URLRequest = new URLRequest("?");** replacing *?* with the URL, or file path, of the SWF file you want to load.

⑤ Create an instance of the Loader class by typing **var swfLoader:Loader = new Loader();**.

⑥ Type **this.addChild(swfLoader);**.

⑦ Type **swfLoader.load(mySwfPath);**.

You can test your movie **Ctrl** + **Enter** (**⌘** + **Enter**) to see the image load.

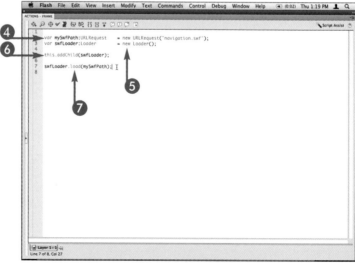

PERFOM AN ACTION AFTER LOADING IS COMPLETE

⑧ Type **swfLoader.contentLoaderInfo. addEventListener(Event.COMPLETE, onComplete);** to listen for the COMPLETE event.

⑨ Type **function onComplete(evt:Event) { trace("SWF load has finished!"); }**.

● Make sure your function name is the same as the function name you specified in the addEventListener call.

Test your movie using the Simulate Download option.

Note: *See Chapter 15 to learn how to simulate a download.*

● Your Flash movie loads the SWF file.

● The Output window opens and displays the result of your trace() statement.

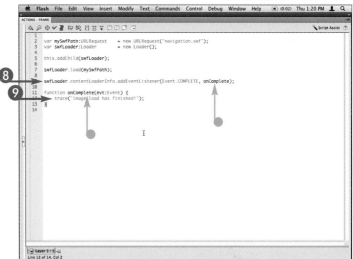

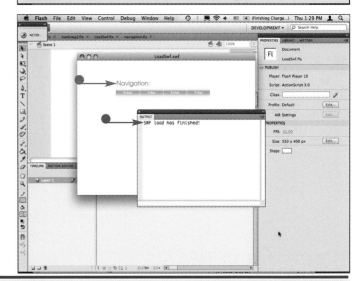

TIPS

How do I reposition and adjust the properties of my loaded SWF?

You can adjust any properties of the loaded SWF by targeting your Loader instance. In this case, you could add the lines swfLoader.x = 100; and swfLoader.alpha = 0.5; to move the loaded movie to an x-position of 100 and to set the alpha to 50 percent. Because the Loader class inherits from DisplayObject, you can see a list of possible properties by clicking the **Add New Item To the Script** button (⊕), and clicking **flash.display**, **DisplayObject**, and then **Properties**.

What actions can I use in my event handler?

You can use any actions you want in the event handler. Many times you will want a Timeline to play once a SWF is loaded using the play() action. Or you may want to have elements on the Stage invisible until your SWF loads. You can set the properties of other elements in your handler as well.

You can create data files in the XML format using a text editor like TextMate or TextEdit (Mac) or NotePad or WordPad (Windows). Be sure to save your XML file as plain text, to avoid file formatting issues.

XML is composed of opening tags and closing tags, or tag pairs. For example, <address> is an opening tag and </address> is a closing tag. Tags may also have attributes. <address street="Broadway"></address> is a tag pair with an attribute named street with a value of Broadway. To learn more about XML, go to www.w3.org/XML/.

Create an XML File

① Open a text editor from your programs or applications.

Note: You can use Notepad on Windows, and TextEdit on OS X.

② Click **File**.

③ Click **New**.

A new document opens.

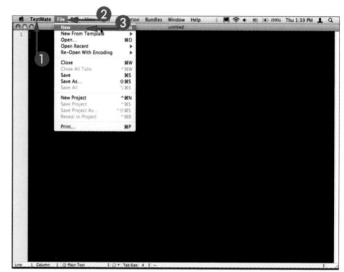

④ Type **<?xml version="1.0" encoding="UTF-8"?>**.

⑤ Create an opening tag named beatles by typing **<beatles>**.

⑥ Create a closing tag named beatles by typing **</beatles>**.

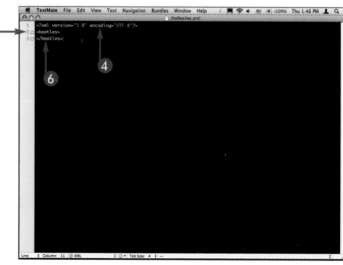

⑦ Between your opening and closing tags type several **<member>** tags with attributes as shown.

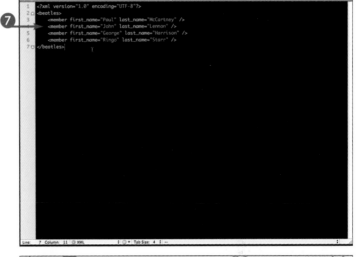

⑧ Click **File**.

⑨ Click **Save As**.

⑩ Click here and type a name for your file.

This examples uses theBeatles.xml.

*Note: Your XML file must be saved as plain text. In TextEdit, you can make your file plain text by clicking **Format**, and then **Make Plain Text**.*

⑪ Click here and select UTF8 (recommended).

⑫ Click **Save**.

TIPS

Can I put comments in my XML file?

Yes. You can add notes to yourself and to other people working on your project right inside the XML file as comments. The syntax for adding a comment in XML is `<!-- This is a comment -->`.

Can I use empty element tags with Flash?

Yes. In the example, you could replace this tag pair:

```
<member first_name="Paul"
last_name="McCartney"></member>
```

with this:

```
<member first_name="Paul" last_name=
"McCartney"/>
```

and achieve the same result.

Load Data from an XML File

You can load external data into your Flash movies from XML files. It only requires a few lines of ActionScript to get useable data from your external XML document into your Flash movie.

Load Data from an XML File

1. Create an XML file and place it in the same folder as your Flash movie.

   This example uses the XML file theBeatles.xml created in the section "Create an XML File."

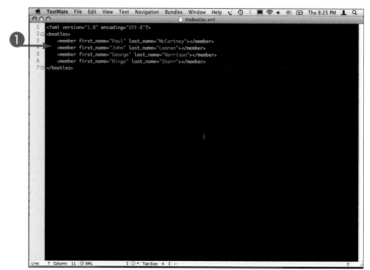

2. Click a keyframe in Flash.

3. Press F9 (Option+F9).

   The Actions panel opens.

4. Create instances of URLLoader and URLRequest.

5. Type the name of your XML file in quotation marks between the parentheses of your new URLRequest();

6. Declare a variable to hold your XML object.

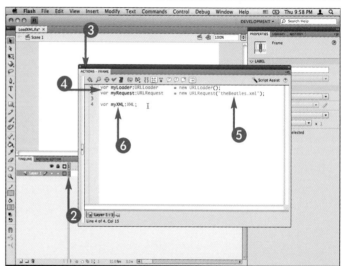

7 Add an event listener to your `URLLoader` instance.

In this example, the `URLLoader` should listen for `Event.COMPLETE`.

8 Create the callback function for your event listener.

● Make sure your callback function has the same name as referenced in your event listener.

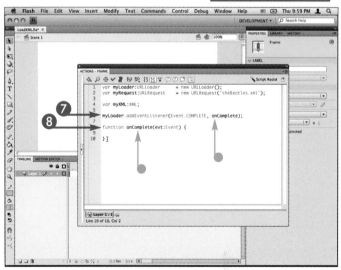

9 Inside the curly braces of your callback function, type **myXML = new XML (evt.target.data);** to pass your loaded data to the XML object.

10 Type **trace(myXML.member.attribute ("first_name")[0]);** to print the `first_name` attribute of the first XML element to the Output window.

11 Repeat step **10** to print the first name of other attributes by increasing the index number.

● The index number is at the end of the line.

12 On a new line after your callback function, Load your request.

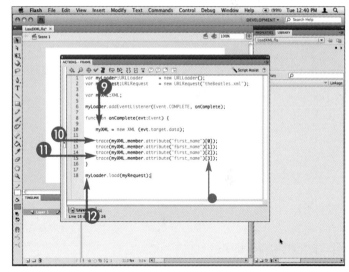

What is "evt.target.data" in my callback function?

Events in Flash pass along a reference to the object that sent the event, called the target. In this example, `evt.target.data` is equivalent to `myLoader.data` because the `myLoader` object is the target.

Load Data from an XML File *(continued)*

In ActionScript 3, XML is loaded using the URLLoader class and an event listener. Your URLLoader performs the loading operation. Then, you need to set up your event listener to know when the loading is complete. After you know the load is complete, you can use your XML data in your scripts.

⑬ Add comments to your code to make it more understandable by typing your notes after a double slash:

```
// this is a comment.
```

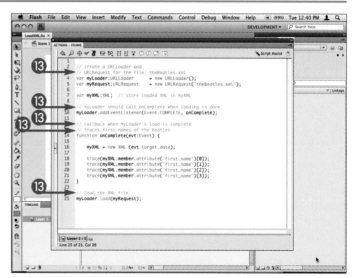

⑭ Click the **Check Syntax** button (✓).

⑮ Click **OK** in the message box that appears.

If your script contains errors, the Compiler Errors window opens with descriptions of any errors.

⑯ Click **Control**.

⑰ Click **Test Movie** to test your movie.

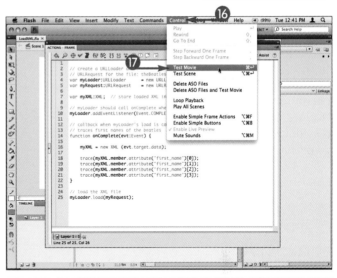

● The value of `first_name` for each "member" in your XML file displays in the Output window.

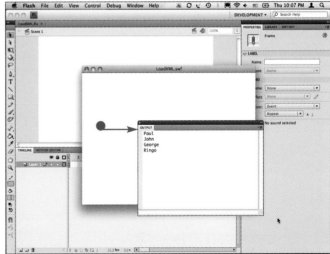

What properties of my loaded XML document can I access?

If the Toolbox is not open, you can open it in the Actions panel by clicking 🔲. Click **flash.xml, XMLDocument,** then **Properties**. The **Toolbox** lists all classes, methods, and properties available in ActionScript. You can try adding your own `trace()` statements to your script to see what the different properties expose.

When I preview my movie in a browser, a security warning appears. Why?

If your Flash publish settings are set to Access network only a security warning is displayed. You can change the Local Playback Security setting in the Flash tab of the Publish Settings window.

Use XML to Create Dynamic Text

You can use dynamic text fields in your Flash movie to display text loaded from an external XML document. This can be extremely useful if you want to update text content frequently on a Flash-based Web site.

① Click the **Text** tool (T).

② Click and drag on the Stage to create a text box.

③ Open the **Properties** panel.

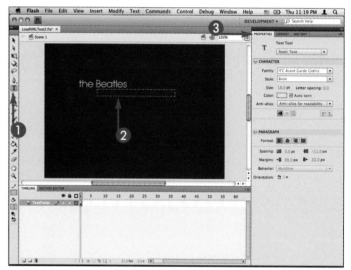

④ Set your text field to be **Dynamic Text**.

⑤ Type an instance name for your text field.

In this example, `tf_member1` is the instance name.

⑥ Repeat steps **2** to **5** to create multiple text fields on the stage.

In this example, four text fields are being created. The fields are given the instance names `tf_member1`, `tf_member2`, `tf_member3`, and `tf_member4`.

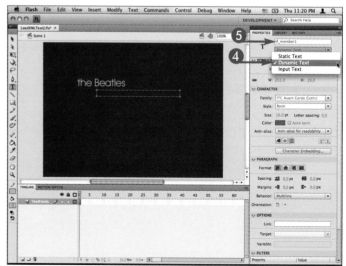

7 Create a new layer in the Timeline for your ActionScript by clicking the **New Layer** button ().

8 Click the first keyframe of your new layer to select it.

9 Click **Window**.

10 Click **Actions**.

The Actions panel opens.

You can also press F9 (Option + F9).

11 Create Instances of URLLoader and URLRequest.

12 Type the name of your XML file in quotation marks between the parentheses of your new URLRequest();.

In this example, the file theBeatles.xml is used. This file was created in the section "Create an XML File."

13 Declare a variable to hold your XML object.

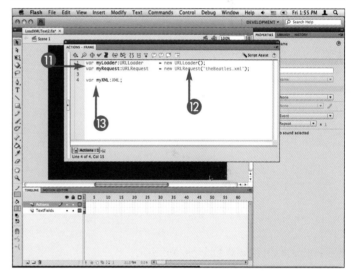

TIP

Can I use an XML feed from the Internet as data for my Flash movie?
Because RSS and ATOM feeds are XML, you can load feed data into your Flash movie and use the data in your project. You can try loading an XML feed like http://rss.cnn.com/rss/cnn_topstories.rss and using the feed data in your Flash movie.

continued

You can set your dynamic text in ActionScript by assigning a value to the .text property of your text field. For example: myField.text = "Peanut"; makes a text field with the instance name *myField* display the word Peanut.

Use XML to Create Dynamic Text *(continued)*

⑭ Add an event listener to your URLLoader instance.

In this example, the URLLoader should listen for Event.COMPLETE.

⑮ Write the callback function for your event listener.

● Your callback function should have the same name as referenced in your event listener.

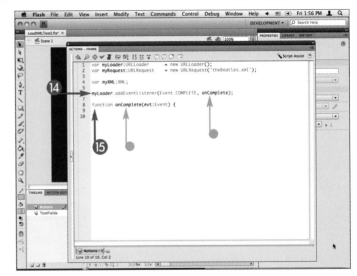

⑯ Inside your callback function, type **myXML = new XML (evt.target.data);** to populate your XML object with the loaded data.

⑰ Assign text values to your text fields by setting the `.text` property of each field.

⑱ Tell the loader instance to load the request.

⑲ Press Ctrl+Enter (⌘+Enter).

Flash tests your movie and your dynamic text appears.

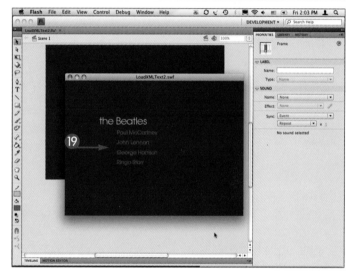

 TIP

Can I use HTML in my dynamic text fields?
Yes. Instead of assigning a value to the `.text` property, you can use the `.htmlText` property. In this example, you can try:

```
this.tf_member4.htmlText = "<a
href='http://www.ringostarr.com'>Ringo Starr</a>";
```

Test your movie again. Ringo Starr is a clickable HTML link.

```
this.tf_member4.htmlText="<a
href='http://www.ringostarr.com
'>RingoStarr</a>";
```

Use XML to Create a JPEG Gallery

You can use information in your XML files to do more than just print text to the screen or output window. You can put filenames and URLs in your XML and use that information to dynamically load other assets. This example demonstrates how to use XML to load images for a photo gallery.

Use XML to Create a JPEG Gallery

① In a text editor, create a new XML file named gallery.xml.

Note: To learn how to create and name an XML file, see the section, "Create an XML File."

② Create the opening and closing tags `<gallery></gallery>`.

Note: To learn how to create opening and closing tags, see the section, "Create an XML File."

③ Add `<image>` tags that include both `title` and `filename` attributes.

④ Save your XML file.

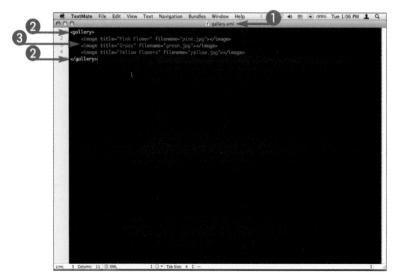

⑤ Place JPEG image files in the same directory with filenames corresponding to the `filename` attributes in your XML file.

6 Open Flash if it is not already open.

7 Place an instance of the `UILoader` component on the Stage with the instance name myUILoader.

Note: See Chapter 11 to learn about adding components.

8 Create an instance of a button on the Stage with the instance name nextButton.

Note: See Chapter 8 to learn about creating button symbols.

9 Create a dynamic text field and give it the instance name title.

Note: See the section "Use XML to Create Dynamic Text" to learn about creating dynamic text fields.

10 Click on the first keyframe on the Timeline to select it.

11 Click **Window**.

12 Click **Actions**.

The Actions panel opens.

You can also press F9 (Option + F9).

continued

309

TIP

Can I collapse a function in the Actions panel?
Yes. Click and drag in the Actions window the script that you want to collapse, and click the **Collapse Selection** button (⊟). Collapsing actions does not delete them, but hides them from view.

XML is a great way to manage
text and image content for a
Flash-based Web site. You can
also use XML to create a
gallery of SWF files, or to
create several buttons that
each load a particular file.

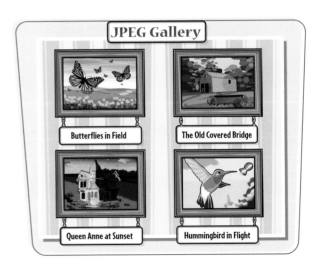

Use XML to Create a JPEG Gallery *(continued)*

⑬ Create Instances of `URLLoader`
and `URLRequest`.

⑭ Type the name of your XML file in
quotation marks between the
parentheses of your new
URLRequest();

⑮ Declare a variable to hold your
XML object.

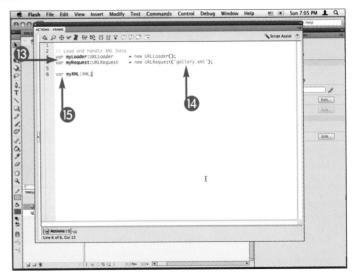

⑯ Type **myLoader.addEventListener
(Event.COMPLETE, onComplete);**
to create your event listener for your
XML load.

⑰ Type the **onComplete** callback
function.

⑱ Load your request.

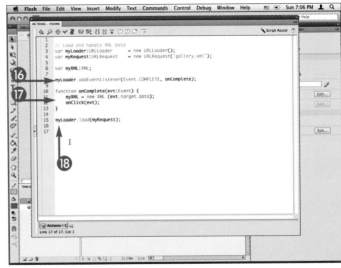

⑲ Type **nextButton.addEventListener (MouseEvent.MOUSE_DOWN, onClick);** to create an event listener for your button.

⑳ Type **var currentImage:Number = 0;** to store the number of your current image.

㉑ Type your **onClick** function to handle button clicks.

㉒ In your event handler, set the `currentImage` variable back to `0` if there are no more image tags in the XML.

㉓ Set the `.text` property of your dynamic text field to the `title` attribute of your XML.

㉔ Create another `URLRequest` from the `filename` attribute of your XML by typing **var imageRequest = new URL Request(myXML.image.attribute("filename")[currentImage]);**.

㉕ Load your `URLRequest` with your `UILoader` instance.

㉖ Add 1 to your `currentImage` variable to prepare for the next button click.

Note: This figure includes comments. Comments are not necessary for the script to function.

㉗ Press Ctrl + Enter (⌘ + Enter) to test your movie, and click your button to cycle through the image gallery.

Flash exports the movie and you can click your button to cycle through the gallery.

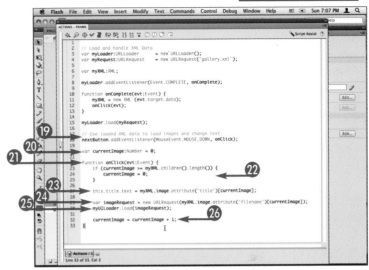

How can I have the gallery load the first image without a click?
You can add script to your `onComplete` function to load the first image and set the first title one of two ways. One way is to copy the script from your `onClick` function. The other way is to call the `onClick` function by typing **onClick(evt);**.

Make a Simple Preloader for Loading an Image

You can use the ProgressBar component to give your users feedback when an image loads. You can also use the Label component to give more detailed progress information.

① Press Ctrl+F7 (⌘+F7).

  The Components panel opens.

② Click and drag a ProgressBar component onto the Stage.

③ Open the Properties panel.

④ Type **myProgressBar** as the instance name.

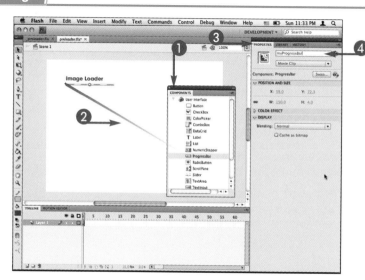

⑤ Click and drag a **Label** component onto the Stage and give it the instance name myProgressLabel.

⑥ Click **Insert**.

⑦ Click **Timeline**.

⑧ Click **Layer**.

  A new layer appears in the Timeline.

⑨ Click the first keyframe of your new layer.

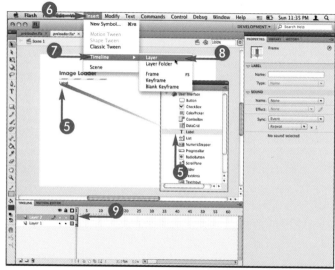

⑩ Press F9 (Option + F9).

The Actions panel opens.

⑪ Create instances of URLRequest and Loader.

⑫ Type **myProgressBar.source = imageLoader.contentLoaderInfo;**.

⑬ Add an EventListener to your ProgressBar.

⑭ Create a callback function for your progress event.

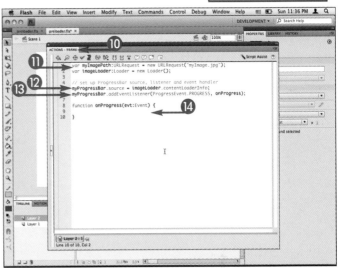

⑮ Get the percent complete from the event.

⑯ Set the .text property of your Label component.

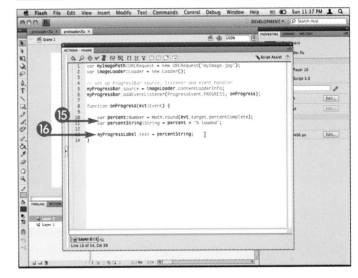

How can I change the color of my Label component?

You can use HTML with your Label component to change the font and color. To change the color, instead of setting the .text property, set the .htmlText property. For example, you could make your Label text red by typing **myProgressLabel.htmlText = "<font color='#FF0000'>" + percentString + "</font>";**.

continued

Because you can't rely on your users' Internet connection speed, pre-loading external content is very important when loading external content over the Internet. You should always give your users visual feedback when something is happening in your movie.

Make a Simple Preloader for Loading an Image *(continued)*

⑰ Add an `Event.COMPLETE` listener to your `Loader` instance.

⑱ Create a callback function for your `Event.COMPLETE` event.

⑲ Inside the callback function, hide the ProgressBar and Label components by setting their `.visible` properties to `false`.

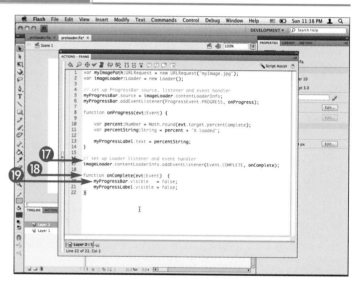

⑳ Outside your callback function type **this.addChild(imageLoader);**.

㉑ On a new line, type **imageLoader.load (myImagePath);** to load the request.

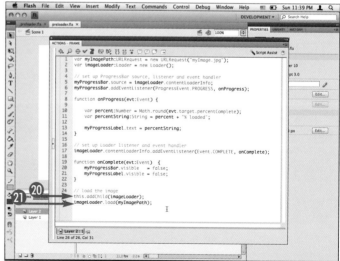

㉒ Click **Control**.

㉓ Click **Test Movie**.

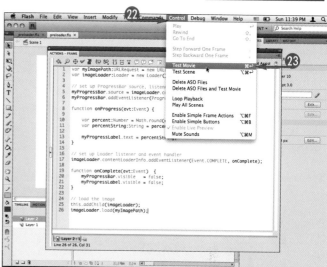

㉔ Click **View** in the player.

㉕ Click **Simulate Download**.

● Flash shows your preloader in action.

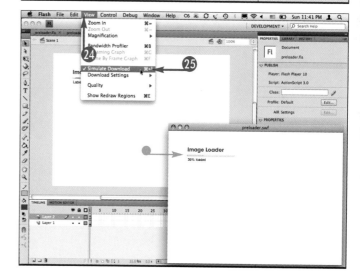

My download simulation is happening too fast to see. Can I slow it down?

Yes. After you test your movie, click **View**, and then **Download Settings**, and select a slower speed for the simulation.

Can I use the ProgressBar component with the UILoader component?

Yes. All components are designed to work either independently or together. You can open the Component Inspector, select your progress bar, and set the source to the instance name of your UILoader. The progress bar automatically tracks your UILoader's download progress.

Publishing Flash Movies

Learn how to publish your Flash movies for sharing with the world. You can create Web pages from your Flash projects or create stand-alone projectors that you can e-mail or burn to CD.

Get to Know the Publish Settings Dialog Box

The Flash Publish Settings dialog box is where you determine how you want to distribute your Flash movie. You can publish as a SWF file, a Web page, an image, or as a self-contained executable. You can open the Publish Settings dialog box by clicking File and then Publish Settings, or you can press Alt+Shift+F12 (Option+Shift+F12).

PUBLISH FORMATS

● Current Profile Menu

This allows you to choose from a menu of saved sets of settings.

● Import/Export Profile

Click this button to export settings as an XML file or to import a previously saved XML file of publish settings.

● Create New Profile

Click this button to create your own custom profile of settings.

● Duplicate Profile

Click this button to create a copy of your current publish profile.

● Rename Profile

Click this button to change the name of your current profile.

● Delete Profile

Click this button to delete the current settings profile.

● Formats, Flash, and HTML Tabs

Click these tabs to view the settings for the types of files you will publish.

● File Types

You can click any or all of the available file formats to export your movie.

● Use Default Names Button

Click this button to reset all filenames to the defaults.

● Publish Destination Button

Click on the folder icon to select a destination where you want to save your file.

● Filenames

You can rename your published files here.

The second tab in the Publish Settings dialog box displays your Flash settings. This tab is where you can adjust image and audio compression levels to create an acceptable file size for your final Flash movie. You can also set security and add metadata to your movie.

FLASH SETTINGS

● **Player Version Menu**

Use this menu to select your target Flash Player version.

● **Script Version Menu**

You can select the version of ActionScript your movie uses here.

● **Image Settings**

Set your default image compression with the slider.

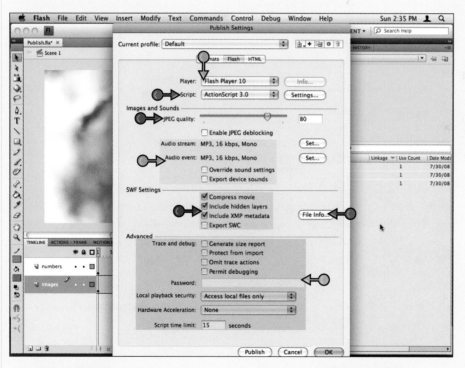

● **Sound Settings**

Set your streaming and event audio compression defaults here.

● **SWF Settings**

Select from these options to compress your movie for smaller file size, include hidden layers, include XMP metadata, and export compiled clips.

● **Advanced Options**

These options are related to security, hardware acceleration, and processing limits.

● **File Info Button**

Click this button to create your XMP metadata.

Publish a SWF File

When you finish your Flash project, you can publish it as a SWF file, to share, or to embed in a Web page. The default publish settings create both a SWF file and an HTML file, so you can view your movie in a browser or upload to a Web server.

Publish a SWF File

① Click **File**.

② Click **Publish Settings**.

The Publish Settings dialog box appears.

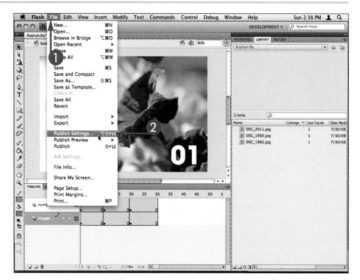

③ Click the **Formats** tab.

④ Select the format types you want to use (☐ changes to ☑).

This example shows Flash (.swf) and HTML (.html) selected.

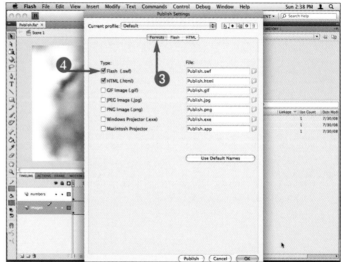

● To change the filename of your SWF file, you can click inside the **File** field and type a new name.

● Click the folder icon (📁) to change the folder where your published file will be placed.

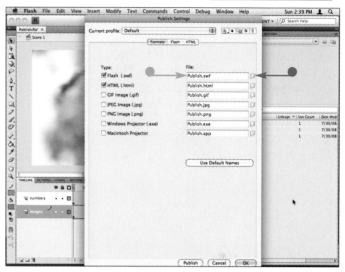

⑤ Click **Publish**.

⑥ Click **OK** to save your publish settings and close the Publish Settings dialog box.

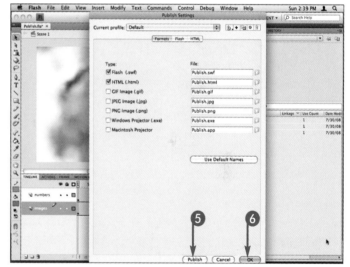

TIPS

After I create my settings, do I need to open the settings window to publish?

You can click **File** and then **Publish** to publish your Flash movie based on your current settings. You can also publish and quickly preview your movie by clicking **File Publish Preview,** and then clicking a preview format. Or you can press Ctrl+F12 (⌘+F12).

What is the difference between Publish and Export?

While you can create SWF files both by publishing and exporting, they have different uses. Export is used to save images or video. Publish is mostly used to create Web pages and stand-alone applications.

When you publish your Flash movie as an image, Flash creates an image of the first frame of the movie. You can use the Export Image command to export an image of any frame of the Timeline.

① Click on a frame in your movie that you want to export as an image.

② Click **File**.

③ Click **Export**.

④ Click **Export Image**.

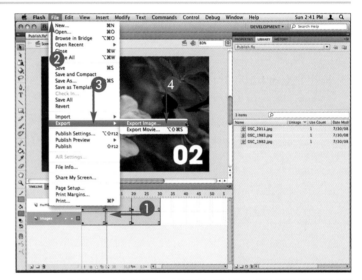

The Export Image dialog box appears.

⑤ Click the **Save as Type (Format)** drop-down menu and select either **GIF** or **JPEG Image**.

● You can type a name for your image here.

● You can click here to choose the destination for your image file.

⑥ Click **Save**.

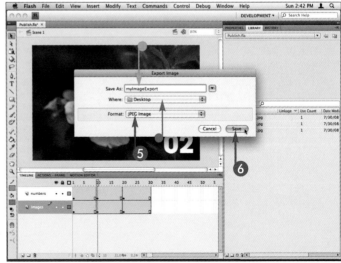

The Export dialog box for the image format you selected appears.

● Set the dimensions of your image here.

● Set your resolution here.

Note: Screen resolution is 72 dpi.

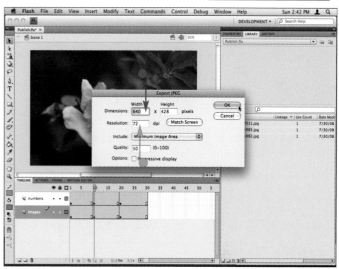

⑦ Click the **Include** drop-down menu and select **Full Document Size**.

⑧ Click **OK**.

Flash Exports a GIF or JPEG image to your selected destination.

TIPS

What is the Minimum Image Area option in the Include menu?

The Minimum Image Area is the height and width of the elements on the Stage, not including the Stage itself. Flash crops to the minimum area unless you select **Full Document Size** from the **Include** menu.

How do I export all of the frames of my Timeline as images?

You can click **File, Export,** and then **Export Movie** to export all the frames of your Flash movie. You then have the option to export an image sequence instead of just a single image.

Export Animation as Video

You can export your Flash animation as QuickTime video that you can use for streaming over the Internet or burning to a DVD. You can also use your QuickTime movie in a video-editing application like Adobe Premiere or Final Cut Pro.

On Windows, you also have the option to export your video in the AVI format.

① Create an animation on the Timeline.

Note: See Chapter 9 to learn how to create Timeline animation.

② Click **File**.

③ Click **Export**.

④ Click **Export Movie**.

The Export Movie dialog box appears.

⑤ Click the **Format** drop-down list and select **QuickTime**.

● You can type a name for your video here.

● You can choose the destination for your video file here.

⑥ Click **Save**.

The QuickTime Export Settings dialog box appears.

⑦ Click **QuickTime Settings**.

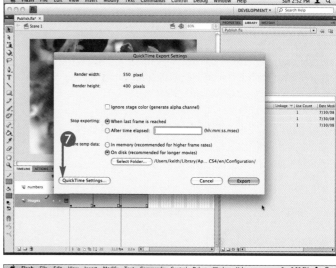

● You can click here to adjust video settings.

● You can click here to adjust audio settings.

● You can click here to select Internet streaming options.

⑧ Click **OK**.

The QuickTime Settings window closes.

⑨ Click **Export**.

Your video is exported.

TIPS

Can I export an animation with an alpha channel for compositing in another progam?

Yes. In the QuickTime Export Settings dialog box, select the **Ignore stage color (generate alpha channel)** option (☐ changes to ☑). Then Flash only exports the elements on the Stage and leaves the background transparent for compositing later.

I exported as an animated GIF and my animation does not appear correctly. Why?

When you export an animated GIF, Flash only exports animation that exists on the main Timeline. Any pieces of animation that are nested within graphic and movie clip symbols do not become part of your exported GIF file.

Publish a Flash Movie as a Web Page

You can save your movie as a Web page. Flash automatically exports your SWF file as well as all the necessary HTML code so that your movie can be viewed in a Web browser like Firefox, Safari, or Internet Explorer.

If you have your own Web site, you can upload your published files for anyone on the Internet to view.

Publish a Flash Movie as a Web Page

① Click **File**.

② Click **Publish Settings**.

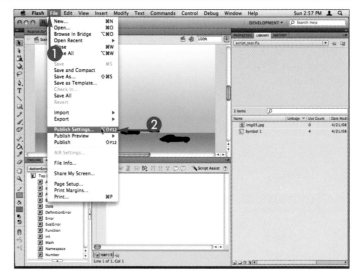

The Publish Settings dialog box appears.

③ Click the **Formats** tab.

④ Select the **Flash (.swf)** option (□ changes to ☑).

⑤ Select the **HTML (.html)** option (□ changes to ☑).

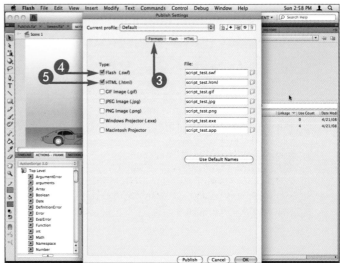

6 Click the **HTML** tab.

Flash displays the options for
your HTML page.

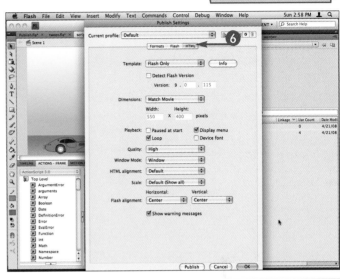

7 Click the **Template** drop-down
menu and select **Flash Only**.

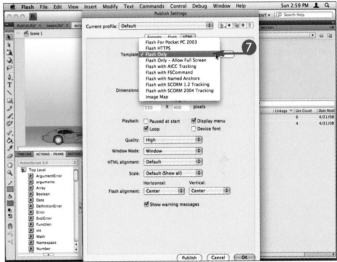

TIPS

Can I make my own HTML templates?

Yes. After you make a template, you need to place the file in Program Files\Adobe\Adobe Flash CS4\en\First Run\HTML (/Applications/Adobe Flash CS4/en/First Run/HTML/). Flash automatically adds your template to the Templates menu after it is placed in the correct folder.

How can I get more information on the included HTML templates?

Click **Info** next to the Template menu to see a dialog box that describes the features of the selected template. The dialog box also displays the filename of the selected template so that you can use it as a starting point for creating your own.

You can change how your Flash movie appears in the HTML page by adjusting the settings in the HTML tab of the Publish Settings dialog box. It is important to remember that changing your HTML settings overrides any previous settings for the file.

Publish a Flash Movie as a Web Page *(continued)*

● You can select the **Detect Flash Version** option (☐ changes to ☑) to integrate version detection into your HTML page.

● You can click the **Dimensions** drop-down menu to set your movie dimensions on the page by pixels or by percent.

● You can select your **Playback** options here. Usually, the defaults are all you need.

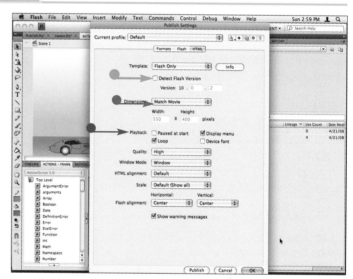

● You can click the **Quality** drop-down menu to adjust the image fidelity in your movie. Set this to High or Best unless you have issues with playback smoothness.

● The options in the **Window Mode** (Windows only) drop-down menu give you the choice of a regular background, transparent background, or opaque background.

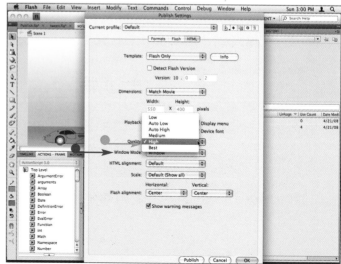

- The options in the **HTML alignment** drop-down menu allow you to set how your Flash movie relates to other elements on the Web page.

- If you choose to change the height and width of your Flash movie, you can click the **Scale** drop-down menu to set how Flash reacts to the new dimensions.

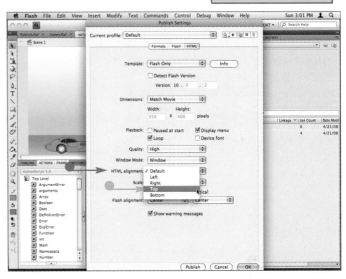

- You can click the **Flash alignment** drop-down menus to set how the Flash movie aligns vertically and horizontally.

⑧ Click **Publish**.

Flash creates the files necessary for you to run your Flash movie in a Web browser.

⑨ Click **OK**.

Your publish settings are saved and the dialog box closes.

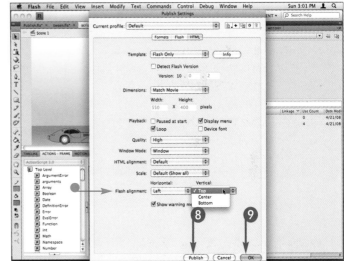

 TIPS

I have an embedded video with full-screen controls, but they don't work. Why?

You must choose an HTML template that enables full-screen support. Click the **Template** menu in your HTML publish settings, and choose **Flash Only – Allow Full Screen**.

How can I make my Flash movie fill the entire browser window?

If you set your HTML dimensions to **Percent,** and then set both the width and height values to 100%, your Flash movie fills the window.

Using the Bandwidth Profiler

You can use the Bandwidth Profiler to help you troubleshoot your movie's playback over the Internet. The Bandwidth Profiler simulates playing your movie back over the Web at estimated connection speeds.

① Click **Control**.

② Click **Test Movie**.

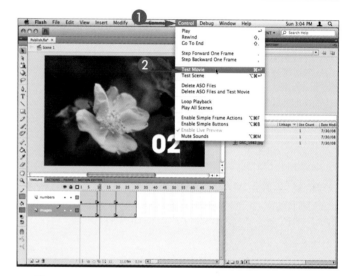

Your Flash movie opens in the player window and begins to play.

③ Click **View**.

④ Click **Bandwidth Profiler**.

You can also press [Ctrl] + [B] ([⌘] + [B]).

In Windows, click **View** from the player menu and then click **Bandwidth**.

The Bandwidth Profiler appears in the Flash Player window.

5 Click **View**.

6 Click **Download Settings**.

7 Click the connection speed you want to test.

In Windows, click **View** from the player menu and then click **Download Settings**.

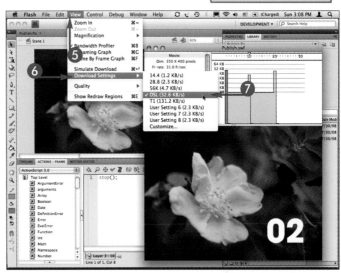

8 Click **View**.

9 Click **Simulate Download**.

In Windows, click **View** from the player menu and then click **Simulate Download**.

Flash simulates the experience of downloading and playing your movie over the Internet.

● The left side of the profiler displays information about your movie file.

● The right side displays a graph of the file size of each frame of your movie.

● During a download simulation, a green bar displays how much of your movie has been downloaded.

Can I test a custom download speed?
Yes. Click **View**, **Download Settings**, and then **Customize**. The **Custom Download Settings** dialog box appears. There you see your current options, all of which are editable. To return to the default set after you make changes, click **Reset**.

Publish a Self-Contained Projector

You can publish your Flash movie as a stand-alone application so that you can share your project without having to worry about plug-ins or browser requirements. You can publish your projector as a Windows executable (.exe) or a Mac application (.app).

PUBLISH THE PROJECTOR

① Click **File**.

② Click **Publish Settings**.

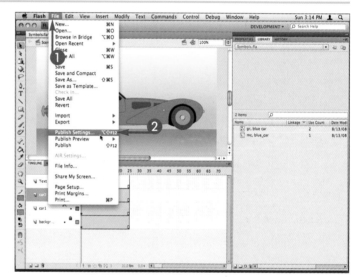

The Publish Settings dialog box appears.

③ Click the **Formats** tab.

④ Select the **Windows Projector (.exe)** or **Macintosh Projector** option (☐ changes to ☑).

⑤ Deselect the default **Flash (.swf)** and **HTML (.html)** options (☑ changes to ☐) because they are not necessary to create a projector.

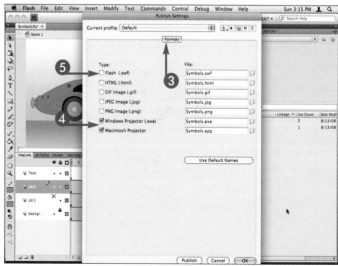

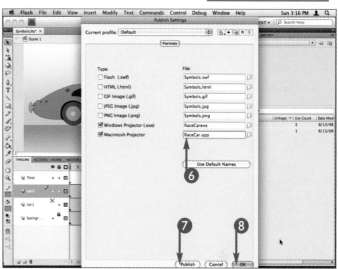

6 Click in the File field and type the name or names of your Projector.

7 Click **Publish**.

Flash publishes your projector.

8 Click **OK**.

RUN YOUR PROJECTOR

1 Double-click your exported projector file to launch it.

In this example, the projector is opened from the Mac OSX Desktop.

● The Flash Player window opens and plays the movie.

2 Click the Close button (●) to exit the projector.

Why use a projector?

You can use a projector to distribute your Flash movies on CD or DVD. If you cannot guarantee that people who receive your CD have the Flash player installed on their computers, a projector is the best publishing option.

If I burn my projector to a CD, how can I make it automatically start when the CD is inserted into the computer?

On Windows, you can add a text file that tells the computer what file to auto-play. Create a new text file in Notepad and type the following:

```
[autorun]
open=myProjector.exe
```

Replace myProjector.exe with your projector's filename. Save as an All Files (*.*) type file named autorun.inf and burn it alongside your projector on a CD.

Flash Keyboard Shortcuts

Window Shortcuts

Keys	Description
Ctrl + F2 (⌘ + F2)	Tools panel
Ctrl + F3 (⌘ + F3)	Properties panel
Ctrl + L (⌘ + L)	Library panel
F9 (Option + F9)	Actions panel
Ctrl + K (⌘ + K)	Align panel
Ctrl + F9 (⌘ + F9)	Swatches panel
Ctrl + I (⌘ + I)	Info panel
Ctrl + T (⌘ + T)	Transform panel
Ctrl + F7 (⌘ + F7)	Components panel
Alt + F7 (Shift + F7)	Component Inspector
F4	Hide Panels

Control Shortcuts

Keys	Description
Enter	Play
Home (Shift + ,)	Rewind
End (Shift + .)	Go to End
.	Step Forward One Frame
,	Step Back One Frame
⌘ + Enter	Test Movie
Ctrl + Alt + B (⌘ + Option + B)	Enable Simple Buttons
Ctrl + Alt + F (⌘ + Option + F)	Enable Simple Frame Actions

Timeline Shortcuts

F5	Insert Frames
Shift + F5	Remove Frames
F6	Insert Keyframe
Shift + F6	Remove Keyframe
F7	Insert Blank Keyframe
Ctrl + Alt + X (⌘ + Option + X)	Cut Frames
Ctrl + Alt + C (⌘ + Option + C)	Copy Frames
Ctrl + Alt + V (⌘ + Option + V)	Paste Frames
Ctrl + Alt + A (⌘ + Option + A)	Select All Frames

View Shortcuts

Ctrl + = (⌘ + =)	Zoom in
Ctrl + - (⌘ + -)	Zoom out
Ctrl + 1 (⌘ + 1)	Zoom to 100%
Ctrl + Alt + Shift + R	Show/Hide Rulers
Ctrl + # (⌘ + ')	Show/Hide Grid
Ctrl + ; (⌘ + ;)	Show/Hide Guides

Commonly Used ActionScript Commands

Common Global Functions and Directives

ActionScript	Description
trace(*message*)	Prints *message* to the Output window.
include "*filename.as*"	Includes the ActionScript file as though it were written in the frame.
import *package.class*	Imports external *class* as defined in *package* for use in ActionScript.
function *name(parameter1, parameter2, etc.):returnType*{}	Creates a method to perform a certain task.

Common ActionScript Statements

ActionScript	Description	Syntax
break	Exits a loop or switch statement.	break;

do while	A *while* loop where the statements are always executed once before the *condition* is evaluated.	do {
		// statements
		}
		while (*condition*);

if, else	Evaluates a condition. Statements inside an *if* block are executed when the *if* statement returns *true*. Statements inside an *else* block are executed when the *if* statement returns *false*.	if (condition)
		
		// statements if the condition is true
		} else {
		
		// statements if the condition is false
		}

for	Starts a loop.	for (var i:Number = 0; i < 10; i++) {
		    trace(i);
		}

return	Returns to the calling function.	function myFunctionName () {
		// statements
		return *value*;
		}

while	Begins a loop while the condition evaluates to true.	while (condition) {
		// statements are executed until condition is *false*.
		}

Common MovieClip Methods

ActionScript	Description	Defined By
gotoAndPlay(*scene, frame*)	Plays the movie clip starting at *frame*.	MovieClip
gotoAndStop(*scene, frame*)	Moves the play head to *frame* and stops.	MovieClip
nextFrame():	Moves the play head forward one frame and stops.	MovieClip
play()	Plays the movie clip.	MovieClip
prevFrame()	Moves the play head to the previous frame and stops.	MovieClip
stop()	Stops the movie clip from playing.	

Useful MovieClip & DisplayObject Properties

ActionScript	Description	Defined By
alpha	The transparency value of the object.	DisplayObject
currentFrame	The number of the frame that the flash play head is located on.	MovieClip
framesLoaded	The number of frames loaded in a streaming SWF file.	MovieClip
mouseX	The x coordinate of the mouse pointer in pixels.	DisplayObject
mouseY	The y coordinate of the mouse pointer in pixels.	DisplayObject
name	The instance name of the object.	DisplayObject
parent	The object that contains the current object.	DisplayObject
root	The main Timeline of a SWF file.	DisplayObject
rotation	Rotation value of the object.	DisplayObject
visible	Whether the object is visible or not.	DisplayObject
width	The number of pixels wide the object is.	DisplayObject
height	The number of pixels high the object is.	DisplayObject
x	X position of the object relative to its container.	DisplayObject
y	Y position of the object relative to its container.	DisplayObject

ActionScript Operators

Arithmetic Operators

Operator	Description
+	Calculates a sum. **trace(3 + 3);** displays **6;**
–	Calculates a difference. **trace(3 - 3);** displays **0.**
*	Calculates a product. **trace(3 * 3);** displays **9.**
/	Performs division. **trace(12 / 3);** displays **4.**
%	Modulus, calculates the remainder of the division of the first number by the second. **trace(5%2);** displays **1.**

Incrementing and Decrementing Operators

Operator	Description
value++	Adds **1** to the value *after* the value is used.
++value	Adds **1** to the value *before* the value is used.
value--	Subtracts **1** from the value *after* the value is used.
--value	Subtracts **1** from the value *before* the value is used.

Assignment Operators

Operator	Description
=	Sets the value of the variable before the operator to the value after the operator. **Var num = 2;** sets the value of **num** to **2.**
+=	Sets the value of the variable before the operator to the value of itself plus the second value. If num = 2 then **trace(num += 3);** displays the value **5;**
-=	Sets the value of the variable before the operator to the value of itself minus the second value. If num = 5 then **trace(num -= 3);** displays the value **2;**
*=	Sets the value of the variable before the operator to the value of itself multiplied by the second value. If num = 5 then **trace(num *= 2);** displays the value **10;**
/=	Sets the value of the variable before the operator to the value of itself divided by the second value. If num =4 then **trace(num /= 2);** displays the value **2;**
%=	Sets the value of the variable before the operator to the value of the remainder itself divided by the second value. If num =5 then **trace(num %= 2);** displays the value **1;**

Comparison Operators

Operator	Description
== (Equal to)	Tests to see if the value before the operator is equal to the value after it. **trace ("6" == 6);** displays **true;**
=== (Strict Equal to)	Tests to see if the value before the operator has the same value and type as the variable after it. **trace(6 === 6);** displays **true;**
!= (Not Equal to)	Tests to see if the value before the operator does not have the same value as the one after it. **trace(6 != 6);** displays **false;**
!== (Strict Not Equal to)	Tests to see if the value before the operator does not have the same value or type as the one after it. **trace("6" !== 6);** displays **true;**
< (Less Than)	Tests to see if the first value is less than the second. **trace(2 < 3);** displays **true;**
> (Greater Than)	Tests to see if the first value is greater than the second. **trace(3 > 2);** displays **true;**
<= (Less Than or Equal to)	Tests to see if the first value is less than or equal to the second. **trace(6 <= 6);** displays **true;**
>= (Greater Than or Equal to)	Tests to see if the first value is greater than or equal to the second. **trace(8 >= 2);** displays **true;**

Index

Index

Index

Index

Index

Read Less–Learn More®

Visual™

There's a Visual book for every learning level...

Simplified®

The place to start if you're new to computers. Full color.

- Computers
- Creating Web Pages
- Mac OS
- Office
- Windows

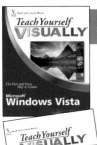

Teach Yourself VISUALLY™

Get beginning to intermediate-level training in a variety of topics. Full color.

- Access
- Bridge
- Chess
- Computers
- Crocheting
- Digital Photography
- Dog training
- Dreamweaver
- Excel
- Flash
- Golf
- Guitar
- Handspinning
- HTML
- Jewelry Making & Beading
- Knitting
- Mac OS
- Office
- Photoshop
- Photoshop Elements
- Piano
- Poker
- PowerPoint
- Quilting
- Scrapbooking
- Sewing
- Windows
- Wireless Networking
- Word

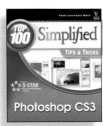

Top 100 Simplified® Tips & Tricks

Tips and techniques to take your skills beyond the basics. Full color.

- Digital Photography
- eBay
- Excel
- Google
- Internet
- Mac OS
- Office
- Photoshop
- Photoshop Elements
- PowerPoint
- Windows

...all designed for visual learners—just like you!

Master VISUALLY®

Your complete visual reference. Two-color interior.

- 3ds Max
- Creating Web Pages
- Dreamweaver and Flash
- Excel
- Excel VBA Programming
- iPod and iTunes
- Mac OS
- Office
- Optimizing PC Performance
- Photoshop Elements
- QuickBooks
- Quicken
- Windows
- Windows Mobile
- Windows Server

Visual Blueprint™

Where to go for professional-level programming instruction. Two-color interior.

- Ajax
- ASP.NET 2.0
- Excel Data Analysis
- Excel Pivot Tables
- Excel Programming
- HTML
- JavaScript
- Mambo
- PHP & MySQL
- SEO
- Vista Sidebar
- Visual Basic
- XML

Visual Encyclopedia™

Your A to Z reference of tools and techniques. Full color.

- Dreamweaver
- Excel
- Mac OS
- Photoshop
- Windows

Visual Quick Tips

Shortcuts, tricks, and techniques for getting more done in less time. Full color.

- Crochet
- Digital Photography
- Excel
- iPod & iTunes
- Knitting
- MySpace
- Office
- PowerPoint
- Windows
- Wireless Networking